# This Mighty Scourge

# *This Mighty Scourge*

## Perspectives on the Civil War

JAMES M. McPHERSON

OXFORD
UNIVERSITY PRESS

2007

# OXFORD

UNIVERSITY PRESS

Oxford University Press, Inc., publishes works that further
Oxford University's objective of excellence
in research, scholarship, and education.

Oxford    New York
Auckland    Cape Town    Dar es Salaam    Hong Kong    Karachi
Kuala Lumpur    Madrid    Melbourne    Mexico City    Nairobi
New Delhi    Shanghai    Taipei    Toronto

With offices in
Argentina    Austria    Brazil    Chile    Czech Republic    France    Greece
Guatemala    Hungary    Italy    Japan    Poland    Portugal    Singapore
South Korea    Switzerland    Thailand    Turkey    Ukraine    Vietnam

Published by Oxford University Press, Inc.
198 Madison Avenue, New York, NY 10016
www.oup.com

Oxford is a registered trademark of Oxford University Press

Library of Congress Cataloging-in-Publication Data
McPherson, James M.
This mighty scourge : perspectives on the Civil War /
James M. McPherson.
p. cm.
Includes bibliographical references and index.
ISBN-13: 978-0-19-531366-6
ISBN-10: 0-19-531366-6
1. United States—History—Civil War, 1861–1865.
I. Title.
E468.M24 2007
973.7—dc22
2006035523

1  3  5  7  9  8  6  4  2

Printed in the United States of America
on acid-free paper

BT    28.10    1/07

TO THE NEXT TWO GENERATIONS:

JENNY, JEFF,
GWYNNE, JAMES,
AND ANNIE

# Contents

Preface ix

Acknowledgments xi

## I SLAVERY AND THE COMING OF WAR

1. And the War Came 3
2. Escape and Revolt in Black and White 21

## II THE LOST CAUSE REVISITED

3. The Confederacy: A House Divided? 43
4. Was the Best Defense a Good Offense?
   Jefferson Davis and Confederate Strategies 51
5. The Saratoga That Wasn't: The Impact of Antietam Abroad 65
6. To Conquer a Peace? Lee's Goals in the Gettysburg Campaign 77
7. The Last Rebel: Jesse James 87
8. Long-Legged Yankee Lies: The Lost Cause Textbook Crusade 93

## III ARCHITECTS OF VICTORY

9. "We Stand by Each Other Always": Grant and Sherman 109
10. The Hard Hand of War 123
11. Unvexed to the Sea: Lincoln, Grant,
    and the Vicksburg Campaign 131

## IV HOME FRONT AND BATTLE FRONT

12. Brahmins at War 145
13. "Spend Much Time in Reading the Daily Papers":
    The Press and Army Morale in the Civil War 155
14. No Peace Without Victory, 1861–1865 167

## V   LINCOLN

15.   To Remember That He Had Lived                                    187

16.   "As Commander-in-Chief I Have a Right to
       Take Any Measure Which May Best Subdue the Enemy"                209

      Notes                                                            223
      Index                                                            253

# Preface

IN 1917 THE BRITISH PACIFIST Viscount John Morley made an astonishing avowal. Writing in the midst of a war that would create many new pacifists, Viscount Morley declared that the American Civil War had been "the only war in modern times as to which we can be sure, first, that no skill or patience of diplomacy would have avoided it; and second, that preservation of the American Union and abolition of negro slavery were two vast triumphs of good by which even the inferno of war was justified."[1]

I don't know whether Viscount Morley ever read Abraham Lincoln's second inaugural address, but his words provide an uncanny echo of Lincoln's message. "Both parties deprecated war," said the American president in 1865, but nevertheless "the war came." After four years of it both sides prayed that "this mighty scourge of war may speedily pass away." But if God willed that it continue until the scourge of war wiped out the scourge of slavery, "the judgments of the Lord, are true and righteous altogether."[2]

The essays in this book address the questions raised by Morley and Lincoln. Why *did* the war come? What were the war aims of each side? What strategies did they employ to achieve these aims? How do we evaluate the leadership of both sides? Did the war's outcome justify the immense sacrifice of lives? What impact did the experience of war have on the people who lived through it? How did later generations remember and commemorate that experience?

During more than forty years of research and writing about the Civil War, I have tried to come to grips with these questions. The chapters that follow reaffirm some of my old interpretations but also offer several new ones. Old or new, my conclusions suggest additional questions that I hope readers will ponder, perhaps arriving at judgments different from mine. I welcome disagreement and dialogue, for that is how scholarship and understanding advance.

Three of these essays are published here for the first time: chapters 6, 11, and 16. The others have appeared in various venues during the past decade, but I have substantially revised and updated most of them for this volume. This experience has been intellectually rewarding and emotionally satisfying; I hope that readers enjoy and learn from these essays as much as I have learned by writing them.

# Acknowledgments

S EVEN OF THE CHAPTERS IN THIS BOOK WERE ORIGINALLY PUBLISHED as review essays in the *New York Review of Books*: chapters 2, 3, 7, 9, 10, 12, and 15. The format and some of the contents of these essays are considerably altered and revised here, and the seven chapters are constructed from what were originally twelve separate review essays of thirty-two books. I own the copyright for these essays, and I am grateful to the *NYRB* for giving me carte blanche to use them in this changed format, and to Robert Silvers for his invitations to review the books that provided the basis for my analyses of several important Civil War issues.

The chapters published herein for the first time (chapters 6, 11, and 16) began life as lectures at the Chambersburg Civil War Seminar, Vicksburg National Military Park, and Princeton University. I thank Ted Alexander, Terry Winschel, and Robert George for invitations to deliver these lectures.

The holders of copyrights for chapters 1, 4, 5, 8, 13, and 14 have kindly given me permission to reprint them herein, as follow:

Ch. 1: *North & South Magazine* (Nov. 2000), "What Caused the Civil War?"

Ch. 4: Gabor S. Boritt, ed., *Jefferson Davis's Generals* (New York, 1999), "Was the Best Defense a Good Offense?"

Ch. 5: Louisiana State University Press, *Inside the Confederate Nation: Essays in Honor of Emory M. Thomas,* ed. Lesley J. Gordon and John C. Inscoe (Baton Rouge, 2005), "The Saratoga That Wasn't."

Ch. 8: University of North Carolina Press, *The Memory of the Civil War in American Culture,* ed. Alice Fahs and Joan Waugh (Chapel Hill, 2004), "Long-Legged Yankee Lies."

Ch. 13: *Atlanta History: A Journal of Georgia and the South* (Spring 1998), "Spend Much Time in Reading the Daily Papers."

Ch. 14: *American Historical Review* (Feb. 2004), "No Peace Without Victory, 1861–1865."

Finally, I am indebted to India Cooper for her skillful copy-editing of the manuscript, which has saved me from innumerable infelicities of punctuation, grammar, and style.

J.M.M.

# I

# Slavery and the Coming of War

# 1

# And the War Came

I N THREE SENTENCES OF HIS SECOND INAUGURAL ADDRESS on March 4, 1865, Abraham Lincoln outlined an interpretation of the causes of secession and of the Civil War. The institution of slavery, he said, created a powerful interest in the states where it existed. "To strengthen, perpetuate, and extend this interest was the object for which the insurgents would rend the Union, even by war. . . . Both parties deprecated war; but one of them would *make* war rather than let the nation survive; and the other would *accept* war rather than let it perish. And the war came."[1]

These sentences have framed arguments about the causes of the Civil War for a century and a half. In the 1860s few people in either North or South would have dissented from Lincoln's insistence in the second inaugural address that slavery "was, somehow, the cause of the war." After all, had not Jefferson Davis, a large slaveholder, justified secession in 1861 as an act of self-defense against the incoming Lincoln administration, whose announced policy of excluding slavery from the territories would make "property in slaves so insecure as to be comparatively worthless . . . thereby annihilating in effect property worth thousands of millions of dollars"?[2] And had not the new vice president of the Confederate States of America, Alexander H. Stephens, said in a speech at Savannah on March 21, 1861, that slavery was "the immediate cause of the late rupture and the present revolution" of Southern independence? The old confederation known as the United States, said Stephens, had been founded on the false idea that all men are created equal. The Confederacy, in contrast, "is founded upon exactly the opposite idea; its foundations are laid, its cornerstone rests, upon the great truth that the negro is not equal to the white man; that slavery, subordination to the superior race, is his natural and normal condition. This, our new Government, is the first, in the history of the world, based on this great physical, philosophical, and moral truth."[3]

After the war, however, Davis and Stephens changed their tune. By the time they wrote their histories of the Confederacy, slavery was gone with the wind—a dead and discredited institution. To concede that the Confederacy had broken up the United States and launched a war that killed 620,000 Americans in a vain attempt to keep four million people in slavery would not confer honor on their lost cause. Therefore they set to work to purge that cause of any association with human bondage. In their postwar view, both Davis and Stephens hewed to the same line: Southern states seceded not to protect slavery but to vindicate state sovereignty. The South, Davis insisted, fought solely for "the inalienable right of a people to change their government . . . to withdraw from a Union into which they had, as sovereign communities, voluntarily entered." The "existence of African servitude," he maintained, "was in no wise the cause of the conflict, but only an incident." Stephens likewise insisted that "Slavery, so called, was but *the question* on which these antagonistic principles . . . of Federation, on the one side, and Centralism, or Consolidation, on the other . . . were finally brought into . . . collision with each other on the field of battle."[4]

Over the years since the war, many Southern whites have preferred to cite Davis's and Stephens's post-1865 writings rather than their claims of 1861. When Ken and Ric Burns's popular PBS video documentary on the Civil War was first broadcast in 1990, it provoked a hostile response from Southerners who did not like the portrayal of their Confederate ancestors as having fought for slavery. "The cause of the war was secession," declared a spokesman for the Sons of Confederate Veterans, "and the cause of secession could have been any number of things. This overemphasis on the slavery issue really rankles us." Among the "any number of things" that caused secession, according to a descendant of a soldier who served in the 27th South Carolina Infantry, were "states rights, agrarianism . . . , aristocracy, and habits of mind including individualism, personalism toward God and man, provincialism, and romanticism"—anything but slavery.[5]

During the first half of the twentieth century the argument that slavery had little to do with the growing polarization between North and South that led to secession found a great deal of support among professional historians. The "Progressive school" dominated American historiography from the 1910s to the 1940s. This school posited a clash between interest groups and classes as the central theme of American history: industry vs. agriculture, capital vs. labor, railroads vs. farmers, manufacturers vs. consumers, and so on. The real issues of American politics revolved around the economic interests of these contesting groups: tariffs, taxes, banks and finance, land policies, subsidies to business or agriculture, and the like. American political history moved in an undeviating line from the clash between Jeffersonian Republicans and Hamiltonian Federalists in the 1790s to similar clashes between New Deal/Fair Deal Democrats and conservative Republicans in the 1930s and 1940s.

The Progressive school explained the causes of the Civil War within this general interpretive framework. The war transferred to the battlefield a long-running contest between plantation agriculture and industrializing capitalism in which the industrialists emerged triumphant. This was not primarily a conflict between North and South. "Merely by the accidents of climate, soil, and geography," wrote Charles A. Beard, doyen of the Progressive school, "was it a sectional struggle"—the accidental fact that plantation agriculture was located in the South and industry mainly in the North.[6] Nor was it a contest between slavery and freedom. Slavery just happened to be the labor system of plantation agriculture, as wage labor was the system of Northern industry. For some Progressive historians, neither system was significantly worse or better than the other—"wage slavery" was as exploitative as chattel bondage. In any case, they said, slavery was not a moral issue for anybody except a tiny number of abolitionists; the abolition of slavery was a mere incident of the destruction of the plantation order by the war. The *real* issues between the North and the South in antebellum politics were the tariff, government subsidies to transportation and manufacturing, public land sales, financial policies, and other types of economic questions on which industrial and planting interests had clashing viewpoints.

This interpretive synthesis, so powerful during the second quarter of the twentieth century, proved a godsend to a generation of mostly Southern-born historians who seized upon it as proof that slavery had little to do with the origins of the Confederacy. The Nashville Fugitives, an influential group of historians, novelists, and poets who gathered at Vanderbilt University and published the famous manifesto *I'll Take My Stand* in 1930, set the tone for the new Southern interpretation of the Civil War's causes. It was a blend of the old Confederate apologia voiced by Jefferson Davis and the new Progressive synthesis created by Charles Beard. The Confederacy fought not only for the constitutional principle of state's rights and self-government but also for the preservation of a stable, pastoral, agrarian civilization against the overbearing, acquisitive, aggressive ambitions of an urban-industrial Leviathan. The real issue that brought on the war was not slavery—this institution, wrote Frank Owsley, a Nashville Fugitive and one of the most influential historians of the South from the 1920s to the 1950s, "was part of the agrarian system, but only one element and not an essential one"—but rather such matters as the tariff, banks, subsidies to railroads, and similar questions in which the grasping industrialists of the North sought to advance their interests at the expense of Southern farmers and planters. Lincoln was elected in 1860 in the interest not of freedom over slavery but of railroads and factories over agriculture and the graces of a rural society. The result was the triumph of acquisitive, power-hungry Northern robber barons over the highest type of civilization America had ever known—the Old South.[7] It was no coincidence that this interpretation emerged during the same period that the novel and movie *Gone with the Wind* became the most popular literary and cinematic successes of all time; history and popular culture on this occasion marched hand in hand.

An offshoot of this interpretation of the Civil War's causes dominated the work of academic historians during the 1940s. This offshoot came to be called revisionism. The revisionists denied that sectional conflicts between North and South—whether such conflicts occurred over slavery, state's rights, industry vs. agriculture, or whatever—were genuinely divisive. The differences between North and South, wrote Avery Craven, one of the leading revisionists, were no greater than those existing at different times between East and West. The other giant of revisionism, James G. Randall, even suggested that they were no more irreconcilable than the differences between Chicago and downstate Illinois.[8]

Such disparities did not have to lead to war; they could have, and should have, been accommodated peacefully within the political system. The Civil War was not an irrepressible conflict, as earlier generations had called it, but a "repressible conflict," as Craven titled one of his books. The war was brought on not by genuine issues but by extremists on both sides—abolitionist fanatics and Southern fire-eaters—who whipped up emotions and hatreds in North and South for their own self-serving partisan purposes. The passions they stirred up got out of hand in 1861 and erupted into a tragic, unnecessary war, which achieved nothing that could not have been accomplished by negotiations and compromise.

Any such compromise in 1861, of course, would have left slavery in place. But the revisionists, like the Progressives and the Vanderbilt agrarians, considered slavery unimportant; as Craven once stated, the institution of bondage "played a rather minor part in the life of the South and the Negro."[9] It would have died peacefully of natural causes in another generation or two had not fanatics forced the issue to armed conflict. This argument hints at another feature of revisionism: While blaming extremists of both sides, revisionists focused most of their criticism on antislavery radicals, even antislavery moderates like Lincoln, who harped on the evils of slavery and expressed a determination to rein in what they called the Slave Power. Their rhetoric goaded the South into a defensive response that finally caused Southern states to secede to get free from the incessant pressure of these self-righteous Yankee zealots. Revisionism thus tended to portray Southern whites, even the fire-eaters, as victims reacting to Northern attacks; it truly was a "war of Northern aggression."

While one or more of these interpretations remain popular among the Sons of Confederate Veterans and other Southern heritage groups, few professional historians now subscribe to them. Of all these interpretations, the state's-rights argument is perhaps the weakest. It fails to ask the question, state's rights for what purpose? State's rights, or sovereignty, was always more a means than an end, an instrument to achieve a certain goal more than a principle. This truth was dramatically illustrated in the dispute over Florida ballots during the presidential election of 2000, when Republicans supposedly in favor of state's rights pressed their case in federal courts while Democrats looked to state courts. In the antebellum South, the purpose of asserting state sovereignty was to protect slavery from the potential hostility of a national majority against Southern interests—mainly slavery. "If Congress can make banks, roads, and canals under the Constitution," said Senator Nathaniel Macon of North Carolina in the 1820s, "they can free any slave in the United States."[10] John C. Calhoun, the South's leading political philosopher, formulated an elaborate constitutional structure of state's-rights theory to halt any use of federal power that might conceivably be construed at some future time as a precedent to act against slavery.

But even for Calhoun, state sovereignty was a fallback position. A more powerful instrument to protect slavery was control of the national government. Until 1861 Southern politicians did this remarkably well. They used that control to defend slavery from all kinds of threats and perceived threats. They overrode the rights of Northern states that passed personal liberty laws to protect black people from kidnapping by agents who claimed them as fugitive slaves. During forty-nine of the seventy-two years from 1789 to 1861, the presidents of the

United States were Southerners—all of them slaveholders. The only presidents to be reelected were slaveholders. Two-thirds of the Speakers of the House, chairmen of the House Ways and Means Committee, and presidents pro tem of the Senate were Southerners. At all times before 1861, a majority of Supreme Court justices were Southerners. This domination constituted what antislavery Republicans called the Slave Power and sometimes, more darkly, the Slave Power Conspiracy.

Historians have often dismissed such labels as another example of the "paranoid style" of American politics. But in an eye-opening book titled *The Slave Power: The Free North and Southern Domination, 1780–1860,* historian Leonard Richards demonstrates convincingly that there *was* a Slave Power. It had no need to function by conspiracy, however, for it could use the constitutional structure of government and the open operation of party politics to exert its domination.[11]

One constitutional source of the South's disproportionate political power was unintentional: the stipulation that each state would be represented by two senators. This provision had been adopted in order to win the support of small states—not slave states—for the Constitution. At the time of the Constitutional Convention, the respective populations of the states lying south of the Mason-Dixon line and those lying north of it were virtually equal, and many Southerners expected their section to grow faster than the North. As time passed, however, the opposite occurred. By 1850, when the number of free and slave states was equal at fifteen each, the free states contained 60 percent of the population and 70 percent of the voters but sent only 50 percent of the senators to Washington. And Southern senators had more than a veto power. Because they could count on several Northern allies, they could in effect deny a veto power to Northern senators on measures concerning slavery.

The South also had disproportionate strength in the House of Representatives. The "three-fifths compromise" adopted by the Constitutional Convention stipulated that three-fifths of the slaves were to be counted as part of a state's population for the purpose of determining the number of seats each state would have in the House. This provision gave slave states an average of twenty more congressmen after each census than they would have had on the basis of the free population alone. The combined effect of these two constitutional provisions also gave slave states about thirty more electoral votes than their share of the voting population would have entitled them to have.

Even more than these constitutional provisions, the functioning of party politics created a Slave Power. The dominant political party most of the time from 1800 to 1860 was the Democratic Republican Party under the Virginia dynasty of Thomas Jefferson and James Madison, which metamorphosed into the Democratic Party under the Tennesseean Andrew Jackson. Southerners controlled this party and used that leverage to control Congress and the presidency. In 1828 and 1832 Jackson won 70 percent of the popular vote for president in the slave states and only 50 percent in the free states. In 1856 the Democrat James Buchanan carried only five of sixteen free states, but his victory in fourteen of the fifteen slave states assured his election—and Southern domination of his administration. As an example of how such leverage could translate into a Slave Power, six of the eight Supreme Court justices appointed by Jackson and his handpicked successor were Southerners, including Chief Justice Roger B. Taney, author of the notorious Dred Scott decision and of other rulings that strengthened slavery.

As Richards makes clear, Southern politicians did not use this national power to buttress state's rights; quite the contrary. In the 1830s Congress imposed a gag rule to stifle antislavery petitions from Northern states. The Post Office banned antislavery literature from the mail if it was sent to Southern states. In 1850 Southerners in Congress plus a handful of Northern allies enacted a Fugitive Slave Law that was the strongest manifestation of *national* power thus far in American history. In the name of protecting the rights of slaveowners, it extended the long arm of federal law, enforced by marshals and the army, into Northern states to recover escaped slaves and return them to their owners.

Senator Jefferson Davis, who later insisted that the Confederacy fought for the principle of state sovereignty, voted with enthusiasm for the Fugitive Slave Law. When Northern legislatures invoked *their* states' rights against this federal law, the Supreme Court with its majority of Southern justices reaffirmed the supremacy of national law to protect slavery (*Ableman vs. Booth*, 1859). Many observers in the 1850s would have predicted that if a rebellion in the name of state's rights were to erupt, it would be the North that would rebel.

The presidential election of 1860 changed the equation. Without a single electoral vote from the South, Lincoln won the presidency on a platform of restricting the future expansion of slavery. "The great revolution has actually taken place," exulted Charles Francis Adams, the son and grandson of the only truly

"Northern" presidents the country had known. "The country has once and for all thrown off the domination of the Slaveholders."[12] Precisely. Slaveholders came to the same conclusion. Gone or going was the South's national power to protect slavery; now was the time to invoke state sovereignty and leave the Union.

The Progressive interpretation of the war's causes carries little more water than the state's-rights explanation. It is quite true, of course, that economic conflicts of interest took place between agrarian and industrial factions. These conflicts emerged in debates over tariffs, banks, land grants, and the like. But these matters divided *parties* (Whig vs. Democrat) and interest groups more than they divided North and South. The South in the 1840s and 1850s had its advocates of industrialization and protective tariffs and a national bank, just as the North had its millions of farmers and its low-tariff, antibank Democratic majority in many states. The Civil War was not fought over issues of the tariff or banks or agrarianism vs. industrialism. These and similar kinds of questions have been bread-and-butter issues of American politics throughout the nation's history, often generating a great deal more friction and heat than they did in the 1850s. But they have not caused any great shooting wars. Nor was the Civil War a consequence of false issues trumped up by demagogues or fanatics. It was fought over real, profound, intractable problems that Americans on both sides believed went to the heart of their society and its future.

In 1858 two prominent political leaders, one of whom expected to be elected president in 1860 and the other of whom *was* elected president, voiced the stark nature of the problem. The social systems of slave labor and free labor "are more than incongruous—they are incompatible," said Senator William H. Seward of New York. The friction between them "is an irrepressible conflict between opposing and enduring forces, and it means that the United States must and will, sooner or later, become either entirely a slaveholding nation, or entirely a free-labor nation."[13] In Illinois, senatorial candidate Abraham Lincoln launched his campaign with a theme taken from the Bible: "A house divided against itself cannot stand." The United States, he said, "cannot endure, permanently, half *slave* and half *free*. . . . It will become *all* one thing, or all the other." The policy of Lincoln's party (and Seward's) was to "arrest the further spread of [slavery], and place it where the public mind shall rest in the belief that it is in course of ultimate extinction."[14]

The slave and free states shared the same language, legal system, political culture, social mores, and religious values, as well as a common heritage of struggle to form the nation. The one institution they did not share was slavery.

Southerners agreed with Lincoln that it was this institution that created the house divided. "On the subject of slavery," declared the *Charleston Mercury* in 1858, "the North and South . . . are not only two Peoples, but they are rival, hostile Peoples." Anticipating Alexander Stephens's speech proclaiming slavery the "cornerstone" of the Confederacy, members of a South Carolina family that contributed four brothers to the Confederate army reacted to the news of Lincoln's election with a determination that "now a stand must be made for African slavery or it is forever lost." In going out of a Union ruled by Yankee abolitionists, "we . . . are contending for all that we hold dear—our Property—our Institutions—our Honor. . . . I hope it will end in establishing a Southern Confederacy who will have among themselves slavery, a bond of union stronger than any which holds the north together."[15]

In language echoed by other seceding states, the South Carolina secession convention justified its action on the ground that, when Lincoln became president, "the Slaveholding States will no longer have the power of self-government, or self-protection, and the Federal Government will have become their enemy." After fighting for two years, a cavalry lieutenant from Mississippi reaffirmed his belief that "this country without slave labor would be completely worthless. We can only live & exist by that species of labor; and hence I am willing to fight to the last."[16]

Slaves were the principal form of wealth in the South—indeed in the nation as a whole. The market value of the four million slaves in 1860 was close to $3 billion—more than the value of land, of cotton, or of anything else in the slave states, and more than the amount of capital invested in manufacturing and railroads combined for the whole United States. Slave labor made it possible for the American South to grow three-quarters of the world's marketed cotton, which in turn constituted more than half of all American exports in the antebellum era. But slavery was much more than an economic system. It was a means of maintaining racial control and white supremacy. Northern whites were also committed to white supremacy. But with 95 percent of the nation's black population living in the slave states, the region's scale of concern with this matter was so much greater as to create a radically different set of social priorities.

These priorities were bluntly expressed by the advocates of secession in the winter of 1860–61. That is the principal finding of one of the most important books on the secession movement to have appeared in recent years, *Apostles of Disunion,* by Charles B. Dew. Growing up in the South of the 1940s and 1950s,

Dew bought the state's-rights interpretation of Civil War causation lock, stock, and barrel. Ancestors on both sides of his family fought for the Confederacy. His much-loved grandmother was a member of the United Daughters of the Confederacy. In his dormitory room at a prep school in Virginia he proudly hung a Confederate flag. And he knew "that the South had seceded for one reason and one reason only: states' rights. . . . Anyone who thought differently was either deranged or a Yankee."[17]

Later, however, as a distinguished historian of the antebellum South and the Confederacy, Dew was "stunned" to discover that protection of slavery and white supremacy was the dominant theme in secession rhetoric. *Apostles of Disunion* is a study of the men appointed by seceding states as commissioners to visit other slave states to persuade them also to leave the Union and join together to form the Confederacy. "I found this in many ways a difficult and painful book to write," Dew acknowledges, but he nevertheless unflinchingly concludes that "to put it quite simply, slavery and race were absolutely critical elements in the coming of the war. . . . Defenders of the Lost Cause need only read the speeches and letters of the secession commissioners to learn what was really driving the Deep South to the brink of war in 1860–61."[18]

Some examples: "The conflict between slavery and non-slavery is a conflict for life and death," a South Carolina commissioner told Virginians in February 1861. "The South cannot exist without African slavery." Mississippi's commissioner to Maryland insisted that "slavery was ordained by God and sanctioned by humanity." If slave states remained in a Union ruled by Lincoln and his party, "the safety of the rights of the South will be entirely gone."[19] If these warnings were not sufficient to frighten hesitating Southerners into secession, commissioners played the race card. A Mississippi commissioner told Georgians that Republicans intended not only to abolish slavery but also to "substitute in its stead their new theory of the universal equality of the black and white races." Georgia's commissioner to Virginia dutifully assured his listeners that if Southern states stayed in the Union, "we will have black governors, black legislatures, black juries, black everything." An Alabamian born in Kentucky tried to persuade his native state to secede by portraying Lincoln's election as "nothing less than an open declaration of war" by Yankee fanatics who intended to force the "sons and daughters" of the South to associate "with free negroes upon terms of political and social equality," thus "consigning her [the South's] citizens to assassinations and her wives and daughters to pollution and violation to gratify the lust of half-civilized Africans."[20]

This superheated rhetoric was the culmination of more than thirty years of proslavery oratory. The centrality of slavery to "the Southern way of life" had long focused the region's politics on defense of the institution. Many Southern leaders in the age of Thomas Jefferson had considered slavery a "necessary evil" that would eventually disappear from this boasted land of liberty. But with the rise of the cotton kingdom, slavery became in the eyes of Southern whites by the 1830s a "positive good" for black and white alike. Proslavery pamphlets and books became a cottage industry. Their main themes were summed up in the title of a pamphlet by a clergyman published in 1850: *Defense of the South Against the Reproaches and Encroachments of the North: In Which Slavery Is Shown to Be an Institution of God Intended to Form the Basis of the Best Social State and the Only Safeguard and Permanence of a Republican Government*. The foremost defender of slavery until his death in 1850 was John C. Calhoun, who noted proudly that "many in the South once believed that slavery was a moral and political evil. That folly and delusion are gone. We see it now in its true light, and regard it as the most safe and stable basis for free institutions in the world" and "essential to the peace, safety, and prosperity" of the South.[21]

The defensive tone of much proslavery rhetoric was provoked by the rise of militant abolitionism in the North after 1830. William Lloyd Garrison, Theodore Weld, Wendell Phillips, Frederick Douglass, and a host of other crusaders branded slavery as a sin, a violation of God's law and of Christian ethics, immoral, inhumane, a defiance of the republican principle of liberty on which the nation had been founded. Although the abolitionists did not get far in the North with their message of racial equality, their argument that slavery was an obsolete and unrepublican institution—a "relic of barbarism," as the new Republican Party described it in its 1856 platform—entered mainstream Northern politics in the 1850s. "The monstrous injustice of slavery," said Abraham Lincoln in 1854, "deprives our republican example of its just influence in the world—enables the enemies of free institutions, with plausibility, to taunt us as hypocrites."[22]

It was not the *existence* of slavery that polarized the nation to the breaking point, however, but rather the issue of the *expansion of slave territory*. Most of the crises that threatened the bonds of union arose over this matter. The first one, in 1820, was settled by the Missouri Compromise, which balanced the admission of Missouri as a slave state with the admission of Maine as a free state and banned slavery in the rest of the Louisiana Purchase north of 36°30'. But once the expansion genie was out of the bottle it could not be put back in again. The debates over the annexation of Texas and the status of territories acquired from Mexico in the 1840s made the Missouri debates a generation earlier look like a love feast.

Revisionist historians described the controversy over slavery in such territories as Kansas and New Mexico as a pernicious abstraction—a quarrel over "an imaginary Negro in an impossible place." It was anything but that. Between 1803 and 1845 the United States nearly tripled in size with the Louisiana Purchase, the acquisition of Florida, and the annexation of Texas. Thomas Jefferson, who began this process, expected the new lands to become an "Empire for Liberty." But every state that came into the Union by 1845 from these territories was a slave state: Louisiana, Missouri, Arkansas, Florida, and Texas plus the southern portions of Alabama and Mississippi. The acquisition of California and the Southwest from Mexico in 1848 opened a vast new region to American settlement and provoked corrosive debates over slavery there and in the Louisiana Purchase territories where slavery was made possible by the Kansas-Nebraska Act of 1854. While slavery seemed unlikely to take root in Nebraska or Oregon, it did exist for a few years in the territories of Kansas, New Mexico, and Utah and in Indian Territory (most of present-day Oklahoma). And one reason for die-hard Southern opposition to the admission of California as a free state in 1850 was a conviction that slavery could flourish in the mines and agriculture of that region.

A key to understanding the urgency of the territorial debate in the 1850s is a recognition that it concerned not only the boundaries of the existing United States but also potential future acquisitions. Many Americans in 1850 had seen the size of the country quadruple in their own lifetimes. There was little reason for them to expect this process to stop. The most likely direction for future expansion was to the south. Southern Democrats pressed for the annexation of Cuba in the 1850s. If they had succeeded, another 400,000 slaves would have entered the Union. Southern adventurers also invaded Nicaragua and northern Mexico in efforts to add these regions to the United States. In 1856 the Tennessee native William Walker proclaimed himself president of Nicaragua and issued a decree reestablishing slavery there before he was overthrown and driven out. Although none of these schemes succeeded, they exacerbated the slavery controversy more than most historians have recognized.

Convinced that the Slave Power in Washington had engineered the annexation of Texas and the Mexican War, the antislavery bloc in Congress determined to flex its muscles. In 1846 David Wilmot of Pennsylvania introduced in the House a resolution banning slavery in all territory that might be conquered from Mexico. By an almost unanimous vote of all Northern congressmen against virtually unanimous opposition from Southern representatives, the resolution passed. Equal representation in the Senate enabled Southerners to block the Wilmot Proviso there. But this issue framed national politics for the next fifteen years.

The most ominous feature of the Wilmot Proviso was its wrenching of the normal pattern of party divisions into a sectional pattern. On most issues before 1846—such as tariffs and a national bank—Northern and Southern Whigs had voted on the same side and Democrats from both sections on the other. On the Wilmot Proviso, however, Northern Whigs and Democrats voted together against a solid alliance of Southern Whigs and Democrats. This became the norm for all votes on any issue concerning slavery—and most of the important national political issues in the 1850s did concern slavery. This sectional alignment in politics reflected a similar pattern in social and cultural matters. In the 1840s the two largest religious denominations, the Methodists and the Baptists, had split into separate Northern and Southern churches over whether a slaveowner could be appointed a bishop or missionary of the denominations.

In 1850 the people living in states that had once been territories but had come into the Union as states since 1790 accounted for more than half of the nation's increase in population. As that process continued, the new territories would shape the future. To ensure a free-labor destiny, antislavery Northerners wanted to keep slavery out of these territories. The Free Soil Party was founded on this platform in 1848. Six years later it evolved into the Republican Party. "We are opposed to the extension of slavery," declared a Free Soil newspaper, because if slavery goes into a new territory "the free labor of the states will not. . . . If the free labor of the states goes there, the slave labor of the Southern states will not, and in a few years the country will teem with an active and energetic population."[23] Eventually the expansion of free territory would make freedom the wave of the future, placing slavery "in course of ultimate extinction," as Lincoln phrased it.

That was just what Southerners feared. The North already had a majority in the House; new free states would give it a majority in the Senate as well as an unchallengeable domination of the electoral college. "Long before the North gets this vast accession of strength," warned a South Carolinian, "she will ride over us rough shod, proclaim freedom or something equivalent to it to our Slaves and reduce us to the condition of Haiti. . . . If we do not act now, we deliberately consign our children, not our posterity, but *our children* to the flames."[24]

This argument appealed as powerfully to nonslaveholders as to slaveholders. Whites of both classes considered the bondage of blacks to be the basis of liberty for whites. Slavery, they declared, elevated all whites to an equality of status by confining menial labor and caste subordination to blacks. "If slaves are freed," maintained proslavery spokesmen, whites "will become menials. We will lose every right and liberty which belongs to the name of freemen."[25] The Northern threat to slavery thus menaced all whites. Nonslaveholders also agreed with slaveholders that the institution must be allowed to go into the territories. Such expansion might increase their own chances of becoming slaveholders.

In another respect that may seem an abstraction today but was very real to antebellum Southern white men, slavery in the territories was a vital issue. For Northerners like Abraham Lincoln to brand slavery a "monstrous injustice" and "unqualified evil" that should be excluded from the territories was to insult Southerners by damning their "peculiar institution" as immoral and unworthy. This impugned their honor, and as Bertram Wyatt-Brown has shown, honor was the central value in white male culture. For them it was not merely the symbol of their manhood and reputation; it was the essence.[26]

To say that a slaveholder could not carry his property to the territories was, according to an Alabama editor, to say "that a free citizen of Massachusetts was a better man and entitled to more privileges than a free citizen of Alabama." Supreme Court Justice Peter Daniel, a Virginian, resented this "insulting exclusiveness . . . which says in effect to the Southern man, Avaunt! You are not my equal, and hence are to be excluded as carrying a moral taint."[27] Such an insult could not be tolerated by men of honor: "Death is preferable to acknowledged inferiority."[28] When Lincoln was elected president by exclusively Northern votes, Southerners, as one newspaper editorial put it, considered the outcome "a deliberate, cold-blooded insult and outrage" that must be replied to by the challenge of secession. "No other 'overt act' can so imperatively demand resistance on our part," declared a North Carolina congressman, "as the simple election of their candidate."[29]

The resistance he had in mind—secession—did not necessarily mean war. When the previously quoted spokesman for the Sons of Confederate Veterans said that "the cause of the war was secession, and the cause of secession could have been any number of things," he was half right and half wrong. The cause of secession was one specific thing: the Southern response to the election of a president and party they feared as a threat to slavery. The cause of the war was indeed secession, but it did not make war inevitable. A series of decisions and actions by men on both sides brought on the war.

The incoming Lincoln administration could have repudiated the platform on which it was elected and granted Southern states every concession they demanded. Or Lincoln could have "let the erring sisters depart in peace," as some in the North advised. But Lincoln and most of the Northern people were not willing to accept the nation's dismemberment. They feared that toleration of disunion in 1861 would create a fatal precedent to be invoked by disaffected minorities in the future, perhaps by the losing side in another presidential election, until the United States dissolved into a dozen petty, squabbling, hostile autocracies. The great experiment in republican government launched in 1776 would collapse, proving the contention of European monarchists and aristocrats that this upstart republic across the Atlantic could not last. "The doctrine of secession is anarchy," declared a Cincinnati newspaper in an editorial echoed across the North. "If the minority have the right to break up the Government at pleasure, because they have not had their way, there is an end of all government."[30]

Even lame-duck President James Buchanan, in his last message to Congress in December 1860, said that the Union was not "a mere voluntary association of States, to be dissolved at pleasure." The founders of the nation "never intended to implant in its bosom the seeds of its own destruction, nor were they guilty of the absurdity of providing for its own dissolution." If secession was legitimate, said Buchanan, the Union became a "rope of sand. . . . The hopes of the friends of freedom throughout the world would be destroyed. . . . Our example for more than eighty years would not only be lost, but it would be quoted as conclusive proof that man is unfit for self-government."[31]

No one held these convictions more strongly than Abraham Lincoln. "Perpetuity . . . is the fundamental law of all national governments," he declared in his inaugural address on March 4, 1861. "No State, upon its own mere motion, can lawfully get out of the Union." Two months later Lincoln told his private secretary that "the central idea pervading this struggle is the necessity that is upon us, of proving that popular government is not an absurdity. We must settle this question now, whether in a free government the minority have the right to break up the government whenever they choose. If we fail it will go far to prove the incapability of the people to govern themselves."[32]

But even this refusal to countenance the legitimacy of secession did not make war inevitable. Moderates on both sides sought a compromise formula. Nothing could stay the course of secession in the seven Lower South states, but the other eight slave states were still in the Union when Lincoln took the oath of office on March 4, 1861. He hoped to keep them there by assurances that he had no right or intention to interfere with slavery in the states and by refraining from hostile action against the Confederate states, even though they had seized all federal property and arms within their borders—except Fort Sumter and three less important forts. By a policy of watchful waiting, of maintaining the status quo, Lincoln hoped to allow passions to cool and enable Unionists to regain influence in the Lower South. But this hope was doomed. Genuine Unionists had all but disappeared in the Lower South. And Fort Sumter became a flash point of contention.

A large brick fortress on an artificial granite island at the entrance to Charleston Bay, Fort Sumter could not be seized by the Confederates as easily as other federal property had been, even though it was defended by only some eighty-odd soldiers. Lincoln came under great pressure from conservatives and Upper South Unionists to yield the fort as a gesture of peace and goodwill that might strengthen Southern Unionism. After leaning in this direction for a time, Lincoln concluded that to give up Sumter would do the opposite; it would demoralize Unionists and strengthen the Confederacy. Fort Sumter had become the master symbol of sovereignty. To yield it would constitute de facto recognition of Confederate sovereignty. It would probably encourage European nations to grant diplomatic recognition to the Confederate nation. It would make a mockery of the national government's profession of constitutional authority over its own property.

The day after his inauguration, however, Lincoln learned that Sumter's garrison would run out of supplies in six weeks or less. The only alternative to surrender seemed to be to send warships to shoot their way into the bay to resupply and reinforce the tiny garrison. But such an apparent act of aggression would divide the North and provoke several more slave states to secede. During a month of indecision in which Lincoln was pushed this way and that by conflicting pressures in this greatest crisis of American history, a third alternative took shape in his mind. He devised an ingenious plan to put the burden of decision for war or peace on Jefferson Davis's shoulders. Giving advance notice of his intentions, Lincoln sent a fleet toward Charleston with supplies and reinforcements. If the Confederates allowed unarmed boats to bring in "food for hungry men," the warships would stand off and the reinforcements would return north. But if Southern artillery fired on the fleet, the ships and fort would fire back. In effect, Lincoln flipped a coin and told Davis: "Heads I win; tails you lose." If Southern guns fired first, the Confederates would stand convicted of starting a war. If they let the supplies go in, the American flag would continue to fly over Fort Sumter. The Confederacy would lose face; Unionists would take courage.

Davis did not hesitate. He considered it vital to assert the Confederacy's sovereignty. He also hoped that the outbreak of a shooting war would force the states of the Upper South to join their fellow slave states. Davis ordered Brigadier General Pierre G. T. Beauregard, commander of Confederate troops at Charleston, to open fire on Fort Sumter before the supply ships got there. At 4:30 A.M. on April 12, Confederate guns opened fire. After a thirty-three-hour bombardment in which the Confederates fired four thousand rounds and the skeleton crew in the fort replied with a thousand, the burning fort lowered the American flag in surrender. And the war came.

# 2

# Escape and Revolt in Black and White

AMONG THE BITTER CONFLICTS that divided North and South and led to war in 1861 were those associated with escaping slaves and Southern attempts to recapture them, which produced the Fugitive Slave Law in 1850. Resistance to capture by fugitives, sometimes aided by Northerners, fanned the flames of Southern anger. In their ordinances of secession, several Southern states cited Northern help to fugitives as one of the grievances that provoked them to leave the Union. The Fugitive Slave Law inspired Harriet Beecher Stowe to write *Uncle Tom's Cabin.* The episode of Eliza escaping with her son across the Ohio River on ice floes to prevent his capture by slavecatchers is one of the most unforgettable images in American letters. And a real-life escaped slave became one of the most famous heroines in American history.

Surveys of freshmen at the State University of New York in Buffalo who registered for the introductory U.S. history course in the 1970s and 1980s revealed that more of them knew of Harriet Tubman than of any other woman who lived before 1900 except Betsy Ross. Tubman also ranked higher on this recognition scale than Thomas Edison, Benjamin Franklin, Patrick Henry, and a host of other prominent persons.[1]

Like Betsy Ross, Tubman had achieved mythical stature because of her conspicuous place in school textbooks and in children's stories about great Americans. The legendary "Moses" of her people, who escaped from slavery in 1849 and returned to Maryland again and again to lead many more slaves to freedom, she also served as a scout during the Civil War and led Union soldiers on raids into the South Carolina interior to liberate hundreds more slaves. For children black and white, Hispanic and Indian, immigrant and native-born, these stories of risk and adventure propelled Tubman ahead of Davy Crockett and Nathan Hale and put her right up there with Meriwether Lewis and William Clark.

It was not always that way. For decades after her death in 1913 at the probable age of ninety (her exact birth date is unknown), Tubman languished in obscurity. In the 1930s the labor activist Earl Conrad (Earl Cohen) decided to write a biography of Tubman. "I looked over the various Negro figures," Conrad explained, "and I came to the conclusion that Harriet was the greatest and the one about whom, for her stature, the least was known. I believed that through presenting Harriet I could show also the contributions of the Negro people."[2] But Conrad could not interest any mainstream publisher in his biography. The black-owned Associated Publishers in Washington finally brought out his *General Harriet Tubman* in 1943. With few reviews and not many more buyers, the book soon went out of print.

Since 1960, however, the greater visibility of black activists and of women in American history has launched a veritable Tubman boom. Conrad's biography was reprinted in 1990. Within a few months of each other, three new biographies were published in 2003–4.[3] At least fifty-four children's and young people's fiction and nonfiction titles about Tubman have appeared in print: six in the 1960s, five in the next decade, six again in the 1980s, twenty-one in the 1990s, and another sixteen from 2000 to 2003. Millions of schoolchildren have watched the educational movie *Freedom Train* and other dramas based on Tubman's life. Dozens of public schools around the country bear her name. She is enshrined in impressive monuments in Boston and in Battle Creek, Michigan. In Canada (where Tubman lived for a time in the 1850s), York University recently opened a digitized Harriet Tubman Resource Centre on the African Diaspora.[4]

Tubman's home in Auburn, New York, where she lived most of her life in freedom, has become a popular tourist site. An annual celebration takes place there on Memorial Day weekend, when high school girls compete for the title of "Miss Harriet Tubman"—an event that would have amused the real Tubman. She would also have been surprised to find herself at the center of a controversy over the National History Standards released in 1994. These standards were attacked as "revisionist" by Lynne Cheney, then the head of the National Endowment for the Humanities, because—among other reasons—they gave equal attention to Harriet Tubman and George Washington. "Overnight, Tubman's name became a 'hot-button' for conservative critics," Catherine Clinton writes in her biography, "and she became a symbolic 'whipping girl' for political correctness."[5]

Little wonder that Tubman had greater name recognition among students at SUNY Buffalo than Francis Scott Key, Thomas Paine, Harriet Beecher

Stowe, and Nathaniel Hawthorne. Yet until the publication of the three biographies by professional scholars in 2003–4, much of what we "knew" about Tubman was encased in myth. Each of these books has particular strengths that complement the others' and add up to a remarkable collective achievement. The most readable and the one that provides the clearest context of slavery and the Civil War is Catherine Clinton's *Harriet Tubman: The Road to Freedom.* The most fully researched study of the details of Tubman's life is Kate Clifford Larson's *Bound for the Promised Land.* And the best account of how Tubman shaped her own image through the autobiographical stories she told her contemporaries is Jean M. Humez's *Harriet Tubman: The Life and the Life Stories,* which reprints much of the documentary evidence on which any biography must be based.

That evidence consists mainly of anecdotes told by Harriet to her earliest biographers, who wrote them down in brief connected narratives published in 1863 and 1865 and a full-length book in 1869. The author of the last, *Scenes from the Life of Harriet Tubman,* was Sarah Bradford, who also collected reminiscences from people who knew Tubman. She twice updated and expanded this work, in 1886 and 1901, both editions carrying the title *Harriet Tubman: The Moses of Her People.*

Missing from sources for Tubman's life are the letters, diaries, and other written accounts in one's own words that form the usual core of evidence for a biography. She remained illiterate all her life, so anything written down as having been said by her was mediated by others. Only four letters from Tubman are known to have survived, and those were dictated to and written by white friends. Many of the incidents of her life as a slave, as a fugitive escaping to freedom, and as the "Moses" who led others out of bondage are derived from her own testimony and often impossible to corroborate from other sources. Problems of evidence present formidable obstacles to biographers intent on sifting reality from myth. All three modern biographies cited here were written by careful scholars with high standards. Even so, there are puzzling anomalies in the story of Tubman's life.

Among these are accounts of young Harriet's physical strength and endurance and of the serious injury she suffered at age thirteen or fourteen. Born a slave on Maryland's Eastern Shore, Harriet was hired out by her owner as early as age five for household chores and child-tending in the homes of other whites. Rebellious even then, she was sometimes starved, abused, or beaten for minor infractions. When she was twelve or thirteen she was sent to work in the fields. A year or two later she sustained a life-threatening head wound when an enraged overseer threw a heavy iron object at an escaping male slave and hit Harriet instead. She recovered, but for the rest of her days she suffered from what her biographers variously term "temporal lobe epilepsy" or "narcolepsy" or possibly "cataplexy." No physician was available to diagnose her malady, and even if one had been available he might not have known what to call it.

Whatever the medical term for her condition, all observers agreed on its symptoms: For the rest of her life Harriet would periodically lose consciousness and appear to fall asleep, sometimes for a minute or two, sometimes longer, and then awaken to carry on as if nothing had happened. Thirty years after the incident had occurred, a friend reported that the injury "still makes her very lethargic. She cannot remain quiet fifteen minutes without appearing to fall asleep. It is not a refreshing slumber, but a heavy, weary condition which exhausts her." During these seizures she often experienced dreams or visions, even hallucinations, sometimes with powerful religious overtones. More than once she said that God had spoken to her.[6]

This injury and the seizures, as well as Harriet's small stature, seem inconsistent with the portrayal by all biographers of her strength and "awesome stamina." She was only five feet tall and probably weighed no more than one hundred pounds. Yet in her later teens and early twenties she worked in a logging camp, in the fields, and in a grist mill loading "huge barrels" of flour onto boats or carts, "drove oxen, carted, and plowed and did all the work of a man," and "would often exhibit her feats of strength to her master's friends."[7] Somehow these accounts of Tubman's physical activities do not seem to add up. Perhaps the inconsistencies can be reconciled, but her biographers do not try to reconcile them or even to recognize that they exist.

Similar questions can be raised about Tubman's remarkable exploits as "Moses." Her own escape in 1849 was aided by what was known as the Underground Railroad, a network of safe houses and free blacks and sympathetic whites (mostly Quakers) in Maryland and Delaware. Traveling at night on foot or hidden in a wagon driven by one of the "conductors" of this metaphorical railroad, hiding during the day in the woods or at one of the "stations," Harriet made her way to Wilmington and then on to free soil in Philadelphia. Hundreds of other slaves followed the same route to freedom—some of them with her help. This trip of more than a hundred miles, usually in winter when the nights were long and hostile whites were less likely to be abroad, required strength, courage, endurance, and adroitness.

But what about her narcoleptic seizures or sudden lapses into unconsciousness? Clinton acknowledges that these "chronic and deep intermittent spells . . . horrified those entrusted to her" during her repeated returns south to bring out more fugitives. Neither Clinton nor the other biographers resolve the seeming paradox of a small woman subject to seizures accomplishing such daring and dangerous feats except to state that the seizures "enhanced her reputation as mystical." Perhaps so, but that seems inadequate as an explanation.[8]

There is no question that Tubman had striking results. The testimony and the records kept by Thomas Garrett, a Quaker merchant in Wilmington who was one of the most prominent "agents" of the Underground Railroad, and by William Still, a black businessman in Philadelphia, who had charge of that station on the "Liberty Line," leave no doubt of Tubman's achievements. But the claim that she led three hundred slaves to freedom is a considerable exaggeration. That number was apparently plucked out of thin air by Sarah Bradford, who included it in her 1869 biography, and it has been cited ever since. The actual number fell somewhere between the fifty-seven documented by Humez, who collated Tubman's own accounts with the few corroborating sources, and the seventy to eighty estimated by Larson from a more expansive reading of the same sources. Tubman made either ten (Humez) or thirteen (Larson) return trips to Maryland for this purpose.[9]

Many of the fugitives she conducted north were her relatives. Tubman had a strong sense of family. During her childhood two sisters were sold to buyers in states farther south. The trauma of that separation affected her deeply. When her owner died in 1849 and rumors spread that the family might be broken up and sold individually to various destinations, Harriet decided to escape. She initially persuaded two brothers to go with her, but they got cold feet and backed out, leaving her to go alone. In 1844 Harriet had married John Tubman, a free black man; in 1851 she returned a third time to Maryland in an attempt to convince him to come north with her but discovered that he had taken another wife. Nevertheless, she returned to the same neighborhood several more times to bring out relatives (including her elderly parents, who by then were free), some of them infants who had to be drugged with laudanum to keep them quiet.

How could she have gotten away with it? The slaveowners in Dorchester County, Maryland, were not complete dunces; they must have noticed a suspicious pattern. Tubman made nearly all her return trips to Maryland after passage of the draconian Fugitive Slave Law of 1850, which was designed to facilitate

the recapture of fugitives in *free* states—never mind the slave states. Thousands
of black people fled to Canada after 1850 for fear of recapture or kidnapping.
The apprehensions of several fugitives in the North and their rendition to slavery
were broadly publicized. So was the escape of several others with the defiant help
of both black and white abolitionists. The Underground Railroad now stretched
all the way to Canada, where Tubman conducted several of the fugitives she had
brought out of Maryland. She herself settled in St. Catharines, Ontario (near Niagara Falls), for a time, but she returned frequently to the United States and traveled through the Northeast raising money to finance her trips to Maryland. In
1858 the prominent Republican politician William H. Seward sold her a small
house and seven acres of land in Auburn, New York, where she lived most of the
rest of her life.

Somehow Tubman was never caught, in either the North or the South. Rumors of a reward for her capture circulated through antislavery circles. The
abolitionist Thomas Wentworth Higginson reported in 1859 that a reward of
$12,000 had been posted in Maryland for her capture. Harriet herself men-
tioned a $10,000 reward on one occasion. By 1867 a white abolitionist inflated
this figure in retrospect to $40,000, which like the three hundred slaves Tub-
man supposedly led to freedom became a frequently cited "fact." That amount
would be equivalent to about a million dollars today. Even the smaller reported
rewards would be equivalent to a quarter-million current dollars. The bounty
hunters who pursued fugitives through the North for the prospect of a hundred dollars or two would almost surely have run down the well-known Tubman if there had been any such reward. After careful research, Kate Larson
concludes that "a reward notice for Tubman's capture has yet to be found."[10]

Whatever the truth about a reward, Tubman's ability to travel in the North
of the 1850s, not to mention the slave states of Maryland and Delaware, cries
out for explanation. On this matter it is instructive to turn to the biography
of another Harriet—Harriet Jacobs.[11] If Tubman's experience illustrates the
physical abuse of slaves and the cruelty of family separation, Jacobs's story illustrates the sexual exploitation of bondswomen. A mulatto slave born in
Edenton, North Carolina, in 1813, Jacobs had an easier childhood than Tubman. Her indulgent mistress taught her to read, but when Harriet was twelve
the mistress died. Willed to a child niece, whose father was a local physician
and a notorious lecher, Harriet became the resisting victim of his sexual appetites when she reached puberty. In desperation she threw herself into the
white arms of a prominent local bachelor lawyer (later a congressman) of

whom she may have been genuinely fond and by whom she had two children. They of course became the legal property of the hated father of her owner. He once again threatened to make Harriet his concubine.

This time she fled, and hid out for almost seven years in the attic of her grandmother, a free Negro, before escaping to the North. Her former lover bought his children but did not immediately free them. They too eventually came north, where all three lived a precarious existence and Harriet was constantly threatened with recapture by her former child owner, now an adult, and her owner's still-vengeful father, the lecherous physician. Jacobs and her children were forced to move from place to place in the North and sometimes to go into hiding. Jacobs worked as a seamstress, governess, and maid for a well-to-do New York family, which bought her freedom in 1853. Her almost-white children had finally been emancipated by their father, so the family could thenceforth live a life free from the fear of reenslavement.

Jacobs decided to follow the example of several other fugitive slaves (nearly all of them men) and write her autobiography. It was published in January 1861 under the pseudonym of Linda Brent with the title *Incidents in the Life of a Slave Girl*. Some contemporaries considered it a novel; others believed it to have been ghostwritten by the white abolitionist Lydia Maria Child, an opinion shared by a number of historians. Through years of research and historical detective work, however, Jean Fagan Yellin discovered not only that Jacobs wrote it herself—with editorial assistance from Child, to be sure—but also that all the events described by Jacobs are corroborated by other evidence. Unlike Harriet Tubman, Harriet Jacobs left a substantial trail of letters and other documents that enabled Yellin to reconstruct the life of an extraordinary woman.

Jacobs's vulnerability to recapture until her Northern employer purchased her freedom raises again the question of how Harriet Tubman, who was more prominent than Jacobs and traveled in the North more openly, was able to escape the bounty hunters. And how could she have returned to the same neighborhood in Maryland so many times? According to Tubman herself, on three occasions she narrowly avoided identification in Maryland by her owner or other whites who knew her. Once she happened to be carrying a newspaper, which she pretended to read. Since her master knew her to be illiterate, he did not look more closely. Another time she was carrying live chickens when she spotted someone who knew her. She dropped the birds and made a big fuss over chasing them down, thereby hiding her face. She said that on another occasion she remained unidentified because, having lived in the North and no longer working in the fields, she had become a shade or two lighter in color. Since several Northern acquaintances described her as "coal black," however, this story seems dubious—and the others not much less so.

Most often, when asked how she could lead frightened fugitives through a hundred miles of slave territory, overcoming fatigue and her own physical infirmity, eluding pursuers and battling inclement weather, she simply answered: "It wasn't me, it was the Lord! I always told him, 'I trust to you. I don't know where to go or what to do, but I expect you to lead me,' and he always did."[12] With no other answers forthcoming, perhaps this one is as good as any.

Tubman lived for half a century after the Emancipation Proclamation, and Jacobs died in her eighty-fourth year, in 1897. These postwar decades seemed anticlimactic for both women. During the Civil War, Jacobs and her daughter worked at a relief center and founded a school for freed slaves in Alexandria, Virginia. Tubman spent part of the war on the South Carolina Sea Islands (between Charleston and Savannah) that were liberated by Union forces in November 1861. She worked as a nurse for black soldiers and as a scout behind enemy lines. Using the skills she had honed in her days as the Moses of fugitive slaves, in June 1863 she guided a raid by three hundred black soldiers up the Combahee River on the South Carolina mainland that destroyed Confederate resources and brought out 750 slaves. A month later, Tubman helped care for wounded men of the 54th Massachusetts Infantry under Colonel Robert Gould Shaw after their assault on Fort Wagner. Although she did not make it into the movie *Glory* about that event, she provided perhaps the most poetic description of it: "And then we saw the lightning, and that was the guns; and then we heard the thunder, and that was the big guns; and then we heard the rain falling, and that was the drops of blood falling; and then we came to get in the crops, it was dead men that we reaped."[13]

Tubman never received regular payments or a pension for her wartime service, despite the support of several army officers and of Secretary of State Seward, who testified to the value of her contributions to the Union war effort. Her quest was tangled in the War Department bureaucracy, which had no record of her employment by the army. After the war a black Union veteran named Nelson Davis boarded at Tubman's house in Auburn. Although he was more than twenty years younger than Harriet, they married in 1869. Davis died of tuberculosis in 1888; the same bureaucracy delayed Harriet's efforts to obtain a widow's pension because Davis had enlisted under the name of Nelson Charles. With help, Harriet finally obtained a pension of eight dollars per month starting in 1892. Her congressman got it increased in 1897 to twenty dollars per month (about $650 in today's money), all the recognition she ever received for her wartime services.

During these years, Tubman took many aged and infirm black people into her Auburn home, supporting them with contributions from numerous white and black friends. In 1908, with financial aid from the African Methodist Episcopal Zion Church, she was able to realize her dream of building a Harriet Tubman Home on adjoining property that she had acquired. Tubman lived out her remaining days in the very institution she founded.

HARRIET TUBMAN MET the notorious white abolitionist John Brown in Canada in 1858. He nicknamed her "General" Tubman because of her command skills in leading fugitives to freedom. Brown outlined to her his plans to foment a slave uprising to overthrow the hated institution of bondage, and asked her help. Until then, writes Catherine Clinton, "Tubman had never been associated with any kind of insurrectionary plots (except for mass escapes), but was clearly ready to shift gears." Had she not fallen ill in the autumn of 1859, she might have accompanied Brown on his Harpers Ferry raid.[14] If she had done so, perhaps she would have added martyrdom to her legend as the Moses of her people.

As Brown was led to the gallows in Charles Town, Virginia, on December 2, 1859, he handed his guard a note: "I John Brown am now quite *certain* that the crimes of this *guilty, land: will* never be purged *away;* but with Blood. I had *as I now think: vainly* flattered myself that without *verry much* bloodshed; it might be done."[15]

This prophecy proved to be more accurate than even Brown could have imagined. Six years later slavery was abolished and four million slaves went free—at the cost in blood of more than 620,000 soldiers who lost their lives in the American Civil War. The act for which Brown and sixteen of his followers, including two of his sons, paid with their lives—an attack on the federal arsenal at Harpers Ferry, Virginia—did much to bring on that war. Was Brown a terrorist who killed innocent victims or a hero-martyr who struck a mighty blow against the accursed institution of slavery? His body has lain a-moldering in its grave for almost 150 years, yet there is today no more consensus on the answers to these questions than in 1859.

John Brown lived the first fifty-five years of his life in relative obscurity. Born in Connecticut in 1800, he grew up in the Western Reserve of northeast

Ohio, a center of antislavery sentiment. His abolitionist father owned a tannery, and young John followed him into that occupation. He also emulated his father in the matter of siring children. Owen Brown had sixteen by two wives, while John Brown fathered twenty children by two wives (the first died in childbirth), of whom eleven lived to adulthood. Although initially successful as a tanner and subsequently as a wool merchant, John Brown lost heavily as a land speculator in the panic of 1837 and subsequently failed in the wool business as well.

According to family tradition, Brown pledged his life to fighting African American bondage after a proslavery mob murdered the abolitionist Elijah Lovejoy in Illinois in 1837. As early as the 1840s Brown began to evolve a plan to lead a raiding party into the Virginia mountains. There he hoped to attract slaves from lowland plantations to his banner and arm them to defend the mountain passes against counterattacks. With his mobile "army" of freed slaves he would move south along the Appalachians, inspiring slaves to escape until the whole execrable system of bondage collapsed.

Brown discussed this plan with Frederick Douglass as well as Harriet Tubman and other black leaders, who admired his determination if not his sagacity. Brown was unusual for his time in his ability to rise above race prejudice and mix with blacks as equals. In 1849 he moved to a farm at North Elba near Lake Placid in the Adirondacks, where the wealthy abolitionist Gerrit Smith had donated thousands of acres to black farmers to create an exemplary interracial rural community. Brown settled part of his family there and became a sort of white patriarch of the settlement, which struggled in vain to achieve prosperity in that land of poor soil and a short growing season.

Brown himself rarely stayed home in North Elba. He spent much of his time winding up his bankrupt wool business and arranging for escaped slaves to go to Canada. In 1854 a new occupation presented itself when Congress passed the Kansas-Nebraska Act repealing the earlier prohibition of slavery in that portion of the Louisiana Purchase north of 36°30'. A product of the growing national power of proslavery Southern Democrats, this legislation set off a violent conflict between proslavery and antislavery settlers in Kansas Territory. In 1855 Brown joined six of his sons and one son-in-law who had taken up claims near Osawatomie, just fifteen miles west of the Missouri border. Brown became captain of a militia company formed to defend free-soil settlers from proslavery "border ruffians" who regularly attacked across the state line from Missouri. In May 1856 Brown's company was on its way to defend the town of

Lawrence when they learned that the border ruffians had burned the town. Next day they also learned of the brutal caning of Massachusetts's antislavery senator Charles Sumner on the floor of the Senate by South Carolina representative Preston Brooks.

For Brown these events were the last straw. He was a strict Calvinist who believed in a God of wrath and justice. In appearance and character he was an Old Testament warrior prophet transplanted to the nineteenth century. He considered himself God's predestined instrument to strike a blow for freedom. "We must show by actual work," he said, "that there are two sides to this thing and that they [proslavery forces] cannot go on with impunity." He told his company to prepare for a "radical retaliatory measure." When one of them advised caution, Brown exploded: "Caution, caution, sir. I am eternally tired of hearing that word caution. It is nothing but the word of cowardice."[16] The next night Brown led four of his sons and two other men to carry out their retaliatory measure for the earlier murders of five free-soil settlers. Brown's party seized five men—who were proslavery activists but had not participated in the murders—from their homes along Pottawatomie Creek and split open their skulls with broadswords.

This shocking massacre went unpunished by legal process. Indeed, Brown's connection with it was unproven until years later. But most Kansans were confident they knew who had done it. Guerrilla warfare raged along the border for months, during which scores of men were killed, including one of Brown's sons.

The Kansas wars distracted Brown from his plan to invade Virginia, but he never lost sight of this purpose. For the next three years he shuttled back and forth between Kansas, the Northeast, and settlements of former slaves in Canada to raise money and recruit volunteers. He organized a convention of blacks in Chatham, Ontario, in May 1858 to adopt a provisional constitution (written by Brown) for the African American republic he intended to establish among the ex-slaves he freed. During his visits to New England, Brown attended antislavery meetings but came away disgusted with what he considered empty rhetoric. "Talk! talk! talk!" he expostulated. "That will never free the slaves. What is needed is action—action."[17]

As the proslavery faction in the governing Democratic Party grew stronger and the Supreme Court issued the Dred Scott decision legalizing slavery in all territories, some abolitionists came over to Brown's viewpoint. Six of them formed a cabal self-described as the "Secret Six" who raised money for Brown in New England and New York. Ostensibly intended for Kansas, these funds were used instead to buy arms and supplies for Brown's invasion of the South and for pikes to arm the slaves he would free. Brown planned to capture the arsenal at Harpers Ferry, where he would seize more arms and start his campaign south along the Appalachian chain.

In the summer of 1859 Brown rented a farm across the Potomac from Harpers Ferry and began to gather his seventeen white and five black recruits. He hoped for more blacks, but even Brown's determined dedication and undoubted charisma could not persuade some potential recruits to take part in an apparently suicidal enterprise. Brown pleaded with his friend Frederick Douglass to join the raid. "I want you for a special purpose," he told Douglass. "When I strike, the bees will begin to swarm, and I shall want you to help hive them."[18] Douglass refused, and tried to dissuade Brown. He knew that Harpers Ferry was a military trap. Situated at the confluence of the Shenandoah and Potomac rivers and surrounded by commanding heights, the town could be cut off by troops that controlled those heights and the two bridges. And so it proved.

Brown considered himself a skilled military leader, and some of his guerrilla activities in Kansas seemed to demonstrate that skill. But his attack on Harpers Ferry the night of October 16–17, 1859, was poorly thought out. With the advantage of surprise he managed to capture the undefended armory and arsenal. He also sent patrols to seize hostages and a few slaves. But he neglected to plan an escape route if things went wrong. He did nothing about laying in supplies or establishing a defensive line against an inevitable counterattack. The nineteen men who invaded the town carried no rations. After his initial success, Brown did not seem to know what to do next. He stopped the night train heading to Baltimore but then inexplicably let it proceed after a few hours—to spread the alarm.

Brown continued to sit tight, apparently waiting for slaves to flock to his banner. Few did. But at daylight the local residents began shooting at the raiders, who fired back. Militia from the surrounding areas seized the bridges, cutting off any chance of escape. Several men on both sides were killed in the fighting on October 17, including two of Brown's sons. His remaining men retreated to the strongly constructed fire-engine house, where they made their last stand. That night a detachment of U.S. Marines arrived from Washington, commanded by none other than Army Lieutenant Colonel Robert E. Lee, who interrupted his leave at Arlington to accept this duty. After Brown refused a summons to surrender, the marines attacked and carried the engine house, killing two more raiders and wounding Brown. Thirty-six hours after it began, John Brown's war to liberate the slaves was over. No slaves were freed. The whole effort seemed a miserable failure.

But that was not the end of the story. Indeed, it was only the beginning. Nothing became John Brown's life like his leaving of it. In death he became much larger than life. As the words of the Union army's favorite song expressed it, even though John Brown's body lay a-moldering in the grave, his soul kept marching on—right down to our own time. The symbolism and power of John Brown's legend and legacy are the principal themes of the large literature about him, fiction and nonfiction alike.[19]

Ten of Brown's men were killed during the raid and seven were captured, including Brown. All seven were tried and convicted of murder, treason, and attempting to incite a slave insurrection. All seven would be hanged by the state of Virginia. Anticipating that Brown's execution would make him a martyr, several Virginia officials explored the possibility of declaring him insane and putting him away in an asylum. Affidavits from Ohio, where various relatives of Brown had lived for years, testified that "insanity is hereditary in that family. His mother's sister died with it, and a daughter of that sister has been two years in a Lunatic Asylum. A son and daughter of his mother's brother have also been confined in the lunatic asylum, and another son of that brother is now insane and under close restraint."[20]

In 2005 a clinical psychologist, Kenneth Carroll, reviewed the evidence from Brown's life and testimony at his trial and concluded that, in modern terminology, he probably suffered from bipolar disorder, with his behavior manifesting more of the manic than the depressive.[21] Whatever the validity of that diagnosis today, it went nowhere in 1859. When Brown's defense counsel (assigned by the state) suggested an insanity plea, Brown indignantly rejected it as "a miserable artifice and pretext." His calm demeanor, acceptance of responsibility for his acts, and rational—even eloquent—statements during and after his trial belied the notion of insanity. Virginia's Governor Henry A. Wise, who grew to admire Brown's character while despising what he stood for, pronounced Brown "remarkably sane if quick and clear perception, if assumed rational premises and consecutive reasoning from them . . . if memory and conception and practical common sense, and if composure and self-possession are evidence of a sound state of mind."[22]

Brown also discouraged rumored plots by Northern abolitionists to try a forcible rescue. "I do not know that I ought to encourage any attempt to save my life," he remarked. "I am worth inconceivably more to hang than for any other purpose." His execution would "do vastly more toward advancing the cause I have earnestly endeavored to promote than all [I] have done in my life before."[23]

These statements raise an intriguing question: Did Brown deliberately court martyrdom? Was the practical failure of the Harpers Ferry raid, at some subconscious or even conscious level, intentional? How else are we to explain the otherwise inexplicable decision by Brown to remain in the trap while his adversaries gathered to spring it? In his stimulating biography of Brown, David S. Reynolds suggested that at some point during the early hours of the raid, Brown realized that it had failed. Slaves were not flocking to his banner—the bees were not swarming. "The reality of the situation had hit him," wrote Reynolds. "His long-anticipated revolution of blacks was not happening." So "he resolved to stay in Harpers Ferry" even though his followers urged him to take to the mountains as originally planned, with or without freed slaves.[24]

At whatever point he recognized that he was "worth inconceivably more to hang than for any other purpose," that profound truth eventually became clear. At first, however, reaction to news of the raid was mainly one of shock and dismay even in antislavery circles. Horace Greeley of the *New York Tribune* declared that Brown had attacked slavery "in a manner that seems to us fatally wrong." This "deplorable affair," wrote Greeley, was "the work of a madman." The foremost white abolitionist, William Lloyd Garrison, branded Brown's raid "a misguided, wild, and apparently insane, though disinterested and well intended effort."[25] While some black leaders praised Brown as a hero willing to give his life for black freedom, their influence on white opinion was negligible.

But soon the tide began to turn. The biographer David Reynolds maintains that it was the Transcendentalist writers Henry David Thoreau and Ralph Waldo Emerson who nudged Northern opinion in a more positive direction. In public speeches they praised Brown as the embodiment of pure spiritual intuition that transcended the corrupt institutions of a society built on human bondage. Emerson caused a sensation with his pronouncement that Brown was a "new saint, than whom none purer or more brave was ever led by love of men into conflict and death,—the new saint awaiting his martyrdom, and who, if he shall suffer, will make the gallows glorious as the cross."[26]

Brown's own words and demeanor during the trial, and especially between his sentencing on November 2 and execution a month later, gave substance to

Emerson's image in the eyes of many in the North. The peroration of Brown's impromptu speech to the court at the time of his sentencing did more than anything else to transform him from criminal madman to heroic martyr:

> This Court acknowledges, too, as I suppose, the validity of the law of God. I see a book kissed, which I suppose to be the Bible, or at least the New Testament, which teaches me that all things whatsoever I would that men should do to me, I should do even so to them. It teaches me, further, to remember them that are in bonds as bound with them. I endeavored to act up to that instruction. I am yet too young to understand that God is any respecter of persons. I believe that to have interfered as I have done, as I have always freely admitted I have done, in behalf of His despised poor, I did no wrong, but right. Now, if it is deemed necessary that I should forfeit my life for the furtherance of the ends of justice, and mingle my blood further with the blood of millions in this slave country whose rights are disregarded by wicked, cruel, and unjust enactments, I say, let it be done.[27]

Not everyone in the North shared Emerson's sentiment that Brown's execution would make the gallows as glorious as the cross—quite the contrary. Democrats and conservatives denounced Brown as a lunatic and murderer. They did their best to tar Republicans like Abraham Lincoln with the brush of Brown's fanaticism. Lincoln's rival, Stephen A. Douglas, declared that Brown's raid was the "natural, logical, inevitable result of the doctrines and teachings of the Republican party."[28] Republicans scrambled to dissociate themselves from Brown. In his famous Cooper Union speech on February 27, 1860, Lincoln exclaimed in vexation: "Harper's Ferry! John Brown!! John Brown was no Republican, and you have failed to implicate a single Republican in his Harper's Ferry enterprise."[29]

Nevertheless, among many Republicans a sort of "praise the man but not the deed" posture arose. John A. Andrew, who was elected the following year as governor of Massachusetts, said that "whether the enterprise of John Brown and his associates in Virginia was wise or foolish, right or wrong . . . John Brown himself is right." On the Sunday before Brown's sentencing, America's foremost clergyman, Henry Ward Beecher of Brooklyn, preached a sermon in which he said: "Let no man pray that Brown be spared. Let Virginia make him a martyr. Now he has only blundered. His soul was noble; his work miserable. But a cord and a gibbet would redeem all that, and round up Brown's failure with a heroic success." When Brown in his cell read these words, he wrote in the margin: "good."[30] On the eve of Brown's hanging, the moderate Massachusetts *Springfield Republican* newspaper remarked editorially that "no event . . . could so deepen the moral hostility of the people of the free states to slavery as this execution. This is not because the acts of Brown are generally approved, for they are not. It is because the nature and the spirit of the man are seen to be great and noble."[31]

On the day Brown was hanged in Virginia, church bells tolled in many Northern towns. Guns fired salutes. Prayer meetings adopted memorial resolutions. Thousands observed a moment of silence in homage to the martyr. This outpouring of apparent Northern sympathy for Brown sent a more powerful shock wave of outrage across the white South even than the raid itself had done. The distinction between disapproval of Brown's act and admiration for his character was lost in the South, where whites could see only that the North "has sanctioned and applauded theft, murder, treason," in the words of *De Bow's Review,* the South's leading periodical. Could the slave states afford any longer "to live under a Government, the majority of whose subjects or citizens regard John Brown as a martyr and a Christian hero?" asked another newspaper editor.[32]

These events gave a great boost to secession sentiment in the South. "I have always been a fervid Union man," wrote a North Carolinian in December 1859, "but I confess the endorsement of the Harpers Ferry outrage . . . has shaken my fidelity and . . . I am willing to take the chances of every possible evil that may arise from disunion, sooner than submit any longer to Northern insolence." During the election campaign of 1860, John Brown's ghost stalked the South. The prospect of a Republican president spread fear that an abolition-minded North would turn loose more people like John Brown upon the South. When one South Carolinian heard the news of Lincoln's election, he remarked: "Now that the black radical Republicans have the power I suppose they will Brown us all."[33]

The war that John Brown's raid helped to provoke ultimately fulfilled his prophecy that slavery would be purged only with blood. As Merrill Peterson's excellent study of Brown's image makes clear, his soul marched through the slave states with Northern armies bringing the nation a new birth of freedom. The army's favorite marching song, "John Brown's Body," was turned into "The Battle Hymn of the Republic" by Julia Ward Howe (whose husband had been one of the Secret Six) after she had heard soldiers singing it. The last verse of "Battle Hymn" recalled Emerson's words about Brown's martyrdom making the gallows as glorious as the cross: "As he died to make men holy, let us die to make men free." And a powerful passage in Lincoln's second inaugural address evoked the stark augury of John Brown's last words. If God willed that the Civil War continue, said Lincoln, "until all the wealth piled by the bond-man's two hundred and fifty years of unrequited toil shall be sunk, and until every drop of blood drawn with the lash, shall be paid by another drawn with the sword, as was said three thousand years ago, so still it must be said 'the judgments of the Lord, are true and righteous altogether.' "[34]

During the post-Reconstruction decades of reconciliation between North and South, the popular memory of John Brown as symbol of a war for freedom faded, except among African Americans. The white South's image of Brown as a terrorist and murderer became more prevalent. Stephen Vincent Benét's epic *John Brown's Body* (1928) was a partial exception to this trend, but even Benét's portrayal of Brown was ambivalent. More typical of the time was Robert Penn Warren's biography *John Brown: The Making of a Martyr* (1929). Warren was a member of the Nashville Fugitives—the Southern writers and artists at Vanderbilt University who deplored the materialist values of "Yankee" America and looked to the Old South as their lodestar. He wrote that John Brown "possessed to a considerable degree that tight especial brand of New England romanticism which manifested itself in stealing Guinea niggers, making money, wrestling with conscience, hunting witches . . . or being an Abolitionist." Brown's antislavery war in Kansas, wrote Warren, was a mere "pretext for brigandage." His celebrated speech to the court that sentenced him to death was a tissue of red-herring falsehoods: "It was all so thin that it should not have deceived a child, but it deceived a nation."[35]

Such attitudes prevailed in the writings of white historians until the 1960s. In the first volume of his centennial history of the Civil War, for example, Bruce Catton wrote that "John Brown was a brutal murderer if ever there was one, and yet to many thousands he had become a martyr."[36] But even as Catton wrote these words, historical interpretations of slavery, abolitionism, and John Brown were changing, in part because of the civil rights movement. The perspective of many white historians and novelists began to merge with that of most blacks, for whom John Brown was a white hero who not only believed in and practiced racial equality but also gave his life for black freedom.

One of Brown's early biographers was the black intellectual W.E.B. Du Bois, founder of the NAACP. On the fiftieth anniversary of Brown's execution, Du Bois wrote: "Jesus Christ came not to bring peace but a sword. So did John

Brown. Jesus Christ gave his life as a sacrifice for the lowly. So did John Brown."[37] In 1906 the second annual meeting of Du Bois's Niagara Movement (forerunner of the NAACP) took place at Harpers Ferry. The delegates made a pilgrimage to "John Brown's Fort," the engine house where he made his last stand and which became a shrine for many African Americans. Black artists, poets, and musicians in the twentieth century celebrated Brown's heritage. For the militant Black Power movement in the 1960s John Brown was, as one partisan said, "the only good white the country's ever had." Malcolm X told whites that "if you are for me—when I say *me* I mean us, our people—then you have to be willing to do as old John Brown did."[38]

Martin Luther King Jr. was one of the few black civil rights leaders who refused to pay homage to Brown, whose methods contradicted King's commitment to nonviolence. This issue raises troubling questions. In 1859 many Northerners separated Brown's means from his ends and disapproved one while approving the other. But in the post-9/11 world it is not so easy to separate means and ends. David Blight, a Yale historian who certainly sympathizes with those who wanted to end slavery, nevertheless asks: "Can John Brown remain an authentic American hero in an age of Timothy McVeigh, Osama Bin Laden, and the bombers of abortion clinics?" Indeed, McVeigh and antiabortionists have invoked the precedent of John Brown. Paul Hill, convicted of murdering an abortion physician, declared that Brown's "example has and continues to serve as a source of encouragement to me." And John Burt, who bombed an abortion clinic in Florida, observed that "maybe like Harpers Ferry, where John Brown used violence to bring the evils of slavery into focus, these bombings may do the same thing on the abortion issue."[39]

Was John Brown a terrorist? For James N. Gilbert, an expert on criminal justice and author of an essay in *Terrible Swift Sword,* the answer is yes. Brown was "undoubtedly a terrorist to his core," Gilbert writes. His actions fit a modern definition of terrorism as "the unlawful use or threat of violence against persons or property to further political or social objectives." Another essay in the same anthology, however, by the political scientist Scott John Hammond, makes the provocative suggestion that if John Brown was a terrorist, so was Robert E. Lee. "We must ask which of the two acted on higher principle," writes Hammond, "which violated the greater law, which one carries more blood on his hands, and who between them is a more genuine American hero."[40]

Must we choose between John Brown and Robert E. Lee? Were both terrorists, or neither? The answer hinges on the word "unlawful" quoted in the preceding paragraph, which comes from the Vice President's Task Force on Combating Terrorism. Both Brown and Lee saw themselves as soldiers in a just war and therefore claimed that their acts were not unlawful but justified under the laws of war. Brown professed to act under the government of God; Lee acted under the government of the Confederate States of America. Whether both or neither was a legitimate government I leave to the reader.

The question of terrorism troubles David Reynolds, a thoughtful biographer who admires Brown. His book's subtitle maintains that Brown struck the blow that killed slavery and, by the example and inspiration of his racial egalitarianism, seeded the modern civil rights movement. Yet Reynolds repeatedly describes Brown's "terrorist tactics," his "terrorist campaigns against slavery" that "would trigger the Civil War." The Pottawatomie massacre in particular was "an act of terrorism."[41]

How can Reynolds reconcile these descriptions with his obvious empathy for Brown in a world where the word "terrorist" lurks just below "Nazi" in the lexicon of evil? To quote the aphorism that "one man's terrorist is another man's freedom fighter" is not enough, as Reynolds recognizes. Rather, he suggests that it is wrong to compare Brown to modern terrorists like McVeigh, Bin Laden, or the suicide bombers in Israel and Iraq, whose goals are negative and destructive. Brown was a terrorist for freedom "who used violence in order to create a society devoid of slavery and racism." Slavery was "a uniquely immoral institution . . . qualitatively different from all other social issues, since it deprived millions of their rights as Americans and their dignity as human beings."[42] This institution was so deeply rooted in American society that it required the huge violence of the Civil War to root it out.

For Reynolds, Brown's terrorism was the requisite prelude to this necessary violence, and was further justified by his "deep wells of compassion for a race whose suffering he felt on his very nerve-endings."[43] Whether this is another way of saying that the end justifies the means is a question for readers to decide. Meanwhile, even though John Brown has long since "gone to be a soldier in the army of the Lord," in the words of the original John Brown song, his soul seems likely to keep marching on through eternity.

# II

# The Lost Cause Revisited

# 3

# The Confederacy: A House Divided?

T HE FIELD OF CIVIL WAR HISTORY has produced more interpretive disputes than most other historical subjects. Next to debates about the causes of the war, arguments about how or why the North won, or the Confederacy lost (the difference in phraseology is significant), have generated some of the most heated but also most enlightening scholarship since the centennial commemorations of the war.[1] And the debates continue today as we approach the sesquicentennial anniversary of the war from 2011 to 2015.

Interpretations tend to fall into one of two broad categories: internal or external. Internal explanations are mainly concerned with the Confederacy and usually phrase the question with some variation of "Why did the South lose?" External interpretations look at both the Union and Confederacy and often phrase it as "Why (or how) did the North win?"

Robert E. Lee himself offered an external explanation in his farewell to the Army of Northern Virginia at Appomattox: The army, he wrote sadly, "has been compelled to yield to overwhelming numbers and resources." Given the North's greater population and superior economic capacity, this has remained a popular interpretation. The novelist/historian Shelby Foote reiterated it in the PBS television documentary *The Civil War*. "The North fought that war with one hand behind its back," he declared. If necessary "the North simply would have brought that other arm out from behind its back. I don't think the South ever had a chance to win that war."[2]

The "overwhelming numbers and resources" that supposedly made Northern victory inevitable were as apparent to Southern leaders in 1861 as to Lee in 1865 or Foote in 1990. Yet they went to war confident of success. Do we therefore judge them guilty of criminal folly or colossal arrogance for bringing on a bloody war they could not win? As they have pondered this question, many students of the Civil War have concluded that "overwhelming numbers and resources" was not the answer after all. Other nations had won or defended their independence against greater proportionate odds than the Confederacy faced in 1861. Southerners often cited the examples of the Netherlands against mighty Spain in the sixteenth century, Greece against the Ottoman Empire in the 1820s, and of course the fledgling United States against the world's greatest naval power in 1783. Two of the Confederacy's leading military commanders maintained after the war that the Southern people had not been "guilty of the high crime of undertaking a war without the means of waging it successfully," in the words of General Joseph E. Johnston. And General Pierre G. T. Beauregard added: "No people ever warred for independence with more relative advantages than the Confederates."[3] Americans who remember the war in Vietnam are painfully aware that overwhelming numbers and resources do not guarantee victory.

Recognition of this truth has coincided with the emergence of social history as the most dynamic field of American historical scholarship. The lives of previously neglected people—women, minorities, immigrants, workers, the poor—have become the principal subjects of much historical writing in which categories of class, gender, race, and ethnicity are used to analyze the divisions among Americans. Much of this writing emphasizes the alienation of these groups from mainstream white male Anglo-Saxon Protestant culture and the conflicts that resulted from their challenges to its domination. The effects of such studies can be seen in the search for "internal" explanations of Confederate defeat. Several important books and essays have portrayed a Confederacy riven by internal conflicts and discontent that inhibited unity, undermined morale, prevented the development of Confederate nationalism, and doomed the South to defeat. Nonslaveholders (two-thirds of Southern white males), women, and the slaves themselves have received a great deal of scholarly attention, most of it arguing that many members of these groups turned against a war to preserve a patriarchal society based on slavery and ruled by the planter class.[4]

Much of the ammunition for these internal explanations was furnished by a small book first published in 1944, long out of print until it was republished in 1972 and again in 1997: *Behind the Lines in the Southern Confederacy*, by Charles W. Ramsdell. The author, a white Southerner who admired and honored the Confederate military effort, maintained that the failure of Southern leaders to solve the problems of economic mobilization and war finance produced widespread shortages, runaway inflation, transportation breakdowns, and charges of corruption that alienated the home-front population, especially nonslaveholders, from the war effort. These failures "so weakened and demoralized the civilian population that it was unable to give effective support to the armies," wrote

Ramsdell. The Confederacy therefore began "to crumble, or break down *within,* long before the military situation appeared to be desperate."[5]

Two-fifths of the people in the Confederate states were slaves, who would seem to have had a greater stake in a Northern victory that would bring them freedom than in a Confederate victory that would keep them in slavery. Another two-fifths were members of nonslaveholding white families, whose commitment to a war to defend slavery had been weak in the first place, according to some historians, and grew weaker as the conflict took an increasing toll. And even among white slaveholding families, women who willingly subscribed to an ethic of sacrifice in the war's early years became increasingly disillusioned, maintains historian Drew Gilpin Faust, as the lengthening conflict robbed them of husbands, sons, lovers, and brothers. Many white women turned against the war and spread this disaffection among their menfolk in the army; in the end, writes Faust, "it may well have been because of its women that the South lost the Civil War."[6]

If all this is true—if the slaves and some nonslaveholding whites opposed the Confederate war effort from the outset and others including women of slaveholding families eventually turned against it—one need look no further to explain Confederate defeat. In *The South vs. the South: How Anti-Confederate Southerners Shaped the Course of the Civil War,* however, William W. Freehling does not go this far. He says almost nothing about women as a separate category, and he acknowledges that many nonslaveholding whites had a racial, cultural, and even economic stake in the preservation of slavery and remained loyal Confederates to the end. But he maintains that, properly defined, half of all Southerners opposed the Confederacy and that this fact provides a sufficient explanation for Confederate failure.

Freehling defines the South as all fifteen slave states and Southerners as all people—slave as well as free—who lived in those states. This distinction between "the South" and the eleven states that formed the Confederacy is important but too often disregarded by those who casually conflate the South and the Confederacy. Admittedly, some 90,000 white men from the four Union slave states (Kentucky, Missouri, Maryland, and Delaware) fought for the Confederacy, but this number was offset by a similar number of whites from Confederate states (chiefly Tennessee and the part of Virginia that became West Virginia) who fought for the Union.

But Freehling's central thesis that "white Confederates were only half the Southerners" raises problems. This arithmetic works only if virtually all black Southerners are counted against the Confederacy. At times Freehling seems to argue that they should be so counted. At other times he is more cautious, maintaining that "the vast majority" of Southern blacks "either opposed the rebel cause or cared not whether it lived or died."[7] Freehling does not make clear how important he considers that qualifying phrase "or cared not." In any event, let us assume that all three million slaves who remained in the Confederacy (as well as the one million in the border states and in conquered Confederate regions) sympathized with the Union cause that would bring them freedom. Nevertheless, their unwilling labor as slaves was crucial to the Confederate economy and war effort, just as their unwilling labor and that of their forebears had been crucial to building the antebellum Southern economy. These Confederate slaves worked less efficiently than before the war because so many masters and overseers were absent at the front. Unwilling or not, however, they must be counted on the Confederate side of the equation, which significantly alters Freehling's 50/50 split of pro- and anti-Confederates in the South to something like 75/25.

Freehling draws on previous scholarship to offer a succinct narrative of the political and military course of the war, organized around Lincoln's slow but inexorable steps toward emancipation, "hard war," and the eventual mobilization of 300,000 black laborers and soldiers to work and fight for the Union. Without them, the North might not have prevailed, as Lincoln himself acknowledged on more than one occasion.

Leaving aside (temporarily) the question of whether class, gender, and racial divisions in the South provide a sufficient explanation for Confederate defeat, another "internal" interpretation merits consideration. William C. Davis's *Look Away! A History of the Confederate States of America* attributes that defeat to poor leadership at several levels, both military and civilian, as well as to factionalism, dissension, and bickering among men with outsize egos and thin skins. In this version of Confederate history, only Robert E. Lee and Stonewall Jackson remain unstained.

For any believer in the myth of the Lost Cause, or any admirer of heroic Confederate resistance to overwhelming odds, the story told by Davis (no relation to the Confederate president) makes depressing reading. It is a story of conflicts not on the battlefields of Manassas or Shiloh or Gettysburg or Chickamauga or the Wilderness—they are in the book but offstage, as it were—but between state governors and the Confederate government in Richmond, between quarreling cabinet officers, between Jefferson Davis and prominent generals or senators or newspaper editors or even his vice president, Alexander H. Stephens.

William C. Davis acknowledges the significance of internal stresses within the Confederacy caused by galloping inflation and the inability of an unbalanced agricultural society under siege to control it, of shortages and hunger and a growing bitterness among large elements of the population, and of slave defections to the enemy. But his principal focus is the jealousies and rivalries of Confederate politicians. While he does not explicitly address the question of why the Confederacy lost the war, his implicit answer lies in the assertion that "the fundamental flaw in too many of the big men of the Confederacy . . . [was] 'big-man-me-ism.' "[8]

There are, however, some problems with this interpretation. In two senses it is too "internal." First, by focusing only on the Confederacy it tends to leave the impression that only the Confederacy suffered from these corrosive rivalries, jealousies, and dissensions. But a history of the North during the Civil War would reveal similar problems, mitigated only by Lincoln's skill in holding together a diverse coalition of Republicans and War Democrats, Yankees and border states, abolitionists and slaveholders—which perhaps suggests that Lincoln was the principal reason for Union victory.

In any event, *Look Away!* is also too "internal" because the author is too deeply dependent on his sources. It is the nature of newspaper editorials, private correspondence, congressional debates, partisan speeches, and the like to emphasize conflict, criticism, argument, complaint. It is the squeaky wheel that squeaks. The historian needs to step back and gain some perspective on these sources, to recognize that the well-greased wheel that turns smoothly also turns quietly, leaving less evidence of its existence for the historian.

If we were to accept all the internal interpretations of Confederate defeat at face value, we could scarcely understand how the Confederacy could have lasted four weeks, let alone four years. These home-front problems and divisions have been exaggerated out of proportion, writes Gary Gallagher, and "have mesmerized historians for too long. The time is ripe to consider the more complex and fruitful question of why white southerners fought as long as they did." In a dozen essays gathered into two volumes, that is precisely what Gallagher does.[9]

He does not slight the problems of slave defections to the Yankees, class tensions among whites, feuds among Confederate leaders, and other internal divisions. But he correctly places these in the context of and in comparison with similar or even more corrosive dissensions in the North. For example, while the bread riots of 1863 exposed threatening fissures in the Confederacy, draft riots in the North, especially in New York City, betrayed ugly class and ethnic divisions that posed a greater danger to the Union war effort. What impresses Gallagher is the comparative degree of white unity and strength of purpose in the Confederacy despite class fault lines. Confederate armies, especially Robert E. Lee's Army of Northern Virginia, became the lodestar of Southern nationalism that sustained Confederate morale and determination even in the face of defeat and the destruction of resources in 1864–65.

At their peak of strength in 1862–63, Confederate armies pursued an "offensive-defensive" strategy that held out the best hope for success and came remarkably close to achieving it on more than one occasion. Two Confederate armies invaded Maryland and Kentucky in September 1862 in an effort to win these border states for the Confederacy, gain British and French diplomatic recognition and mediation, and sway the congressional elections in the North. In drawn battles at Sharpsburg, Maryland (Antietam), and Perryville, Kentucky, this Confederate threat was repulsed, but as Wellington said of the battle of Waterloo, it was a near thing. Again in the summer of 1863 the Army of Northern Virginia seemed poised to win a victorious peace until the third day at Gettysburg—another near thing.

Plenty of evidence exists to sustain the theme of Confederate determination even in the face of extreme adversity. A Union officer who was captured at the battle of Atlanta on July 22, 1864, and spent the rest of the war in Southern prisons wrote in his diary on October 4 that from what he had seen in the South "the End of the War . . . is some time hence as the Idea of the Rebs giving up until they are completely subdued is all Moonshine they submit to privations that would not be believed unless seen."[10] Confederate armies suffered proportional casualty rates twice as high as Union armies and several times greater than American armies in any other war this country has fought. Yet the Confederacy kept fighting until it almost literally had nothing left to fight with in 1865.

Why, then, did the South lose? There is no simple answer to that question, but Gallagher points in the right direction: "Defeat in the military sphere, rather than dissolution behind the lines, brought the collapse of the Confederacy."[11] The question cannot be answered by large generalizations implying that the outcome was inevitable. It can be answered only by a narrative and analysis of unfolding events on the battlefields and the home fronts—in both North and South—that give due weight to such factors as political and military leadership, economic mobilization, logistics, strategy, war aims, morale, social strains and cohesion, diplomacy, and the sometimes fickle fortunes of battle.

In the fall of 1863, for example, Confederate leaders made an important de-cision to transfer two divisions from Virginia to Georgia, where they helped win a tactical victory at Chickamauga. Northern leaders recaptured the initia-tive with a smashing victory at Chattanooga after an even more ambitious transfer by railroad of four divisions to that city. These movements, like others during the war, involved a complex interplay of contingencies belying general-izations that imply inevitability to the outcome.[12]

When the imprisoned Union captain predicted that the "Rebs" would not give up "until they are completely subdued," he was right. That moment came in April 1865, when the large and well-equipped Union armies finally brought the starving, barefoot, and decimated ranks of Confederates to bay. Gallagher revives the "overwhelming numbers and resources" explanation for Confeder-ate defeat, shorn of its false aura of inevitability. Numbers and resources do not prevail in war without the will and skill to use them. The Northern will wavered several times, most notably in response to Lee's victories in the sum-mer of 1862 and winter-spring of 1863 and the success of Lee's resistance to Grant's offensives in the spring and summer of 1864. Yet Union leaders and armies were learning the skills needed to win, and each time the Confederacy seemed on the edge of triumph, Northern victories blunted the Southern mo-mentum: at Sharpsburg and Perryville in the fall of 1862; at Gettysburg and Vicksburg in July 1863; and at Atlanta and in Virginia's Shenandoah Valley in September 1864. Better than any other historian of the Confederacy, Gallagher understands the importance of these contingent turning points that eventually made it possible for superior numbers and resources to prevail. He under-stands as well that the Confederate story cannot be written except in counter-point with the Union story, and that because of the multiple contingencies in these stories, Northern victory was anything but inevitable.

What stands out for Gallagher after considering these factors is the deter-mined persistence of the Confederate effort in a war to defend a society based on slavery, an effort repugnant to the sensibilities of our time. "It defies mod-ern understanding," he concludes, "that any people—especially one in which nonslaveholding yeomen formed a solid majority—would pour energy and re-sources into a fight profoundly tainted by the institution of slavery. Yet the Confederate people did so. Until historians can explain more fully why they did, the story of the Civil War will remain woefully incomplete."[13]

In recent years a number of superb studies of Southern communities and states in the crucible of war have shown how Confederate determination was rooted in events at the local or regional level. Several of these studies focus on Virginia and Virginia communities.[14] A fine example is Brian Steel Wills's *The War Hits Home,* a fascinating account of the home front and battle front in southeastern Virginia, especially the town of Suffolk and its hinterland just inland from Norfolk. No great battles took place there, but plenty of skirmishing and raids by combatants on both sides kept the area in turmoil. Confederates controlled this region until May 1862, when they were compelled to pull back their defenses to Richmond. Union forces occupied Suffolk for the next year, staving off a halfhearted Confederate effort to recapture it in the spring of 1863. The Yankees subsequently fell back to a more defensible line nearer Norfolk, leaving the Suffolk region a sort of no-man's-land subject to raids and plundering by the cavalry of both armies.

Through it all most white inhabitants remained committed Confederates, while many of the slaves who were not removed by their owners to safer territory absconded to the Yankees, adding their weight to the Union side of the scales in the balance of power discussed by Freehling. White men from this region fought in several of Lee's regiments, suffering casualties that left many a household bereft of sons, husbands, or fathers. Yet their Confederate loyalties scarcely wavered; indeed they grew stronger in a determination to win a victory that would validate and justify their sacrifices.

Northern occupation forces at first tried a policy of conciliation in the region, hoping to win the Southern whites back to the Union. When this failed, they moved toward a harsher policy here as they did elsewhere, confiscating the property and liberating the slaves of people they now perceived as enemies to be crushed rather than deluded victims of secession conspirators to be converted.

Wills does not make a big point of it, but he does note that his findings stand "in sharp rebuttal" to the arguments of historians who portray a weak or divided white commitment to the Confederate cause as the reason for defeat. "These people sought to secure victory until there was no victory left to win."[15] In the end, the North did have greater numbers and resources, wielded with a skill and determination that by 1864–65 matched the Confederacy's skill and determination. Only then did Northern victory become inevitable.

# 4

# Was the Best Defense a Good Offense? Jefferson Davis and Confederate Strategies

W HEN GENERALS JOSEPH E. JOHNSTON and Pierre G. T. Beauregard wrote that the Confederacy had possessed more than sufficient resources to win the Civil War, their thinly veiled message was that responsibility for failure rested on the shoulders of Jefferson Davis. The former Confederate president, who endured several such accusations in the postwar years, did not deign to reply to them directly in the twelve hundred pages of his own memoirs, *The Rise and Fall of the Confederate Government.* Instead, he declared loftily that he would tell the truth in full confidence "that error and misrepresentations have, in their inconsistencies and improbabilities, the elements of self-destruction, while truth is in its nature consistent and therefore self-sustaining."[1]

In the spirit of this indirect exchange, Davis's relationships with his generals have framed much of the analysis of Confederate defeat. His feuds with Johnston and Beauregard, and his supposed favoritism toward Generals Braxton Bragg and John Bell Hood, are often portrayed as major causes of disasters in the Western theater, where the Confederacy lost the war. At the same time, Davis's personal rapport with General Robert E. Lee, for which most historians give Lee the principal credit, helps explain the Confederacy's relative success in the Eastern theater. The "dysfunctional partnership" between Davis and Johnston, according to Johnston's biographer Craig Symonds, "was an unalloyed disaster for the cause they served" and responsible in large measure "for the failure of the Confederate war effort." In the end, this and other rifts between Davis and his Western-theater generals more than outweighed the positive results gained by the "powerful team" of Lee and Davis.[2]

The focus on personal relations between Davis and his generals in much historical writing reflects another facet of the emphasis on "internal" explanations for Confederate defeat. It ignores the truth that similar problems plagued command relationships in the North. If Davis had Joe Johnston, Lincoln had George B. McClellan and George G. Meade; if Davis had Beauregard, Lincoln had John C. Frémont; if Davis looked bad by sticking too long with Bragg, Lincoln looked bad by successively appointing and then dismissing John Pope, Ambrose E. Burnside, and Joseph Hooker over the course of a year during which the morale of the Army of the Potomac sank to a point perilously close to collapse.

Although the personalities and the relationships among the commanders in chief and their principal army commanders in both Confederacy and Union had an important impact on the outcome of the war, a focus on strategy rather than personalities might yield a better understanding of the Confederacy's defeat.

A review of the larger context of Confederate military strategy will prove helpful. During the last two millennia, studies of military leadership have usually concentrated on victorious generals and their strategies. One thinks of Hannibal, Julius Caesar, Alexander the Great, Marlborough, Frederick the Great, Napoleon Bonaparte, Wellington, and Helmuth von Moltke. In the case of the American Civil War, the focus of much professional study of strategy and leadership, particularly by British military historians but also by some Americans, has been on Ulysses S. Grant, William T. Sherman, and Lincoln. One thinks of J.F.C. Fuller and John Keegan on Grant, Basil H. Liddell Hart on Sherman, Colin Ballard on Lincoln, and also of T. Harry Williams, Kenneth P. Williams, Herman Hattaway, and Archer Jones.[3] The purpose of such studies has often been to derive some positive lessons, some formula for success, from their campaigns.

Two exceptions to this emphasis on victors are the numerous studies of German generals and their strategies in both world wars and studies of Confederate generals in the Civil War, especially Robert E. Lee and Stonewall Jackson. These exceptions, however, at least partly prove the rule; that is, even though the Germans and the Confederates lost their wars in the end, they won a good many victories along the way and exhibited an operational or tactical brilliance that has made their campaigns fit subjects for studies to divine the secrets of their successes—and perhaps also of their failures.

Karl von Clausewitz's dictum that war is the continuation of politics (or policy) by other means is so often cited that it has become almost a cliché. Because of its familiarity, however, historians sometimes gloss over the distinction that Clausewitz drew between politics and other means while blurring the continuity between them. To unpack the meaning of Clausewitz's aphorism, we need to define each of its components. *Policy* refers to the war aims—the political objectives—of a nation in time of war. *National strategy* refers to mobilization

of the political, economic, diplomatic, and psychological as well as military resources of the nation to wage war. *Military strategy* refers to the employment of
a nation's armed forces to achieve its war aims. In the Confederacy, as in the
Union, the formulation of policy was the province of the president and Congress, who were also responsible for carrying out national strategy. Military
strategy is planned and carried out by commanders of the armed forces. The
president is the crucial link among all three components by virtue of his powers and responsibilities as commander in chief.

In theory there should be congruity among policy, national strategy, and
military strategy. That seems an obvious commonsense observation. But in
practice they sometimes diverge. Wars have a tendency to take on a character
and momentum that become increasingly incompatible with the original war
aims. And in many wars, sharp disagreements about policy develop within the
polity, giving military commanders mixed and confusing signals about national strategy, which inhibits their ability to devise the correct military strategy. That is what happened to United States policy in Vietnam. President Lyndon Johnson's refusal to consider a tax increase to finance the war also
introduced an incongruity between national strategy and the requirements of
military strategy. In other wars, conflict between military strategy as defined
by generals and policy as defined by civilian leadership can cause a nation to
fight at cross-purposes. In the Korean War, President Harry Truman insisted
on a limited war, while General Douglas MacArthur wanted to fight an unlim-
ited one. Truman finally had to fire MacArthur, producing a sense of frustration among many Americans who, like MacArthur, desired to overthrow Com-
munism in North Korea and perhaps in China as well.

The most successful wars in American history have been those with a close
congruity between policy and strategies. The war aim of the American Revolution was independence; national and military strategy achieved this goal, no
more and no less. The policy goals of the Mexican War were the Rio Grande
border for Texas and the acquisition of New Mexico and California; when
these were assured, the United States stopped fighting despite the clamor of
some expansionists for "all Mexico." In World War II the war aims of the Allies
were not merely the liberation of Europe and Asia from Fascist conquest but
also the overthrow of Fascist governments in the Axis nations themselves.
These aims required a national strategy of total mobilization and a military
strategy of total war to achieve a policy goal of unconditional surrender; that
was precisely the type of war that the Allies waged. During the first Persian

Gulf War (1990–91) the policy was to drive Iraq's army out of Kuwait; when that was done, the coalition forces stopped fighting.

During the Civil War, Northern war aims as well as national and military strategies changed as the conflict expanded from a limited war intended to restore the antebellum status quo into a "hard war" intended to destroy enemy resources including slavery and to mobilize those resources on the Union side, to bring an end to the social order sustained by slavery, and to give the United States a "new birth of freedom." Lincoln's genius as commander in chief was his ability to shape and define this expanding policy and to put in place, after three rocky years, a military strategy and military leaders to carry it out.

Jefferson Davis as commander in chief suffers by comparison with Lincoln, in part because the Confederacy lost the war and in part because of his flaws of personality and leadership. Davis was thin-skinned and lacked Lincoln's ability to work with critics for a common cause. Lincoln was reported to have said of McClellan in the fall of 1861 that "I will hold McClellan's horse if he will only bring us success."[4] It is hard to imagine Davis saying the same of Joseph E. Johnston. Because of dyspepsia and neuralgia that grew worse under wartime pressures and left him virtually blind in one eye, Davis was wracked by pain that exacerbated his waspish temper. Even his wife, Varina, noted that "if anyone disagrees with Mr. Davis he resents it and ascribes the difference to the perversity of his opponent."[5] Lincoln was more eloquent than Davis in expressing his country's war aims, more successful in communicating them to his people. Nothing that Davis wrote or spoke during the war has resonated down through the years like the peroration of Lincoln's first inaugural address, the peroration of his annual message to Congress on December 1, 1862, the Conkling letter of August 26, 1863, the Gettysburg Address, or the second inaugural address.

In his first message to the Confederate Congress after the outbreak of war, however, Davis did define Confederate war aims clearly and concisely: "We seek no conquest, no aggrandizement, no concession of any kind from the States with which we were lately confederated; all we ask is to be let alone."[6] This policy suggested a defensive military strategy. It was grounded in an important fact, so obvious that its importance is often overlooked: The Confederacy began the war in firm control of nearly all the territory it claimed. This is rarely the case in civil wars or revolutions, which typically require rebels or revolutionaries to fight to gain control of land or government or both. With a functioning government and a strong army already mobilized or mobilizing in May 1861, the Confederacy embraced some 750,000 square miles in which not a single enemy soldier was to be found save at Fort Monroe at Hampton Roads and on three islands off the coast of Florida. All the Confederacy had to do to win the war was to defend what it already had.

The nearest comparison to the Confederacy's initial situation was that of the United States on July 4, 1776. And like the leaders of that first American war of secession, Davis seems initially to have envisaged a "thoroughly defensive, survival-oriented" military strategy, in the words of historian Steven Woodworth.[7] Like the Roman general Quintus Fabius in the Second Punic War, or George Washington in the American Revolution, or the Russian general Mikhail Kutuzov in 1812, Confederate commanders would have to trade space for time, keep the army concentrated and ready to strike enemy detachments dangling deep in Southern territory, and above all avoid the destruction of Confederate armies. Such a defensive strategy of attrition might wear out the will or capacity of the enemy to continue fighting, as the Americans and Russians had done in 1781 and 1812.

What did it matter if this Fabian strategy yielded important cities and territory? Americans in the Revolution lost New York, Philadelphia, Charleston, Savannah, Williamsburg, and Richmond, yet won their independence in the end. On one occasion during the Civil War, Davis articulated such a strategy. "There are no vital points on the preservation of which the continued existence of the Confederacy depends," he maintained. "Not the fall of Richmond, nor Wilmington, nor Charleston, nor Savannah, nor of all combined, can save the enemy from the constant and exhaustive drain of blood and treasure which must continue until he shall discover that no peace is attainable unless based on the recognition of our indefeasable rights."[8]

But Davis said this in November 1864, after more than three years of war had forged a fierce Confederate nationalism that had sustained the will to fight despite the loss of territory and cities—though not for long after the subsequent loss of the cities named by Davis. In 1861, however, Confederate nationalism was still fragile. Southern states had seceded individually on the principle that the sovereignty of each state was superior to that of any other entity. The very name of the new nation, the *Confederate* States of America, implied an association of still-sovereign states. This principle was recognized in the Confederate Constitution, which was ratified by "each State acting in its sovereign and independent character."[9]

An example of Davis's respect for state sovereignty was his policy of brigading Confederate troops by state—something infrequently done in the Union army. Given the existence of this initial provincialism, if Davis had tried to pursue a purely Fabian strategy in 1861 by concentrating Confederate armies in Virginia and Tennessee, for example, and leaving other areas open to enemy incursion, the Confederacy might have fallen to pieces of its own accord. Popular and political pressures compelled Davis to scatter small armies around the perimeter at a couple of dozen points in 1861.

The danger of such a dispersal, labeled by T. Harry Williams as a cordon defense and by Craig Symonds as an extended defense, was that an enemy superior in numbers might break through this thin gray line somewhere, cutting off and perhaps capturing one or more of these small armies and penetrating as far into Confederate territory as if it had been left undefended.[10] That is precisely what happened in late 1861 and early 1862 in western Virginia, Missouri and Arkansas, Kentucky and Tennessee, coastal North and South Carolina, southern Louisiana, and even northern Alabama. In a rare confession (made, to be sure, in a private letter), Davis wrote in March 1862: "I acknowledge the error of my attempt to defend all of the frontier."[11]

He need not have been so hard on himself. Under the circumstances of 1861 he had little choice. The governors of North and South Carolina, or Mississippi and Arkansas and Alabama, not to mention the citizen soldiers from those states who had sprung to arms to defend home and family, would not have allowed him to strip their states of troops to fight in Virginia or Tennessee. Such parochialism (if that is the correct word) would remain a problem for Davis and the commanders of his principal armies during most of the war. But the experiences of 1861 and early 1862 did drive home the lesson of a need for some degree of concentration to meet the main enemy threats.

Underlying this principle of concentration was the advantage of interior lines. From 1861 to 1864 the Confederates repeatedly used their interior lines in both the Eastern and Western theaters to achieve at least a partial concentration of forces to strike at invading Federal armies. The first and one of the most famous examples was the transfer by rail of most of Joseph Johnston's small army from the Shenandoah Valley to Manassas in July 1861 to repel General Irvin McDowell's attackers at Bull Run and drive them in a rout back to Washington.

Nine months later, when confronted with a buildup of McClellan's forces on the Peninsula, the Confederates again used interior lines to transfer most of Johnston's army from Centreville to Yorktown. As Craig Symonds points out, this campaign revealed a difference between Davis and Johnston concerning the relationship between interior lines and concentration. Davis wanted to leave a substantial force along the Rappahannock River to protect that region against Union forces south of Washington—thus retaining part of his concept of an extended defense. Johnston wanted to concentrate nearly all Confederate units in Virginia against McClellan, as near to Richmond as possible, even at the risk of temporarily yielding other parts of Virginia to the enemy. After disposing of McClellan, Johnston said, the main Confederate army could then recapture these other regions.[12]

That is what eventually happened in the summer of 1862, but not under the command of Johnston, who was wounded at Seven Pines and replaced by Robert E. Lee on June 1. Part of the army of 90,000 men that Lee concentrated in front of Richmond by the last week of June 1862, the largest single Confederate army of the war, was drawn from the Shenandoah Valley. During the previous two months, Stonewall Jackson had brilliantly executed another operation that emulated a successful American strategy in the Revolution: a concentration of superior numbers in a mobile force to strike separated enemy outposts or detachments. George Washington had done this at Trenton and Princeton, and other American commanders had done the same in the Carolinas during the Revolution. Jackson borrowed a leaf from their book and struck smaller Union detachments at McDowell, Front Royal, and Winchester and then turned on his pursuers to check them at Cross Keys and Port Republic.

Jackson's men then became part of Lee's concentrated army that drove McClellan away from Richmond in the Seven Days—although Jackson himself did not perform up to expectations in that campaign. In the next one, however, he exceeded expectations. Jackson carried out Lee's bold exploitation of interior lines to concentrate against Pope along the Rappahannock as McClellan was withdrawing from the Peninsula. Using a favorite strategic operation of Napoleon's, *les manoeuvres sur la derrière*—a wide flanking movement to get into the enemy's rear—Jackson then marched around Pope's flank, destroyed his supply base at Manassas, and held out until the Confederates reconcentrated to win the second battle of Manassas.

Confederates in the Western theater also practiced the strategy of concentration in 1862. After the Federals had broken through the cordon defense of the other Johnston—Albert Sidney—at several points in Kentucky and Tennessee and had captured 20 percent of his troops at Fort Donelson, Johnston retreated all the way to Corinth, Mississippi. There he concentrated his scattered forces for a counterthrust at Shiloh. Although this effort did not produce a Confederate victory and it cost Johnston his life, Shiloh nevertheless set the Federals back on their heels for a time. The Confederate Army of Mississippi, now commanded by Beauregard, was finally forced to evacuate Corinth at the end of May 1862, just as Joseph Johnston's army in Virginia had evacuated Yorktown several weeks earlier. But these retreats set the stage for offensive operations later in the summer under new commanders (Lee in Virginia and Bragg in Kentucky) that took the armies across the Potomac and almost to the Ohio River by September.

These campaigns accomplished a startling reversal of momentum in the war. They also represented a new phase in Confederate strategy, which has been variously labeled offensive-defensive, offensive defense, or defensive-offensive. Davis himself described it as offensive-defensive and contrasted it with what he called "purely defensive operations."[13] This confusion of nomenclature perhaps reflects a confusion about the precise nature of this strategy and about whether Davis favored it, opposed it, or both favored and opposed it at different times with varying emphasis on the offensive or defensive elements of it, according to circumstances.

The effort to sort out these variables is hindered by the failure of the principals—Davis, Lee, Beauregard, Bragg, and others—to define systematically what they meant by offensive-defensive or purely defensive. We must tease out the meaning by a study of what they said and did in particular campaigns. One way to approach this matter is by way of an analogy from football, in which most coaches would agree that the best defense is a good offense. Of course Lee knew nothing about modern American football, but he would have understood the slogan. Indeed, he could almost have invented it. "There is nothing to be gained by this army remaining quietly on the defensive," he wrote on the eve of the Gettysburg campaign. "We cannot afford to keep our troops awaiting possible movements of the enemy. . . . Our true policy is . . . so to employ our own forces, as to give occupation to his at points of our selection." (In other words, we can win only if we keep our opponent off balance with an imaginative offense.) A year later Lee told General Jubal Early that "we must destroy this army of Grant's before he gets to the James River. If he gets there, it will become a siege and then it will be a mere question of time."[14]

One source of confusion about the meaning of an offensive-defensive strategy sometimes results from a failure to distinguish between strategy and tactics. When Davis or Lee or any other commander spoke of the offensive-defensive— or words to that effect—were they referring to strategy or tactics or both? They did not always offer a clear answer. Several combinations of offensive or defensive tactics and strategy are possible; Lee's campaigns demonstrated all of them. The Seven Days and Gettysburg illustrate the operational offensive in both strategy and tactics, but the Seven Days served the defensive purpose of relieving the threat to Richmond. Fredericksburg was a defensive battle in both strategy and tactics. Antietam culminated an offensive campaign, but the Confederates fought there mainly on the tactical defensive. Second Manassas was part of a strategic offensive and was both defensive and offensive in tactics. From Spotsylvania to the end of the war, Lee's army fought almost entirely on the defensive both strategically and tactically, although Jubal Early's raid down the Valley and into Maryland was an offensive diversion in aid of an essentially defensive strategy in Virginia.

The same variables characterized Western campaigns and battles. The first day at Shiloh was a Confederate offensive both strategically and tactically, as was the second day at Chickamauga. Every battle during the Vicksburg campaign was defensive both in strategy and tactics for the Confederates, as was each of Johnston's fights during the Atlanta campaign. After John Bell Hood succeeded Johnston, he promptly launched three tactical offensives to serve the strategic defense of Atlanta. Hood's later invasion of Tennessee was a strategic offensive that came to grief both in the tactical offensive at Franklin and the tactical defensive at Nashville.

What determined these variables was the strategic and tactical situation at a given time and place. When Davis contrasted the offensive-defensive with the purely defensive, he was probably speaking of both strategy and tactics in different combinations according to circumstances. Failure to sort out these circumstances and the resultant variables accounts for much of the confusion and ambiguity about Confederate strategy.

Lee's biographer Emory Thomas and historian Steven Woodworth have both clarified and muddied these waters in their writings on Confederate strategy. Both authors detect a difference of emphasis between Davis and Lee, neatly spelled out by Woodworth in his book with the double-entendre title *Davis and Lee at War*: "For Davis, the war could be won simply by not losing, for Lee . . . it could be lost simply by not winning." That is why Davis seemed at times to favor what he called "purely defensive operations," a Fabian strategy that would conserve the Confederacy's resources by compelling the enemy to consume his own by repeatedly attacking. The North would thereby suffer heavy casualties, eroding the will of the Northern people to sustain an increasingly costly effort to destroy the Confederacy.[15]

Yet from the time Lee took command of what he named the Army of Northern Virginia, Davis apparently approved all of the general's operations that have come to be known by the label of offensive-defensive: the attack on McClellan in the Seven Days; the shift of operations to northern Virginia culminating in Second Manassas; the invasion of Maryland; the counterthrust against Hooker at Chancellorsville followed by the invasion of Pennsylvania; and even the detachment of Early to raid down the Shenandoah Valley to the very outskirts of Washington. And let us not forget the Western theater, or theaters: Albert Sidney Johnston and Beauregard launched an offensive at Shiloh; Bragg and Edmund Kirby Smith invaded Kentucky; Bragg subsequently counterattacked William S. Rosecrans at Murfreesboro and Chickamauga; Hood counterattacked Sherman around Atlanta and then launched raids against Sherman's communications in north Georgia preparatory to an invasion of Tennessee, while General Sterling Price moved north in an ambitious invasion of Missouri.

If Davis opposed these offensives, we have little record of it. On the contrary, we have plenty of evidence of his approval, especially of Lee's and Hood's operations. With respect to Davis's cordial relations with Lee, both Thomas and Woodworth suggest that Lee charmed and smooth-talked Davis into such support so skillfully that, as Thomas expresses it in his biography of Lee, "Davis was unaware of the difference between himself and Lee." Indeed, the "difference was not apparent during the war" and has also eluded most historians.[16] Thomas finds the "dissonance" between Davis and Lee most salient in Lee's two most ambitious offensive efforts to conquer a peace, the invasion of Maryland in September 1862 and of Pennsylvania nine months later.

Yet curiously, Thomas also notes that Davis "was delighted with Lee's invasion" of Maryland.[17] If so, that helps explain why their dissonance was not apparent to Davis at the time or to most historians since. In any event, it is quite true that during the Gettysburg campaign Davis held some troops in the Richmond area instead of combining them with brigades from North Carolina under the command of Beauregard to conduct a diversionary action near Culpeper and draw Federal forces away from Pennsylvania, as Lee had requested. Davis did so for the very good reason that, as Lee headed north, 16,000 Union troops on the Peninsula commanded by General John A. Dix were threatening Richmond from the east in a brief campaign that has been all but ignored, while Beauregard had his hands full dealing with a major Federal effort against Charleston.

Although Davis and Lee appeared to be in accord on most matters of strategy, Thomas and Woodworth are nevertheless on to something in their focus on areas of disagreement. As Thomas explains, the difference in strategic outlook was a subtle matter of which word—offensive or defensive—should receive the greater emphasis in the concept of an offensive-defensive strategy.[18] There is an unacknowledged irony here, however, if Woodworth is correct that Davis really preferred a "thoroughly defensive, survival-oriented grand strategy." These words describe Joseph E. Johnston's strategy almost perfectly. But of course it was with Johnston that Davis quarreled most bitterly. So thoroughly defensive and survival-oriented was Johnston's strategy during the Atlanta campaign that historian Richard McMurry was not being altogether facetious when he said that Johnston would have fought the crucial battle of that campaign on Key West.[19] If Davis's choice of Hood to replace Johnston is any clue to his strategic leaning, it was more to the offensive than the defensive, for Hood was one of the most offensive-minded of the generals who came up under Lee's tutelage.

A related issue in a discussion of Confederate strategy concerns the East vs. West debate. In May 1863 the top Confederate leadership confronted a crucial decision about allocation of resources and effort between the Eastern and Western theaters. Lee had just won a renowned victory at Chancellorsville, but the Confederacy faced a dangerous situation at Vicksburg and in middle Tennessee. General James Longstreet and some others proposed the detachment of two divisions from Lee's army to reinforce Bragg for an offensive-defensive campaign against Rosecrans in middle Tennessee, which might also relieve the pressure against Vicksburg. In such a scenario, Lee would have to remain on the defensive-defensive in Virginia, a prospect he did not relish. Instead he counseled Davis to turn him loose on an offensive into Pennsylvania while the Western armies remained on the defensive. The result of Davis's decision to support Lee's plan was the loss of Vicksburg and middle Tennessee while the Army of Northern Virginia limped home after suffering a crippling 25,000 or more casualties at Gettysburg.

Was this a strategic blunder or bad luck? Was Lee's preoccupation with Virginia a consequence of parochialism that limited his vision to the East while the war was being lost in the West? Did his preference for both an offensive strategy and offensive tactics, especially at Gettysburg, bleed his army to death? Did Lee gain too much influence over Davis on these matters to the detriment of a sound strategic vision for all theaters that would have conserved Confederate manpower and eroded the Northern will through a defensive strategy of attrition?

These are important questions, and several influential historians have answered them in the affirmative.[20] But ultimately these questions are unanswerable. We just do not know what would have happened if Longstreet had taken two divisions to Tennessee in May 1863, if Lee had not invaded Pennsylvania, or if Lee himself had gone west to take command in that troubled theater as Davis asked him to do in August 1863 and again after the debacle at Chattanooga in November.

What we do know is that Lee was far from alone in perceiving Virginia as the most important theater. Most people in North and South alike, as well as European observers, shared that view. While it may be true that the Confederacy lost the war in the West, it is also clear that Lee's victories in the East came close on several occasions to winning the war, or at least to staving off defeat. The Confederacy was tottering on the edge of disaster when Lee took command on June 1, 1862, with the enemy six miles from Richmond and a huge amount of the Western Confederacy under Union control after a long string of Northern victories in that theater. Within a month Lee's offensive-defensive strategy during the Seven Days battles had dramatically reversed the equation in the eyes of most observers, whose view was focused on Virginia.

During the next two months Lee's and Jackson's offensive-defensive strategy came close to winning European diplomatic recognition. Antietam prevented that, but Confederate successes during the next nine months, again mainly in the East, reopened this possibility and discouraged so many Northern voters with the prospect of ever winning the war that the Democrats made great gains in congressional elections and potentially threatened the Lincoln administration's ability to continue the war. Lee and his offensive-defensive strategy appeared invincible. Gettysburg proved that it was not, but the lingering legacy of invincibility made Meade so cautious that the Army of the Potomac accomplished little for the next ten months.

Again in the summer of 1864 it was principally Lee and his army that almost caused the North to throw in the towel and caused Lincoln to conclude in August that he would not be reelected and the Union might not be preserved. To be sure, Lee's strategy and tactics were now mainly defensive, but the event that did more than anything else to convince many Northerners of the war's hopelessness was an offensive stroke—Early's raid toward Washington. As late as February 1865 Secretary of War Edwin M. Stanton and Senator Charles Sumner agreed that "peace can be had only when Lee's army is beaten, captured, or dispersed." So long as that army remained "in fighting condition, there is still a hope for the rebels," but "when Lee's army is out of the way, the whole Rebellion will disappear."[21] And so it proved; Appomattox was the actual if not literal end of the war.

A final observation. The subject of this essay has been Confederate strategies. There is an inevitable tendency to get so wrapped up in the subject at hand as to neglect part of the context. In the discussion of whether Davis's relations with Johnston, Beauregard, Lee, Hood, or Bragg helped or hurt the Confederate cause, whether more emphasis on the West or a more Fabian defensive strategy might have won the war, it is easy to forget that such matters did not occur in a vacuum. The Union army's command relationships and strategies both shaped and responded to Confederate command relationships and strategies. An anecdote in conclusion will help make this point. Several million words, or so it sometimes seems, have been written about which Confederate general was responsible for losing the battle of Gettysburg. When someone thought to ask George Pickett after the war who he thought was responsible for that Confederate defeat, he reflected for a moment and famously replied: "I always thought the Union army had something to do with it."

# 5

# The Saratoga That Wasn't: The Impact of Antietam Abroad

$T$HE CAMPAIGN AND BATTLE OF ANTIETAM had consequences that reached far beyond the mountains and valleys and fields of western Maryland where the fighting took place. Indeed, the battle's reverberations were heard across the Atlantic in London and Paris. Like the secessionists of 1776 who founded the United States, the secessionists of 1861 who founded the Confederate States counted on foreign aid to help them win their independence. In the Revolution they got what they hoped for after the battle of Saratoga. French recognition of the fledgling United States and subsequent financial and military support were crucial to American success. In the Civil War the Confederates failed to achieve foreign recognition, which might have been crucial to Confederate success if it had happened. The outcome of the fighting near Sharpsburg was the main reason it did not happen; in that respect Antietam could be described as a failed Saratoga.

The principal goal of Confederate foreign policy in 1862 was to win diplomatic recognition of the new Southern nation by foreign powers. Both North and South—one in fear and the other in hope—understood the importance of this matter. As early as May 21, 1861, Union secretary of state William H. Seward had instructed the American minister to Britain, Charles Francis Adams, that if the British government extended diplomatic recognition to the Confederacy, "we from that hour, shall cease to be friends and become once more, as we have twice before been forced to be, enemies of Great Britain."[1]

Even if diplomatic recognition did not provoke a third Anglo-American war, Southerners expected it to be decisive in their favor. "Foreign recognition of our independence will go very far towards hastening its recognition by the government of the United States," declared the *Richmond Enquirer* in June 1862. "Our independence once acknowledged, our adversaries must for very shame disgust themselves with the nonsense about 'Rebels,' 'Traitors,' &c" and "look upon our Independence . . . as *un fait accompli.*" Confederate secretary of state Judah

P. Benjamin believed that "our recognition would be the signal for the immediate organization of a large and influential party in the Northern States favorable to putting an end to the war." Moreover, "in our finances at home its effects would be magical, and its collateral advantages would be immeasurable."[2]

Benjamin was not just whistling "Dixie." Judging from the strenuous efforts by Union diplomats to prevent recognition and from the huge volume of news and editorial coverage of the issue in Northern newspapers, foreign recognition of the Confederacy would have been perceived in the North as a grievous and perhaps fatal blow. It would have conferred international legitimacy on the Confederacy and produced great pressure on the United States to do the same. It would have boosted Southern morale and encouraged foreign investment in Confederate bonds. Recognition would also have enabled the Confederacy to negotiate military and commercial treaties with foreign powers.

This question, however, presented the South with something of a catch-22. Although Napoleon III of France wanted to recognize the Confederacy from almost the beginning, he was unwilling to take that step except in tandem with Britain. (All other European powers except perhaps Russia would have followed a British and French lead.) British policy on recognition of a revolutionary or insurrectionary government was coldly pragmatic. Not until it had proved its capacity to sustain its independence, almost beyond a peradventure of a doubt, would Britain risk recognition. The Confederate hope, of course, was for help in *gaining* that independence.

Most European observers and statesmen believed in 1861 that the Union cause was hopeless. In their view, the Lincoln administration could never reestablish control over 750,000 square miles of territory defended by a determined and courageous people. And there was plenty of sentimental sympathy for the Confederacy in Britain, for which the powerful *Times* of London was the foremost advocate. Many Englishmen professed to disdain the braggadocio and vulgar materialism of money-grubbing Yankees. They projected a congenial image of the Southern gentry that conveniently ignored slavery. Nevertheless, the government of Prime Minister Viscount Palmerston was anything but sentimental. It required hard evidence of the Confederacy's ability to survive, in the form of military success, before offering diplomatic recognition. But it would also require Union military success to forestall that possibility. As Lord Robert Cecil told a Northern acquaintance in 1861: "Well, there is one way to convert us all—Win the battles, and we shall come round at once."[3]

In 1861, however, the Confederacy had won most of the battles—the highly visible ones, at least, at Manassas, Wilson's Creek, and Ball's Bluff. And by 1862 the cutoff of cotton exports from the South to Britain and France by the Southern embargo and Northern blockade was beginning to hurt the economies of those countries. Henry Adams, private secretary to his father in the American legation at London, wrote in January 1862 that only "one thing would save us and that is a decisive victory. Without that our fate here seems to me a mere matter of time." In February the *New York Tribune* acknowledged the critical foreign-policy stakes of the military campaigns then impending: "If our armies now advancing shall generally be stopped or beaten back, France, England, and Spain will make haste to recognize Jeff's Confederacy as an independent power." Only Union victories—"prompt, signal, decisive—can alone prevent that foreign intervention on which all the hopes of the traitors are staked."[4]

Northern arms did win signal and decisive victories during the next several months that more than fulfilled the *Tribune*'s hopes, starting with Forts Henry and Donelson and Roanoke Island in February, followed by Pea Ridge and New Bern in March. In London the Confederate envoy James Mason conceded that news of the fall of Forts Henry and Donelson "had an unfortunate effect on the minds of our friends here." Charles Francis Adams informed Seward in March that as a consequence of Northern success, "the pressure for interference here has disappeared." At the same time, Henry Adams wrote to his brother in the army back home that "times have so decidedly changed since my last letter to you. . . . The talk of intervention, only two months ago so loud as to take a semi-official tone, is now out of the minds of everyone."[5] The London *Times* ate crow, admitting it had underestimated "the unexpected and astonishing resolution of the North." Even Napoleon's pro-Southern sentiments seemed to have cooled. From Paris the American minister wrote in April that "the change in condition of affairs at home has produced a change, if possible more striking abroad. There is little more said just now as to . . . the propriety of an early recognition of the south."[6]

News from America took almost two weeks to reach Europe. In mid-May Henry Adams returned to the legation from a springtime walk in London to find his father dancing across the floor and shouting, "We've got New Orleans." Indeed, Henry added, "the effect of the news here has been greater than anything yet." It must have been, to prompt such behavior by the grandson of John Adams and son of John Quincy Adams. While Adams was dancing, James Mason was writing dispiritedly to Jefferson Davis that "the fall of New Orleans will certainly exercise a depressing influence here for intervention."[7]

Mason did not stop trying, however. He urged Lord John Russell, the British foreign secretary, to offer England's good offices to mediate an end to a war "ruinous alike to the parties engaged in it, and to the prosperity and welfare of Europe." Such an offer, of course, would be tantamount to recognizing Confederate independence. In a blunt reply, Russell pointed out that "the capture of New Orleans, the advance of the Federals to Corinth, to Memphis, and the banks of the Mississippi as far as Vicksburg" meant that "Her Majesty's Government are still determined to wait." Nevertheless, Mason worked his contacts with members of Parliament, who planned to introduce a motion in the House of Commons calling for recognition of the Confederacy. But Palmerston wrote in June that "this seems an odd moment to Chuse for acknowledging the Separate Independence of the South when all the Seaboard, and the principal internal Rivers are in the hands of the North. . . . We ought to know that their Separate Independence is a Truth and a Fact before we declare it to be so."[8]

Therefore, as Charles Francis Adams informed Seward, even among skeptics in Britain "the impression is growing stronger that all concerted resistance to us will before long be at an end." The danger of foreign recognition, Adams had earlier noted, "will arise again only in the event of some decided reverse."[9] Indeed it would, and such reverses were soon to occur as the pendulum of battle swung toward the Confederacy in the summer of 1862.

On May 30 and June 6, 1862, Union arms climaxed four months of victories with the occupation of Corinth, Mississippi, and the capture of Memphis. General George B. McClellan's Army of the Potomac advanced to within six miles of Richmond. But even as these events took place, the Confederate team of Stonewall Jackson and Robert E. Lee was beginning to strike back. Jackson's famous "foot cavalry" outmarched enemy forces in the Shenandoah Valley and won a series of victories that pumped up sagging Southern morale. Robert E. Lee took over the Army of Northern Virginia on June 1 and began planning a counteroffensive against McClellan, which he launched on June 26. By July 2 the Army of the Potomac had been driven back to Harrison's Landing on the James River in the Seven Days battles, plunging Northern morale to the lowest point in the war thus far. In the Western theaters also, the Union war machine stalled in the summer of 1862 and then went into reverse as Confederate forces raided through Tennessee and prepared to invade Kentucky.

These Confederate successes reopened the question of foreign recognition. They confirmed the widespread belief in Europe that the North could never subdue the South. The cotton "famine" was beginning to hurt workers as hundreds of textile mills in Britain and France shut down or went on short time. Unemployment soared. Seward's earlier assurance that Union capture of New Orleans would lead to a resumption of cotton exports from that port was not fulfilled, as Confederates in the lower Mississippi Valley burned their cotton rather than see it fall into Yankee hands. Only a trickle of cotton made it across the Atlantic in 1862. The conviction grew in Britain and France that the only way to revive cotton imports and reopen the factories was to end the war. Pressure built in the summer for an offer by the British and French governments to mediate peace negotiations on the basis of Confederate independence.

When news of Jackson's exploits in the Shenandoah Valley reached Europe (much magnified as it traveled), the government-controlled press in France and anti-American newspapers in Britain began beating the drums for intervention. The Paris *Constitutionnel* insisted in June that "mediation alone will succeed in putting an end to a war disastrous to the interests of humanity." In similar language the London *Times* declared that it was time to end this war that had become "a scandal to humanity."[10] The "humanity" the *Times* seemed most concerned about was textile manufacturers and their employees. The American minister to France, citing information coming to him from that country as well as from across the Channel, reported "a strenuous effort . . . to induce England and France to intervene. . . . I should not attach much importance to these rumors, however well accredited they seem to be, were it not for the exceeding pressure which exists for want of cotton."[11] In mid-June the *Richmond Dispatch* headlined one story "Famine in England—Intervention Certain." Northern newspapers published many alarmist news stories and editorials about "British Intervention," "Foreign Intervention Again," and "The Intervention Panic"—all before news of the Seven Days battles reached Europe.[12]

Southerners hoped and Northerners feared that the Seven Days would greatly increase the chances of intervention. "We may [now] certainly count upon the recognition of our independence," wrote the Virginia fire-eater Edmund Ruffin. The *Richmond Dispatch* was equally certain that this "series of brilliant victories" would "settle the question" of recognition.[13] Under such headlines as "The Federal Disasters in Virginia—European Intervention the Probable Consequence," Northern newspapers regardless of party affiliation warned that "we stand at the grave and serious crisis of our history. The recent intimations from Europe look to speedy intervention in our affairs."[14]

Although perhaps not so critical as this rhetoric might suggest, the matter was indeed serious. "Let us hope that the North will listen at last to the voice of reason, and that it will accept mediation before Europe has recognized the Confederacy," declared the Paris *Constitutionnel*. On July 16 Napoleon III granted an interview to Confederate envoy John Slidell. The "accounts of the defeat of the Federal armies before Richmond," said the emperor, confirmed his opinion that the "re-establishment of the Union [was] impossible." Three days later Napoleon sent a telegram to his foreign minister, who was in London: "Ask the English government if it does not believe the time has come to recognize the South."[15]

The English seemed willing—many of them, at least. The *Times* stated that if Britain could not "stop this effusion of blood by mediation, we ought to give our moral weight to our English kith and kin [i.e., Southern whites], who have gallantly striven so long for their liberties against a mongrel race of plunderers and oppressors." The breakup of the United States, said the *Times* in August, would be good "riddance of a nightmare." The London *Morning Post*, semi-official voice of the Palmerston government, proclaimed bluntly in July that the Confederacy had "established its claim to be independent."[16]

Even pro-Union leaders in Britain sent dire warnings to their friends in the North. "The last news from your side has created regret among your friends and pleasure among your enemies," wrote John Bright to Senator Charles Sumner of Massachusetts on July 12. "I do not lose faith in your cause, but I wish I had less reason to feel anxious about you." Richard Cobden likewise sounded an alarm with Sumner: "There is an all but unanimous belief that you cannot subject the South to the Union. . . . Even they who are your partisans & advocates *cannot* see their way to any such issue."[17] From France, Count Agenor-Etienne de Gasparin, who despite his title was a friend of the Union, wrote to Lincoln that only a resumption of Northern military victories could stem the tide toward European recognition. Lincoln took this opportunity to reply with a letter expressing his determination to stay the course. Yet, he added in a tone of frustration, "it seems unreasonable that a series of successes, extending through half-a-year, and clearing more than a hundred thousand square miles of country, should help us so little, while a single half-defeat should hurt us so much."[18]

Unreasonable it may have been, but it was a reality. A pro-Confederate member of Parliament introduced a motion calling for the government to cooperate with France in offering mediation. Scheduled for debate on July 18, this motion seemed certain to pass. The mood at the American legation was one of despairing resignation. The current was "rising every hour and running harder against us than at any time since the *Trent* affair," reported Henry Adams.[19]

But in a dramatic moment, Prime Minister Palmerston temporarily stemmed the current. Seventy-seven years old and a veteran of more than half a century in British politics, Palmerston seemed to doze through parts of the interminable debate on the mediation motion. Sometime after midnight, however, he lumbered to his feet and in a crisp speech of a few minutes put an end to the debate and the motion (the sponsor withdrew it). Parliament should trust the cabinet's judgment to act at the right time, said Palmerston. That time would arrive when the Confederacy's independence was "firmly and permanently established." One or two more Southern victories, he hinted, might do the job, but until then any premature action by Britain might risk rupture with the United States.[20]

This did not end the matter. James Mason wrote the following day that he still looked "speedily for intervention in *some form*." In Paris on July 25 John Slidell declared himself "more hopeful than I have been at any time since my arrival in Europe."[21] The weight of both the British and French press still leaned strongly toward recognition. And just before he left England in August for a tour of the Continent with Queen Victoria, Foreign Secretary Russell arranged with Palmerston for a cabinet meeting when he returned in October to discuss mediation and recognition.

During the next six weeks, prospects for the Confederacy grew ever brighter. Stonewall Jackson won another victory at Cedar Mountain on August 9. Lincoln and his new general in chief Henry W. Halleck decided, over McClellan's protest, to withdraw the Army of the Potomac from the Virginia Peninsula southeast of Richmond to reinforce the newly created Army of Virginia under General John Pope along the Rappahannock River. Lee decided to strike before most of these reinforcements could arrive. In a complicated set of maneuvers he sent Jackson's corps on a long flanking march to get into Pope's rear, then reunited the army near the Manassas battlefield of the previous year. On August 29–30 the Army of Northern Virginia withstood a series of disjointed attacks by Pope and then counterattacked to win one of the most decisive victories of Lee's career. Lee decided to make this triumph a springboard for an invasion of Maryland to win that state for the Confederacy and perhaps to conquer a peace on previously Union soil. At the same time, two Confederate armies were in Kentucky carrying out what appeared to be a successful invasion of that state as well. On September 4 the Army of Northern Virginia began crossing the Potomac River into Maryland.

The news of Second Manassas and of Lee's invasion accelerated the pace of intervention discussions in London and Paris. Benjamin Moran, secretary of the American legation in London, reported that "the rebels here are elated beyond measure" by tidings of Lee's victory at Manassas. Moran was disgusted by the "exultation of the British press. . . . I confess to losing my temper when I see my bleeding country wantonly insulted in her hour of disaster." Further word that Lee had invaded Maryland produced in Moran "a sense of mortification. . . . The effect of this news here, is to make those who were our friends ashamed to own the fact. . . . The Union is regarded as hopelessly gone."[22] The French foreign secretary told the American minister in Paris that these events proved "the undertaking of conquering the South is impossible." The British chancellor of the exchequer, William Gladstone, said that it was "certain in the opinion of the whole world except one of the parties . . . that the South cannot be conquered. . . . It is our absolute duty to recognise . . . that Southern independence is established."[23]

Gladstone was not a new convert to this position. The real danger to Union interests came from the potential conversion of Palmerston. After Second Manassas he seemed ready to intervene in the American war. The Federals "got a very complete smashing," he wrote to Russell (who was still abroad with the queen), "and it seems not altogether unlikely that still greater disasters await them, and that even Washington or Baltimore might fall into the hands of the Confederates." If something like that happened, "would it not be time for us to consider whether . . . England and France might not address the contending parties and recommend an arrangement on the basis of separation?" Russell needed little persuasion. He concurred, and added that if the North refused to accept mediation, "we ought ourselves to recognise the Southern States as an independent State."[24]

On September 24 (before news of Antietam arrived in England), Palmerston informed Gladstone of the plan to hold a cabinet meeting on the subject when Russell returned in October. The proposal would be made to both sides: "an Armistice and Cessation of the Blockades with a View to Negotiation on the Basis of Separation," to be followed by diplomatic recognition of the Confederacy.[25] But Palmerston and Russell agreed to take no action "till we see a little more into the results of the Southern invasion. . . . If the Federals sustain a great defeat . . . [their] Cause will be manifestly hopeless . . . and the iron should be struck while it is hot. If, on the other hand, they should have the best of it, we may wait a while and see what may follow."[26]

Little more than a week later, the news of Antietam and of Lee's retreat to Virginia arrived in Europe. These reports came as "a bitter draught and a stunning blow" to friends of the Confederacy in Britain, wrote American legation secretary Moran. "They express as much chagrin as if they themselves had been defeated."[27]

The London *Times* certainly was stunned by the "exceedingly remarkable" outcome of Antietam. "An army demoralized by a succession of failures," in the words of a *Times* editorial, "has suddenly proved at least equal, and we may probably say superior, to an army elated with triumph and bent upon a continuation of its conquests." Calling Lee's invasion of Maryland "a failure," the normally pro-Southern *Times* admitted that "the Confederates have suffered their first important check exactly at the period when they might have been thought most assured of victory."[28] Other British newspapers expressed similar sentiments. The Union victories at South Mountain (a preliminary battle three days before Antietam) and Antietam restored "our drooping credit here," reported American minister Charles Francis Adams. Most Englishmen had expected the Confederates to capture Washington, and "the surprise" at their retreat "has been quite in proportion. . . . As a consequence, less and less appears to be thought of mediation and intervention."[29]

Adams's prognosis was correct. Palmerston backed away from the idea of intervention. The only favorable condition for mediation "would be the great success of the South against the North," he pointed out to Foreign Secretary Russell on October 2. "That state of things seemed ten days ago to be approaching," but with Antietam "its advance has been lately checked." Thus "the whole matter is full of difficulty," and nothing could be done until the situation became more clear. By October 22 it *was* clear to Palmerston that Confederate defeats had ended any chance for successful mediation. "I am therefore inclined to change the opinion I wrote you when the Confederates seemed to be carrying all before them, and I am [convinced] . . . that we must continue merely to be lookers-on till the war shall have taken a more decided turn."[30]

Russell and Gladstone, plus Napoleon of France, did not give up easily. The French asked Britain to join in a proposal for a six-month armistice in the American war during which the blockade would be lifted, cotton exports would be renewed, and peace negotiations would begin. France also approached Russia, which refused to take part in such an obviously pro-Confederate scheme.

On November 12 the British cabinet also rejected it after two days of discussions in which Secretary for War Sir George Cornewall Lewis led the opposition to intervention. In a letter six days later to King Leopold of Belgium, who favored the Confederacy and supported intervention, Palmerston explained the reasons for Britain's refusal to act. "Some months ago," wrote Palmerston, when "the Confederates were gaining ground to the North of Washington, and events seemed to be in their favor," an "opportunity for making some communication" appeared imminent. But "the tide of war changed its course and the opportunity did not arrive."[31]

Most disappointed of all by this outcome was James Mason, who was left cooling his heels by the British refusal to recognize his own diplomatic status as well as that of his government. On the eve of the arrival in London of news about Antietam, Mason had been "much cheered and elated" by initial reports of Lee's invasion. The earl of Shaftesbury, Prime Minister Palmerston's son-in-law, had told Mason that "the event you so strongly desire," an offer of mediation and recognition, "is very close at hand." Antietam dashed these hopes and soured Mason on the "obdurate" British; he felt "that I should terminate the mission here."[32] He decided to stay on, but never again did his mission come so close to success as it had in September 1862.

Another consequence of Antietam with an important impact abroad was Lincoln's issuance of a preliminary Emancipation Proclamation. During the war's first year the North had professed to fight only for Union. Even as late as August 1862, in his famous public letter to *New York Tribune* editor Horace Greeley, Lincoln had said that if he could save the Union without touching slavery he would do it. This position alienated many potential British friends of the Union cause. Since "the North does not proclaim abolition and never pretended to fight for anti-slavery," wrote one of them, "how can we be fairly called upon to sympathize so warmly with the Federal cause? . . . If they would ensure for their struggle the sympathies of Englishmen, they must abolish slavery."[33]

In his letter to Greeley, however, Lincoln had also said that if he could save the Union by freeing some or all of the slaves, he would do that. In fact, he had already decided to take this fateful step and had so informed his cabinet on July 22. Secretary of State Seward persuaded him to withhold the proclamation "until you can give it to the country supported by military success." Otherwise, in this time of Northern despair over the military reverses in the Seven Days battles and elsewhere, the world might view such an edict "as the last measure of an exhausted government, a cry for help . . . our last *shriek*, on the retreat."[34]

The wait for a military victory to give the proclamation legitimacy and impetus proved to be a long and discouraging one. But Antietam brought the waiting to an end. Five days after the battle, Lincoln issued a proclamation warning Confederate states that unless they returned to the Union by January 1, 1863, their slaves "shall be then, thenceforward, and forever free."[35]

Europeans responded to this preliminary proclamation with some skepticism. But when January 1 came and Lincoln fulfilled his promise, a historic shift in European—especially British—opinion took place. "The Emancipation Proclamation has done more for us here than all our former victories and all our diplomacy," wrote Henry Adams from London. "It is creating an almost convulsive reaction in our favor all over this country." Huge mass meetings in every part of Britain—some fifty of them in all—adopted pro-Union resolutions.[36] The largest of these meetings, at Exeter Hall in London, "has had a powerful effect on our newspapers and politicians," wrote Richard Cobden, one of the most pro-Union members of Parliament. "It has closed the mouths of those who have been advocating the side of the South. Recognition of the South, by England, whilst it bases itself on Negro slavery, is an impossibility." Similar reports came from elsewhere in Europe. "The anti-slavery position of the government is at length giving us a substantial foothold in European circles," wrote the American minister to the Netherlands. "Everyone can understand the significance of a war where emancipation is written on one banner and slavery on the other."[37]

Antietam was unquestionably the most important battle of the Civil War in its impact on foreign relations. Never again did Britain and France come so close to intervention; never again did the Confederacy come so close to recognition by foreign governments. In the Revolution, the battle of Saratoga brought French intervention, which was the key to ultimate American victory. In the Civil War, Antietam turned out to be the Saratoga that failed.

# 6

## To Conquer a Peace? Lee's Goals in the Gettysburg Campaign

GENERAL ROBERT E. LEE WROTE two official reports on the Gettysburg campaign: a preliminary after-action account on July 31, 1863, and a final report on January 20, 1864. In these documents he summarized the five main objectives of his invasion of Pennsylvania:

1) To draw the Union Army of the Potomac away from the Rappahannock River line.
2) To take the initiative away from the enemy and disrupt any offensive plans General Joseph Hooker might have had for the rest of the summer.
3) To drive Union occupation forces out of Winchester and the lower Shenandoah Valley.
4) To draw Union forces away from other theaters to reinforce Hooker.
5) To take the armies out of war-ravaged Virginia and to provide the Army of Northern Virginia with food, forage, horses, and other supplies from the rich agricultural countryside of Pennsylvania.[1]

If Lee's goals were indeed limited to these five objectives, the Gettysburg campaign was a Confederate success. Lee did seize the initiative from Hooker; he did draw him away from the Rappahannock and disrupt any possible Union offensive in Virginia for the rest of the summer. The campaign did clear the lower Shenandoah Valley of enemy troops under General Robert Milroy and in fact captured four thousand of them. During the three to four weeks the Army of Northern Virginia was in Pennsylvania it lived very well off the enemy's country. And according to Kent Masterson Brown's book *Retreat from Gettysburg,* the Confederates seized enough food and forage and animals in Pennsylvania to keep the army supplied for months to come. The fifth objective Lee mentioned was achieved with qualified success: The only Union forces drawn from elsewhere during the campaign were five brigades from the Washington defenses—although after the battle some Northern units *were* shifted from the southern Atlantic coast to reinforce the Army of the Potomac.

The implication in Lee's reports that his goals in the Gettysburg campaign were limited, and largely achieved, is at least partly consistent with some modern studies of the campaign. They challenge the traditional view that Gettysburg was a disastrous Confederate defeat that shattered Lee's hopes for a war-winning victory on Northern soil. They also reject the notion that Gettysburg was a crucial turning point toward ultimate Union victory in the war. According to historians who question these traditional interpretations, Lee's incursion into Pennsylvania was a raid, not an invasion. A smashing victory over the Army of the Potomac would have been a nice bonus, but it was not the main goal of the raid. The Union victory at Gettysburg was merely defensive, and the Army of Northern Virginia got away with its spoils and lived to fight another day—indeed, many other days, as the war continued for almost two more years. It was only in retrospect and in memory that Gettysburg became the climactic battle and turning point of the war.[2]

Some of these arguments are self-evidently correct. The war did go on for almost two more years, and the Confederacy still had a chance to win it as late as August 1864 by wearing out the Northern will to continue fighting. Rebel foraging parties did scour hundreds of square miles of south-central Pennsylvania for whatever they could find and take—including many African Americans carried back to Virginia into slavery.

But we might ask whether all these spoils were worth the 28,000 or more casualties suffered by Confederates in the campaign as a whole, including the nightmare retreat. Of this number at least 18,000 men were gone for good from the Army of Northern Virginia—dead, imprisoned, or so badly wounded that they could never fight again. And we might also ask whether, even though Gettysburg was not a decisive turning point toward imminent Union victory, it might have been a decisive turning point away from a Confederate victory that could have demoralized the Army of the Potomac and the Northern people and might also have neutralized the loss of Vicksburg.

But what about Lee's official reports that set forth no such ambitious purpose for his invasion—or raid? To disagree with Lee is not to question his integrity. He told the truth in his reports. But he appears not to have told the whole truth. There is a considerable amount of evidence that he had more sweeping goals for his invasion of Pennsylvania than he described.

We need first to provide a context for this evidence. A fundamental assumption underlay Lee's military strategy, not only in the Gettysburg campaign but also in the war as a whole. Lee believed that the North's greater population and resources would make Union victory inevitable in a prolonged war of attrition, so long as the Northern people had the will to employ those superior resources. The only way the Confederacy could achieve its independence, Lee thought, was to win battlefield victories while the South had the strength to do so, victories that would if possible cripple the enemy's main army and demoralize the Northern people to the point they became convinced that continuing to fight was not worth the cost in lives and resources. Lee believed that these battlefield victories could not be won by sitting back and waiting for the enemy to take the initiative. The only time he did that, before 1864 at least, was at Fredericksburg in December 1862, a defensive Confederate victory that Lee found frustrating because the defeated enemy was able to pull back over the Rappahannock without further harm. Even at Antietam, where the Confederates fought a tactically defensive battle except for localized counterattacks, the battle itself was the culmination of Lee's strategic offensive. During the battle—indeed, the day after it as well—Lee looked for ways to take the tactical offensive even with his exhausted and depleted army. And following his retreat across the Potomac after Antietam, Lee still wanted to recross into Maryland farther upriver to continue his offensive, and expressed frustration over the army's inability to do so.

From the moment he took command of the Army of Northern Virginia, Lee had sought openings for a knockout blow. After driving McClellan back to the James River at the cost of 20,000 Confederate casualties in the Seven Days battles, Lee did not bask in his victory but instead lamented that "our success has not been as great or as complete as I could have desired. . . . Under ordinary circumstances the Federal Army should have been destroyed."[3]

Destroyed!! This Napoleonic vision continued to be Lee's guiding star for the next year. Just as Napoleon had destroyed enemy armies at Austerlitz and Jena-Auerstadt, forcing Austria, Russia, and Prussia to sue for peace on his terms, Lee hoped for similar if perhaps less spectacular results from the Seven Days, from the invasion of Maryland in 1862—and from the invasion of Pennsylvania in 1863.

In the Antietam and Gettysburg campaigns Lee linked his military initiatives to proposals for parallel political initiatives to achieve the goal of Confederate independence. After his victory at Second Manassas, Lee believed the enemy army was "much weakened and demoralized," he wrote to Jefferson Davis. Now was the time to give them that knockout blow. Braxton Bragg's and Edmund Kirby Smith's armies were invading Kentucky at the same time that Lee's men crossed the Potomac into Maryland. In a Napoleonic proclamation to his troops on September 6, 1862, Lee declared: "Soldiers, press onward! Let the armies of the East and West vie with each other in discipline, bravery, and activity, and our brethren of our sister States [Maryland and Kentucky] will soon be released from tyranny, and our independence be established on a sure and abiding basis."[4]

Lee was an avid reader of Northern newspapers smuggled across the lines. From them he gleaned not only bits of military intelligence but also—and more important in this case—information about Northern politics and the growing disillusionment with the war among Democrats and despair among Republicans. One of Lee's purposes in the Maryland invasion was to intensify this Northern demoralization in advance of the congressional elections in the fall of 1862. He hoped that Confederate military success would encourage antiwar candidates. If Democrats could gain control of the House, it might cripple the Lincoln administration's ability to carry on the war. On September 8 Lee outlined his ideas on this matter in a letter to Davis. "The present posture of affairs," Lee wrote, "places it in [our] power . . . to propose [to the Union government] . . . the recognition of our independence." Such a proposal, coming when "it is in our power to inflict injury on our adversary . . . would enable the people of the United States to determine at their coming elections whether they will support those who favor a prolongation of the war, or those who wish to bring it to a termination."[5]

This desire to influence the Northern elections was one reason Lee gave serious thought to resuming the campaign in Maryland even after Antietam. That was not to be. Democrats did make significant gains in the 1862 congressional elections, although Republicans managed to retain control of Congress. But morale in the Army of the Potomac and among the Northern public plunged to rock bottom in the early months of 1863 after the disaster at Fredericksburg, the fiasco of the Mud March, and the failure of Grant's initial efforts to accomplish anything at Vicksburg. Antiwar Democrats in the North—self-described as Peace Democrats but branded by Republicans as treasonable Copperheads—became more outspoken and politically powerful than ever. Lee followed these developments closely. In February he secretly ordered Stonewall Jackson's skilled topographical engineer, Jedediah Hotchkiss, to draw detailed maps of south-central Pennsylvania from the Cumberland Valley to

Harrisburg and all the way east to Philadelphia. Lee did not give Hotchkiss such an assignment just because he liked to read maps.[6]

About this time Lee also read in Northern newspapers of General George B. McClellan's testimony to the congressional Committee on the Conduct of the War about the finding of Lee's Special Orders No. 191 in the Antietam campaign. This solved the mystery of why McClellan had moved more quickly and aggressively than Lee had anticipated. Stephen Sears suggests that this eye-opening revelation may have convinced Lee that only an unlucky accident had frustrated his ambitious goals for the first invasion of the North. With better luck and tighter security he might succeed on a second try.[7]

By April 1863 Lee was beginning to plan that second invasion. Not only would it sweep Milroy out of the Shenandoah Valley and force Hooker out of Virginia, Lee informed Davis; it would also compel the Federals threatening the coast of the Carolinas and General William S. Rosecrans's Union Army of the Cumberland to divert reinforcements to Hooker. The Army of the Potomac would soon become weaker as the terms of 30,000 of its two-year men who had enlisted in 1861 and nine-month men who had enlisted in 1862 began to expire. Now was the time, said Lee, to strike again with an invasion to force Hooker's reduced army into the open for another blow to discourage Northern opinion. "If successful this year," Lee wrote his wife on April 19, "next fall there will be a great change in public opinion at the North. The Republicans will be destroyed & I think the friends of peace will become so strong that the next administration will go in on that basis."[8] Here indeed was a bold strategic vision. It was not limited to a mere raid to take the armies out of Virginia and obtain supplies.

Before Lee could begin to implement this vision, however, Hooker struck first on the Rappahannock. Lee countered, sent Jackson on his famous flank march, mesmerized Hooker, and forced him to hunker down in his entrenchments north of Chancellorsville by May 5. Intending to throw his knockout punch right there before Hooker could get back over the river as Burnside had done the previous December, Lee was bitterly disappointed when Hooker slipped away on the night of May 5–6.

Even as they mourned Stonewall Jackson's death, Southerners nevertheless celebrated Chancellorsville as a great victory. But to Lee it was another empty triumph that left the enemy to fight another day and also left the two armies once again confronting each other across the Rappahannock as the sand in the Confederacy's hourglass dropped inexorably grain by grain. If the war was ever to be won, Lee believed, 1863 was the year; the South would only get weaker and the North stronger if the conflict went on much longer. The men and horses of the Army of Northern Virginia were on half rations as the Confederacy's economy and rail network continued to deteriorate. Food and forage as well as the opportunity to maneuver the enemy into a position where Lee could fight him to advantage beckoned from Pennsylvania.

But by the time General James Longstreet and his two divisions under Generals John Bell Hood and George Pickett rejoined the Army of Northern Virginia after their sojourn south of the James gathering supplies and threatening the Union lines at Suffolk, Lee had to overcome competing visions of what Confederate strategy should be. Grant was closing in on Vicksburg; Rosecrans threatened General Braxton Bragg's position in middle Tennessee; a Union army/navy task force threatened General P.G.T. Beauregard at Charleston. Longstreet suggested that he take Hood's and Pickett's divisions to reinforce Bragg for an offensive against Rosecrans, which might also force Grant to release his tightening grip on Vicksburg. Secretary of War James Seddon and Postmaster-General John Reagan gained a hearing from Jefferson Davis for their proposal that Longstreet's two divisions go directly to General John C. Pemberton's support at Vicksburg.

In conversations and correspondence during the second and third weeks of May, however, Lee strongly opposed these proposals. It would take too long for Longstreet's men to get to Vicksburg for them to do any good, he said, and it was not clear that Pemberton and Joseph Johnston would know what to do with them if they did get there. Besides, the heat and diseases of a Deep South summer would loosen Grant's grip. Even if Vicksburg fell, a successful invasion of Pennsylvania would more than compensate for that loss. If Longstreet's two divisions went west, Lee warned, he might have to retreat into the Richmond defenses.[9]

Lee won over Davis and Seddon. Most interesting of all, he won over Longstreet, who now agreed with Lee that an invasion of Pennsylvania offered the best opportunity "either to destroy the Yankees or bring them to terms," as Longstreet wrote to Senator Louis Wigfall of Texas on May 13.[10] If the defensive-minded Longstreet could talk like this, it seems even more likely that the offensive-minded Lee went north looking for that Confederate Austerlitz or Jena-Auerstadt. Longstreet later claimed he had extracted a promise from Lee that he would maneuver in such a way as to fight only on the tactical defensive in Pennsylvania. As Stephen Sears comments, however, "that of course was nonsense."[11] Lee might have been willing to fight on the tactical defensive if he could do so on ground or under conditions that gave him the opportunity to win the kind of victory he felt had eluded him at Fredericksburg and Chancellorsville—but he certainly could not have made such a binding promise to Longstreet. And almost everything Lee said or did in Pennsylvania indicated that he had always meant to keep the initiative by attacking.

In any event, plans for the invasion went forward. Davis scraped up some reinforcements for the Army of Northern Virginia, though not as many as Lee had hoped for. Nevertheless, he was confident as his army started north. His reading of Northern newspapers and other intelligence reports convinced him that the Northern people were demoralized. Regiment after regiment of two-year and nine-month men in the Army of the Potomac was being demobilized. On June 23 Confederate division commander Dorsey Pender wrote to his wife: "It is stated on all sides that Hooker has a small army and that it is very much demoralized. General Lee says he wants to meet him as soon as possible."[12] Lee had taken Hooker's measure at Chancellorsville and now spoke of him with thinly veiled contempt as "Mr. F. J. Hooker" in a sarcastic reference to Hooker's "Fighting Joe" nickname in the Northern press.

Lee believed his own army to be "invincible," he told General Hood. "They will go anywhere and do anything if properly led."[13] Proper leadership after Jackson's death and other Chancellorsville casualties was a problem, to be sure. Lee reorganized the army into three corps with Generals Richard Ewell and A. P. Hill as new corps commanders. Their record as division commanders under Jackson gave promise of vigorous, hard-hitting leadership in their new role. And that is precisely what Lee expected of them. Lee went into Pennsylvania as he had gone into Maryland the year before, not merely on a raid for supplies but looking for a fight—perhaps even a war-winning fight. In a conversation with General Isaac Trimble on June 27, when most of the Army of Northern Virginia was at Chambersburg, Pennsylvania, and when Lee believed the enemy was still south of the Potomac, he told Trimble: "When they hear where we are, they will make forced marches . . . probably through Frederick, broken down with hunger and hard marching, strung out on a long line and much demoralized, when they come into Pennsylvania. I shall throw an overwhelming force on their advance, crush it, follow up the success, drive one corps back on another, and by successive repulses and surprises, before they can concentrate, create a panic and virtually destroy the army." Then "the war will be over and we shall achieve the recognition of our independence."[14]

Trimble wrote these words twenty years later, and one might question their literal accuracy—even though Trimble said the conversation was vivid in his memory and he was confident that he quoted Lee almost verbatim. In any case, Trimble surely did not make up Lee's words out of whole cloth. They were consistent with Lee's tactical decisions at Gettysburg even though many of the assumptions underlying his conversation with Trimble turned out to have been wrong: The Army of the Potomac was north of the river, it was not strung out or demoralized, and it was no longer commanded by Mr. F. J. Hooker. Even so, at Gettysburg Lee ordered an attack—again an attack—and again attacks, almost as if to make his predictions to Trimble come true.

As he had done during the invasion of Maryland the previous September, Lee offered some political advice to Jefferson Davis. This advice also was consistent with his prediction to Trimble that a crushing military victory would enable Davis to extract a peace agreement from the United States government that would recognize Confederate independence. Lee's reading of Northern newspapers had convinced him that "the rising peace party in the North," as he described the Copperheads, offered the South a "means of dividing and weakening our enemies." It was true, Lee acknowledged in a letter to Davis on June 10, that the Copperheads professed to favor reunion as the object of the peace negotiations they were clamoring for, while of course the Confederate goal in any such negotiations would be independence. But it would do no harm, Lee advised Davis, to play along with this reunion sentiment to weaken Northern support for the war, which "after all is what we are interested in bringing about. When peace is proposed to us it will be time enough to discuss its terms, and it is not the part of prudence to spurn the proposition in advance, merely because those who made it believe, or affect to believe, that it will result in bringing us back to the Union."[15]

Lee concluded his letter with a broad hint that Davis "will best know how to give effect" to Lee's views. Davis did indeed think he knew a way to offer the olive branch of a victorious peace at the same time that Lee's sword won that victory in the field. About the time he received Lee's letter, Davis also opened one from Vice President Alexander H. Stephens suggesting a mission to Washington under flag of truce. The ostensible purpose would be a negotiation to renew the cartel for prisoner of war exchanges, which had broken down because of the Confederate threat to execute or reenslave captured officers and men of black regiments. But the real purpose would be negotiation of a peace on the basis of Confederate independence. Davis immediately summoned

Stephens from Georgia to Richmond with the intention of sending him into Pennsylvania with the army as a sort of minister plenipotentiary to start negotiations after Lee won a military victory.[16]

Stephens arrived too late to catch up with the troops; and he protested that the enemy would never receive him anyway if he accompanied the army. So Davis sent him under flag of truce to Fortress Monroe, where he arrived on July 2 and had word sent to Lincoln asking permission to come to Washington. The press in Richmond may have gotten wind of this affair. In any case the initial news from Lee's invasion that filtered back from Pennsylvania was highly encouraging. An editorial in the *Richmond Examiner* reflected a widespread sentiment in the South in early July: "The present movement of General Lee will be of infinite value as disclosing the easy susceptibility of the North to invasion. Not even the Chinese are less prepared by previous habits of life and education for martial resistance than the Yankees. We can carry our armies far into the enemy's country, exacting peace by blows leveled at his vitals."[17]

That was precisely what Lee hoped to do. But first, on June 28, he ordered Ewell with two divisions, supported by Longstreet, to move north against Harrisburg. Having already cut the Baltimore & Ohio Railroad, Lee intended to destroy the Pennsylvania Railroad bridge and tracks at Harrisburg in order to cut all the links between the Midwest and Washington, Baltimore, and Philadelphia. Believing that the Army of the Potomac was still south of its namesake river, Lee thought he had time to carry out this demolition before concentrating to carry out a similar demolition of Hooker's army.

But that very evening of June 28 Lee received word from Longstreet's spy James (or Henry—his first name is uncertain) Harrison that the enemy was near the Maryland/Pennsylvania border, much closer and more concentrated than Lee—in the absence of any word from Jeb Stuart—had realized. Recall orders went off to Ewell's divisions, including Jubal Early's on the Susquehanna River east of York, to concentrate at Gettysburg or Cashtown, and Lee headed that way himself on June 29. Two days later the battle of Gettysburg began.

It began without Lee's presence, and in a sense against his wishes and his orders to subordinates not to bring on a battle until the army was concentrated. But once he made the decision to go in with everything he had, about three o'clock on the afternoon of July 1, he did not deviate from his intention to seize and hold the initiative by repeatedly attacking in an attempt to win the kind of victory that would destroy the enemy that had eluded him since the Seven Days battles a year earlier. "The enemy is there," Lee told Longstreet on the morning of July 2 and again the next morning, pointing to Cemetery Ridge, "and I am going to attack him there."

As late as the morning of July 3—perhaps even as late as 3:30 that afternoon—Lee still hoped and planned for a Cannae victory. His orders for July 3 included not only the attack we now call Pickett's Charge—or the Pickett-Pettigrew assault—but also an attack on Culp's Hill and a coup-de-grace strike by Stuart's six thousand cavalry swooping down on the Union rear while Pickett and Ewell punched through the center and rolled up the right.

By 4:00 P.M. on July 3 these hopes had been shattered. A day later a telegram arrived in Washington from the Union naval commander at Hampton Roads (ironically named Samuel Phillips Lee) notifying President Lincoln of Alexander H. Stephens's desire to meet with him. Having already heard the news from Gettysburg, Lincoln sent back a brusque refusal.[18] And the war continued.

# 7

# The Last Rebel: Jesse James

O NE OF THE ENDURING MYTHS of American folklore is that Jesse James was a home-grown Robin Hood who "stole from the rich and gave to the poor," in the words of "The Ballad of Jesse James," which enjoyed a revived popularity among the romantic Left in the 1960s. Supported by Hollywood movies, pulp fiction, and even serious scholarship, this image has dominated our understanding of the post–Civil War James gang and other Western outlaws. The British historian Eric J. Hobsbawm placed James squarely in the category of "social bandit." He was a "primitive rebel," a "noble robber" who championed "a special type of peasant protest and rebellion." He was one of the "peasant outlaws . . . who remain within peasant society, and are considered by their people as heroes, as champions, avengers, fighters for justice."[1]

One problem with this interpretation, noted the eminent historian of the American West Richard White, is that "Jesse James could not be a peasant champion because there were no American peasants to champion." White provides a variation of the primitive-rebel theme, however, by endorsing the idea that "the portrait of the outlaw as a strong man righting his own wrongs and taking his own revenge had a deep appeal to a society concerned with the place of masculinity and masculine virtues in a newly industrialized and seemingly effete order."[2] Another historian, David Thelen, elaborated these themes in his study of rural resistance to modernization in postwar Missouri. The instruments and master symbols of efforts "to convert farming from a traditional way of life into a profitable business" were banks and railroads—the very institutions that the James band robbed. "At the center of popular support for the bandits," writes Thelen, was the belief that by attacking these institutions the robbers "defended traditional values. . . . Jesse James rose to fame following the classical pattern of the world's great social bandits."[3]

James's biographer T. J. Stiles will have none of it. Easiest for him to refute is the Robin Hood myth: "There is no evidence that [the James gang] did anything with their loot except spend it on themselves."[4] Popular stories such as the one that told of Jesse giving a poor widow the mortgage money and then getting it back by robbing the rapacious banker are folklore. The unromantic truth is that Jesse spent much of his ill-gotten gains on fine horseflesh and gambling.

Stiles also disposes easily of the image of social bandits defending the peasantry. The James family owned seven slaves and a substantial farm that grew hemp and tobacco for the market before the Civil War. Most of the other outlaws came from a similar background in Missouri's "Little Dixie," the prosperous counties bordering the Missouri River and containing the greatest concentration of slaves in the state. Rather than being "primitive rebels," the bandits' "families had owned a larger-than-average number of slaves," and "their families and supporters were among the most market-minded farmers in the state."[5]

What about the argument that by robbing banks and trains, the James gang was making a statement against modernizing capitalism? Jesse James would have considered this notion a great joke. He would surely have agreed with a famous bandit of a later generation, Willie Sutton. When someone asked Sutton why he robbed banks, he supposedly replied: "Because that's where the money is." The same was true in Missouri and its neighboring states after the Civil War. As for railroads, Stiles points out that James's train robberies were not directed at the railroads as such but at the express companies that shipped cash and other valuables in the baggage cars. The robbers went after the express company safes because that's where the money was.

But if James was not Robin Hood, or a social bandit, or a rural enemy of capitalism, was he merely a criminal motivated by greed? Certainly not, according to Stiles. The key to understanding James and what he stood for was the Civil War, especially the vicious guerrilla war within the larger war that plagued Missouri. Forced to a decision between Union and Confederacy in 1861, most Missourians chose the Union. But support for the Confederacy was strong in Little Dixie, especially in the counties flanking the Missouri River just east of the Kansas border. In these counties lived most of the men and boys who went into the brush as Confederate guerrillas, including Frank and Jesse James, who were only seventeen and thirteen years old respectively when the war began.

But they grew up quickly under the tutelage of such psychopathic killers as William Clarke Quantrill, "Bloody Bill" Anderson, and Archie Clement. Frank James rode with Quantrill in the raid of August 1863 across the border to Lawrence, Kansas, hated capital of the Free State Party in the antebellum

Kansas wars between proslavery and antislavery forces. The raiders seized all the unarmed males they could find in Lawrence and murdered them in cold blood—nearly two hundred in all. Both Frank and Jesse were with Bloody Bill Anderson in a band of eighty men who rode into Centralia, Missouri, on September 27, 1864. They burned a train, robbed its passengers, and took twenty-three unarmed Union soldiers traveling home on furlough, some of them wounded convalescents, and ruthlessly murdered all but one of them. Chased out of town by Union militia, the guerrillas picked up 175 allies from other bands, ambushed their pursuers, and killed 124 of the 147 militia, including the wounded, whom they shot in the head.

These experiences were Jesse and Frank James's education in a crusade to defend slavery and disunion. A study of the social origins of Missouri's Confederate guerrillas shows that they came from families (like the James family) that were three times more likely to own slaves and possessed twice as much wealth as the average Missouri family. The Younger brothers (Cole, Jim, Bob, and John), who formed the core of the postwar James gang along with Jesse and Frank, were the sons of Jackson County's richest slaveowner.[6] One of the motifs of Jesse James's life grew out of this context. "His entire existence," writes Stiles, "was tightly wrapped around the struggle for—or, rather, against—black freedom."[7] He fought during the war against emancipation and after the war against the Republican Party that freed and enfranchised the slaves.

Persistent Confederate loyalties were the glue that bound the James gang together after the war and motivated their crimes. Wartime bushwhacking turned into Reconstruction banditry. "Like the Ku Klux Klan and other groups of rebel veterans in the Deep South," maintains Stiles, "the bushwhackers served as irregular shock troops in the Confederate resurgence after the war."[8] Many of the banks and express companies struck by the James gang were owned by individuals or groups associated with the "Radicals"—the Republican Party nationally as well as in Missouri.

When Confederate soldiers surrendered at Appomattox and elsewhere, the Civil War of 1861–65 ended, only to start up again in the new form of violent resistance by the Klan and other paramilitary organizations to Reconstruction efforts to enforce the civil and political rights of freed slaves. In Missouri the conflict never really ended at all. Wartime hatreds between Unionist and Confederate Missourians continued at almost the same level through the early years of Reconstruction, when Republicans controlled the state and their militia fought the same guerrilla outlaws they had fought during the war. The James brothers and their friends "began to rebel against Missouri's homegrown Reconstruction with the same methods they had used during the war, ranging from robbery to intimidation to murder."[9]

Bloody Bill Anderson and Quantrill had been killed during the war; Archie Clement, a cold-blooded killer who was young Jesse's hero, met the same fate at the hands of Republican militia in 1866. Jesse vowed revenge; from then on he emerged as the most ruthless of the guerrilla outlaws who were sustained by the support and cover of the same pro-Confederate regions of Little Dixie that had sheltered them and served as their base during the war.

Jesse waged this continuing war with his pen as well as with his six-shooters. He revealed a talent for obfuscation and self-promotion in numerous letters he wrote for publication in newspapers identified with the ex-Confederate faction of the Missouri Democratic Party. In this enterprise he was aided by John Newman Edwards, a journalist who had served as adjutant to Confederate general Joseph Shelby during the war. Vowing never to surrender, Shelby and a few hundred followers, including Edwards, had made their way to Mexico in 1865. There they cultivated the favor of Ferdinand Maximilian, whom Louis Napoleon of France had installed as emperor of Mexico in 1864. When republican forces under Benito Juárez overthrew and executed Maximilian in 1867, Shelby and his men returned to Missouri. Edwards soon took up his editorial pen and used it to glorify James and his gang as knights fighting the good fight against Radicalism.

After one of the James and Younger brothers' most audacious robberies, a heist of the cashbox from the ticket booth at the Kansas City fair, Edwards wrote an editorial titled "The Chivalry of Crime" that foreshadowed the whole noble-outlaw myth. "There are things done for money and for revenge of which the daring of the act is the picture and the crime is the frame," wrote Edwards. "A feat of stupendous nerve and fearlessness that makes one's hair rise to think of it, with a condiment of crime to season it, becomes chivalric; poetic; superb." These guerrilla bandits, claimed Edwards, "might have sat with ARTHUR at the Round Table, ridden at tourney with Sir LANCELOT or worn the colors of GUINEVERE."[10]

Heady stuff, but Jesse James went it one better in a letter to the *Kansas City Times* signed by Jack Shepherd, Dick Turpin, and Claude Duval—famous bandits of European folklore. "Some editors call us thieves," wrote Jesse. "We are not thieves—we are bold robbers. I am proud of the name, for Alexander the Great was a bold robber, and Julius Caesar, and Napoleon Bonaparte." Written during the heated presidential election campaign of 1872, Jesse's letter promoted his self-image as Confederate martyr and Robin Hood. "Just let a party of men commit a bold robbery, and the cry is hang them," he wrote, "but Grant and his party can steal millions, and it is all right. . . . It makes me feel like they were trying to put me on a par with Grant and his party. . . . They rob the poor and rich, and we rob the rich and give to the poor."[11]

By the 1870s Democrats had "redeemed" (their word) Missouri from Republican rule, and the ex-Confederate wing of the party had regained respectability. So long as the James gang carried out its robberies and murders within or close to Missouri, it was able to defy county sheriffs, state militia, bounty hunters, and even the Pinkerton detective agency. When the outlaws ventured farther afield, however, they courted trouble. And nowhere did they find more trouble than in Northfield, Minnesota, 450 miles north of their usual hunting grounds. Why did they go to Northfield in 1876? The answer reveals much about the persistent Confederate ideology and actions of these outlaws.

To Northfield earlier in 1876 had come Adelbert Ames to join his father and brother in running the local flour mill. Ames was no ordinary miller, however. He was a West Point graduate (class of 1861) and a Medal of Honor winner in the Civil War, in which he became one of the best Union division commanders. After the war he was stationed with occupation forces in Mississippi and elected as the first Republican senator from that state in 1870. One of the most idealistic of the "carpetbaggers," Ames was a strong supporter of equal rights for blacks. In 1873 he was elected governor of Mississippi. During the legislative elections of 1875, however, white Mississippians formed "rifle clubs" and carried out the "Mississippi Plan" to win the state for Democrats by violence, intimidation, and murder. Ames appealed for federal troops, but the Grant administration refused. Democrats won the election; a disillusioned Ames left the state and soon went to Northfield.

Ames was everything Jesse James detested: a leader of the victorious army that had crushed James's beloved Confederacy; an idealistic radical who had worked for racial justice; and perhaps worst of all, the son-in-law of notorious (in Southern eyes) Radical Republican congressman Benjamin Butler. When Jesse James learned that Ames had settled in Northfield, he decided to make his biggest political statement yet by robbing the local bank, in which Ames and Butler were rumored to have deposited $75,000. With seven other men including his brother Frank and three of the Younger brothers, Jesse headed north in August 1876.

The robbery attempt on September 7 turned into the worst disaster of James's career as the self-proclaimed Napoleon of crime. The cashier of the bank (a Union veteran) refused to open the vault—for which James murdered him in cold blood—while the citizens of Northfield fought back, killing two of the bandits and wounding all three of the Youngers before the robbers could flee the town. The aroused Minnesota countryside swarmed with posses that captured the three Youngers and killed one other bandit. They also wounded Frank and Jesse, who nevertheless escaped and eventually made their way back to Missouri in an epic feat of endurance. Nevertheless, it was the beginning of the end for Jesse James. Frank temporarily went straight and tried to become a farmer, though he lapsed and joined Jesse in more robberies. Several other members of the old gang were killed or captured. The political climate in Missouri had changed. The ex-Confederate faction made its peace with the Unionist wing of the Democratic Party. Many Democrats now saw James as a liability because he had made Missouri a byword for crime that frightened away investment and immigration. The most famous desperado in America, the sandy-haired Jesse grew a beard, dyed it black, and lived under a false name in Tennessee for a time before returning to Missouri, where there was now a price of $10,000 on his head. He recruited new members for his gang, but none of them had roots in the Civil War guerrilla soil, and they felt none of the loyalty that had so strongly bonded the original guerrilla outlaws. Two of these new recruits, Charley and Bob Ford, betrayed Jesse for the $10,000 reward and shot him dead on April 3, 1882.

After reading this biography, no one can doubt that the driving force of Jesse James's career was persistent Confederate ideology and loyalty. But T. J. Stiles concludes the book with a troubling question that remains unanswered. It is true, he writes, that James was "daring, brave, and capable of astonishing feats of endurance," but "it is also true that most of his homicide victims after the Civil War were unarmed and helpless, as were many of the men he murdered as a teenage guerrilla. So why do so many still worship him as a hero?"[12] Why indeed? The answer lies in what both contemporaries and later commentators have chosen to see in Jesse James—Robin Hood, social bandit, scourge of capitalism—rather than in what he really stood for.

# 8

# Long-Legged Yankee Lies: The Lost Cause Textbook Crusade

WOODROW WILSON WAS THE FIRST native-born Southerner to be elected president (in 1912) since Zachary Taylor in 1848. On July 4, 1913, Wilson had been in office exactly four months when he addressed a huge reunion of Union and Confederate veterans who had come to Gettysburg to commemorate the fiftieth anniversary of that Civil War battle. "How wholesome and healing the peace has been!" Wilson exulted. "We have found one another again as brothers and comrades, in arms, enemies no longer, generous friends rather, our battles long past, the *quarrel forgotten*."[1] The spirit of this joint reunion of Blue and Gray was captured by a photograph of septuagenarian Confederate veterans shaking hands with their Union counterparts across the stone wall where so much death had occurred fifty years earlier at the climax of Pickett's Charge.

This reconciliation of once-bitter enemies was achieved at the cost of justice to the freed slaves and their descendants. Flush with victory in 1865 and determined to secure "the fruits of victory" by planting Yankee institutions and values in the conquered South and empowering black freedpeople in the domain once ruled by the planter class, the Northern people within a generation had yielded the field to the guardians of white supremacy and Confederate memory. The custodians of that memory won their postwar battle to celebrate the South's Lost Cause as a valiant crusade for constitutional liberties and state's rights that was overwhelmed only by brute force. Slavery had little to do with causing the war, in this version of history, and reconciliation of the two sections that had fought a "brothers' war" was a more important consequence than the abolition of slavery. The federal government and the Northern people had long since conceded the power to define race relations in the South to whites, who had proceeded to impose a rigid system of segregation and disfranchisement on black people.

In 1865 Edward Pollard, editor of the *Richmond Examiner* during the Civil War, published a book titled *The Lost Cause: A New Southern History of the War of the Confederates,* and two years later followed it with a second volume titled *The Lost Cause Regained.* These books foreshadowed most of the themes now associated with what many historians describe as "the myth of the Lost Cause." In this use, the word "myth" is not synonymous with "falsehood" (though it may incorporate many untruths) but rather to be understood in its anthropological meaning as the collective memory of a people about their past, which sustains a belief system that shapes their view of the world in which they live.

The Lost Cause myth helped Southern whites deal with the shattering reality of catastrophic defeat and impoverishment in a war they had been sure they would win. They emerged from the war subdued but unrepentant; they had lost all save honor, and their unsullied honor became the foundation of the myth. Having (in their own view) outfought the Yankees, they were eventually ground down by "overwhelming numbers and resources," as Robert E. Lee told his grieving soldiers at Appomattox. This theme was echoed down the years in Southern memoirs, at reunions of Confederate veterans, and by heritage groups like the United Daughters of the Confederacy and the Sons of Confederate Veterans. "Genius and valor went down before brute force," declared a Georgia veteran in 1890. The Confederacy "had surrendered but was never whipped."[2] Robert E. Lee was the war's foremost general, indeed, the greatest commander in American history, while Ulysses S. Grant was a mere bludgeoner whose army overcame its more skilled and courageous adversary only because of those overwhelming numbers and resources.

Not only did Confederate soldiers fight better; they also fought for a noble cause, the cause of state's rights, constitutional liberty, and consent of the governed. Slavery had nothing to do with it. "Think of it, soldiers of Lee!" declared a speaker at a reunion of the United Confederate Veterans in 1904. "You were fighting, they say, for the privilege of holding your fellow man in bondage! Will you for one moment acknowledge the truth of that indictment? Oh, no! That banner of the Southern Cross was studded with the stars of God's heaven. . . . You could not have followed a banner that was not a banner of liberty!"[3]

Similar rhetoric poured forth at the dedications of hundreds of monuments to Confederate soldiers and their commanders planted on courthouse lawns and other public spaces across the South. If the Confederacy had raised proportionately as many soldiers as the postwar South raised monuments, it might not have succumbed to "overwhelming numbers." White children played a conspicuous part in these monument-unveiling ceremonies, so that the rising generation with no personal memories of the war would understand the heroism of their fathers. The climactic such event occurred in 1907 when three thousand children pulled a large wagon containing the statue of Jefferson Davis through two miles of cheering spectators to the site of the colossal Davis memorial on Monument Avenue in Richmond. According to an observer, the children hauled on "two lines of rope over seven hundred feet in length." In recognition of their sacred effort, "souvenir pieces of rope will be kept in their homes by many of the children through the years of the future."[4]

Children were ubiquitous at parades, rallies, and reunions of veterans and heritage groups. Indeed, the very names of the United Daughters of the Confederacy and Sons of Confederate Veterans expressed a determination to keep the Confederate heritage alive among the children of those who fought the war. Katharine Du Pre Lumpkin, born in Georgia as the youngest child of a Confederate veteran, remembered her first attendance at a United Confederate Veterans (UCV) reunion in 1903. The speeches made a great impression on the six-year-old girl, who recalled the occasion a half century later: "Even a child liked to listen, punctuated as they were every few moments with excited handclapping, cheers, stamping of feet, music. And such great men," including an Episcopal bishop who was a Confederate veteran. "Who there would not feel his Lost Cause blessed when so noble a man could tell them, 'We all hold it to be one of the noblest chapters in our history.'"[5]

Lumpkin's father was an officer in the UCV. He took her to many meetings during which she heard him exhort his colleagues to "educate the children! . . . Men of the South, let your children hear the old stories of the South; let them hear them by the fireside, in the schoolroom, everywhere, and they will preserve inviolate the sacred honor of the South." He practiced at home what he preached in public. All the time she was growing up, Lumpkin heard heroic tales of the war. One of her favorite memories was of formal debates that her parents organized among the children. These "debates" somehow always seemed to come out the same way, however, for she remembered "how the plaster walls of our parlor rang with tales of the South's sufferings, exhortations to uphold her honor, recitals of her humanitarian slave regime . . . and, ever and always, persuasive logic for her position of 'States Rights.'"[6]

Lumpkin's father relied on more than oral tradition. He "was ever in search of books to nurture us," she wrote. "One new set, I can recall, had, to be sure, lives of Lee and Jackson, but to our dismay also brought a life of Grant. We children were especially indignant at this affront," so her sister "snatched the Grant book away to hurl it into the woodshed as ignominious trash."[7]

Lumpkin's parents were carrying out the injunction of Sumner A. Cunningham, founder and editor of *Confederate Veteran Magazine,* to create "living monuments" to Southern heroism. In 1909, at the close of a decade in which as many stone or bronze monuments had been dedicated as in all other decades combined, Cunningham noted with sadness that "year by year the ranks of the Confederate veterans are thinning; rapidly, the mothers of the cause are falling into their last sleep, and the time will be, only too soon, when at no convention, no meeting will there be left any who witnessed the great and wonderful struggle for liberty." Statues of Confederate soldiers were, of course, necessary to preserve the memory of this struggle, wrote Cunningham, but "shall no living monuments record the gallant dead?" The children and grandchildren of veterans must be these living monuments. "Let auxiliaries be formed of the eager children. In their fertile minds now is the time of planting if a harvest is to be reaped."[8]

In a grim reminder of those thinning ranks, the National Casket Company had become one of the principal advertisers in *Confederate Veteran Magazine.* This company entered the winning float in a Southern heritage parade in 1908. Two teenagers, one dressed as a Confederate officer and the other as a plantation belle, stood on the float next to a casket atop a large funeral bier with the inscription "Your Sons and Daughters will forever guard the memory of your brave deeds."[9]

Confederate veterans and their wives had been aware of the need for living monuments well before Cunningham's editorial and the National Casket float. Soon after its founding in 1895, the United Daughters of the Confederacy (UDC) began to organize children's auxiliaries, most of which were named, appropriately, Children of the Confederacy. Their purpose, according to a UDC member, was "telling the Truth to Children." The "nobleness, the chivalry, the self-denial, the bravery, and the tireless endurance of the Confederate soldier should be instilled into every Southern child."[10]

The adult leaders of the Children of the Confederacy came up with several creative ways to accomplish this goal. One of the most effective was an "educational game" with fifty-two playing cards bearing portraits of Confederate officers and political leaders, the names of Confederate states and victorious battles (with the definition of Confederate victories stretched a bit), and descriptions of other notable events. Called "The Game of Confederate Heroes," this pastime was a big hit. One woman who often played it with her children commented, "I always feel like weeping when I draw 'Robert E. Lee,' 'The Stars and Bars,' and 'The Cruise of the Shenandoah.' I find this an easy way of familiarizing the children with precious moments, and they all love to play the game."[11]

Another tactic was to have children recite poetry or speeches, supposedly of their own composition, on ceremonial occasions. At a reception in Charleston for Mary Custis Lee, General Robert E. Lee's daughter, the last of several children's speeches was offered by the youngest orator, seven-year-old B. William Walker, grandson of a Confederate general. Walker concluded with these words: Robert E. Lee "was a grand man. He loved God, and loved his country [which country was not specified], he loved all that was good and noble. . . . The name of Robert E. Lee will never die. It is written in history and the book of Life, and will live for ever." Mary Lee was so moved by Walker's eloquence that she swept him up in her arms and kissed him. His response was not recorded.[12]

Alas, a serpent lurked in this Confederate Garden of Eden. The decades flanking 1900 were a period of expansion for public education at what we would today call the middle school and high school levels. Before this time, U.S. history had been part of the curriculum only in an occasional, unsystematic way. But by the 1890s the professionalization of history at the university level had come of age, and American history entered the curriculum in secondary schools. Publishers scrambled to produce textbooks for this new market. Most of their authors and nearly all of their publishers were located in the North—the publishers of nine out of the ten leading U.S. history textbooks before 1900, according to one student of the subject. Their point of view tended to reflect the triumphant nationalism growing out of Union victory in the Civil War.[13]

Here was the serpent in the garden, warned Confederate veterans: Yankee textbooks introducing innocent Southern children to the knowledge of good and evil—mostly Northern good and Southern evil. The shocked chaplain general of the UCV reported that such books caused many Southern youths to "think that we fought for slavery. . . . This is really pathetic," for if schoolbooks continued to "fasten upon the South the stigma of slavery and that we fought for it . . . the Southern soldier will go down in history dishonored." This was only one of the "long-legged Yankee lies" in Northern books that invaded Southern homes, schools, libraries, bookstores, and newsstands with "a horde of war literature so erroneous in statement of principle and fact . . . as to require on [our] part an immediate defense of [our] reputation by a prompt refutation of the errors thus widely sown in the minds of [our] children."[14]

As they had done in 1861, Southerners mobilized to repel this invasion. A principal motive for the UDC's founding was to counter this "false history," which taught Southern children "that their fathers were not only 'rebels' but guilty of almost every crime enumerated in the decalogue. . . . One of our main objects has been to put into the hands of our children a correct history."[15] Both the UDC and UCV formed "Historical Committees" with the twofold purpose to "select and designate such proper and truthful history of the United States, to be used in both public and private schools of the South" and to "put the seal of their condemnation upon such as are not truthful histories."[16]

Having found such unsatisfactory books, the committees should "enter into friendly correspondence with the authors and publishers of such books, with a view to correcting such errors, or supplying such omissions." This friendly correspondence should urge authors to make clear that "the cause we fought for and our brothers died for was the cause of civil liberty" and that Confederates were "a chivalric, intelligent, proud, liberty-loving people" who contended for "the most sacred rights of self-government" against "the clamor of a majority overriding the Constitution and demanding terms so revolting to our sense of justice" as to be intolerable.[17]

Although the Grand Army of the Republic, the Union veterans' organization, also formed committees to promote its version of the war, the UCV and UDC committees were more determined, uncompromising, and persistent. "Friendly correspondence" with Northern publishers had some results. Some publishers issued revised editions of their U.S. history textbooks in an effort to meet Southern criteria. Others put out separate editions for the Southern market.

But for most UCV and UDC history committees, these efforts were unsatisfactory. The books were still written by Yankees, "who are inimical to us, and who have permitted just enough of the truth to creep into their pages to make the lies stick and to place the Confederate soldier, as well as our entire people, in a false light before the world."[18]

Friendly correspondence having proved inadequate, the UCV vowed to "do everything in its power to encourage the preparation of suitable school histories and especially to encourage their publication by the building up of Southern publishing houses." This enterprise enjoyed considerable success. In 1895 the preeminent Southern educator Jabez L. M. Curry compiled a textbook titled *The Southern States of the American Union,* published in Richmond. Unlike

Northern books, which tended to "consign the South to infamy," wrote Curry in the introduction, his book demonstrated that the South was "rich in patriotism, in intellectual force, in civil and military achievements, in heroism, in honorable and sagacious statesmanship." Here was history as it should be written.[19]

Equally exemplary was *A School History of the United States,* first published in 1895, also in Richmond, written by a Virginian whose name announced her credentials: Susan Pendleton Lee. The abolitionists had branded slavery "a moral wrong," she wrote, but the Southern people knew that "the evils connected with it were less than those of any other system of labor. Hundreds of thousands of African savages had been Christianized under its influence—the kindest relations existed between [the slaves] and their owners. . . . The slaves were better off than any other menial class in the world." As for the Ku Klux Klan during Reconstruction, it was necessary "for self-protection against . . . outrages committed by midguided negroes."[20]

Armed with the increasing availability of these and several other textbooks by Southern authors, UCV and UDC committees met with local school boards and administrators to press them to get rid of books that contained long-legged Yankee lies and substitute approved books by Southern writers. The UCV was a powerful lobby in Southern politics, and the UDC enjoyed great prestige in Southern communities. Many school principals and school board members were Confederate veterans or the sons of veterans. The crusade to purge Yankee lies from the schools achieved great success. As early as 1902 *Confederate Veteran Magazine* ran an exultant headline: "False Histories Ousted in Texas."[21] In South Carolina the UCV history committee got a bill introduced in the legislature to ban any "partial or partisan or unfair or untrue book" from every school in the state and to punish anyone who assigned such a book with a $500 fine or one year's imprisonment. The bill did not pass, but school boards and teachers got the message. By 1905 a UCV leader in South Carolina could congratulate his colleagues that "the most pernicious histories have been banished from the school rooms."[22]

Other Southern states were not far behind. In 1904 the Mississippi legislature enacted a law requiring the state textbook commission to choose a uniform series of texts in which "no history in relation to the late civil war between the states shall be used in this state unless it be fair and impartial." Similar laws appeared elsewhere. At least two states, North Carolina and Florida, appropriated funds to subsidize the production of "a Correct History of the United States, Including a True and Correct History of the Confederacy," in the words of Florida's law. Nearly all Southern states created state textbook commissions to prescribe texts for all public schools instead of leaving the choice up to local school systems, as most Northern states did—an interesting application of the state sovereignty these same textbooks maintained that the Confederacy stood for. Whether intended or not, one effect of this pattern of statewide adoptions was to compel national publishers to eliminate anything offensive to the South to avoid a state or regional boycott of their books.[23]

By 1910 the historical committee of the UCV expressed satisfaction with the results of its textbook crusade. "We do not fear the bookmaker now," the committee reported. "Southern schools and Southern teachers have prepared books which Southern children may read without insult or traduction of their fathers. Printing presses all over the Southland—and all over the Northland— are sending forth by thousands ones which tell the true character of the heroic struggle. The influence . . . of the South forbid[s] longer the perversion of truth and the falsification of history."[24]

The serpent had been banished from textbooks but still lingered in trade and reference books that might find their way into the hands of innocent youth. The UCV and UDC led a charge against placing in public and school libraries such works, "which are unkind and unfair to the South, which belittle our achievement, impugn our motives and malign the character of our illustrious leaders." Several state and local chapters formed committees to "recommend to the proper authorities the elimination of any books inculcating false history" from libraries.[25] One target of these committees was the *Encyclopedia Britannica,* which contained an article stating that slavery was exploitative rather than paternal and another maintaining that secession was revolutionary rather than constitutional. "Such a distortion of historical facts," bristled the UCV historical committee, "could emanate only from ignorance or malignity."[26]

No book or author was either too important and powerful or too marginal and obscure to escape the censure of UCV and UDC watchdogs. Two examples come from 1911. A Confederate veteran happened that year to read Woodrow Wilson's *History of the American People.* In a brief reference to the famous naval battle between the USS *Monitor* and the CSS *Virginia* (*Merrimac*), Wilson wrote that the *Monitor* won the showdown. The outraged veteran fired off a letter of protest to Wilson and sent copies to Southern newspapers, which gave it wide publicity. "If this is the way a Virginia born historian writes her history, may God spare us from another such," he told Wilson, who was then governor of New Jersey and soon to run for president of the United States. "When one born of our own soil speaks untruthful history, it cuts deeper and makes a more insidious wound" than the "flaming slanders" of Yankee historians, who everyone knew were full of "overloaded prejudice and ignorance." A chastened Wilson wrote a letter of apology on the official stationery of the New Jersey executive mansion, expressing himself "very much mortified" by his mistake. Wilson's letter was also widely printed in the Southern press.[27]

While this exchange was taking place, a UCV committee discovered in a fourth-grade reader used in South Carolina schools a poem entitled "The Old Sergeant," which included a line describing the Confederate army as a "dark, rebellious host." Using the tactics of friendly correspondence, the UCV persuaded the Northern publisher, D. C. Heath, to replace the poem with the biblical story of Ruth, which the UCV found acceptable.[28]

If friendly correspondence and political activism by adults failed to purge false history, students themselves might take direct action. In 1894 a student in a Tennessee grammar school told her teacher (as a speaker at a UCV reunion described the incident) that "she didn't intend to study Mr. Higginson's history any more, that she had burnt her book up, for 'it made the Yankees win all the battles.' The other little girls in the class who were the daughters of the old soldiers burnt their books, too." Southern newspapers applauded this action; UCV camps passed resolutions of approval; and from Arkansas came a petition bearing five hundred signatures commending the girls, who "dared to take the first step toward writing a history that would do justice to the South."[29]

Two decades later the "historian general" of the UDC, Mildred L. Rutherford, who also described herself as the official state historian of Georgia, recounted an incident that occurred at an unnamed Southern college. The U.S. history text used there portrayed Jefferson Davis in an unflattering light. As Rutherford depicted it, the students "sent a committee to the teacher to request that the textbook be changed." The teacher refused. The students then went to the college president, who backed the teacher. The trustees declined to interfere. So, in Rutherford's words, the students "kindled a bonfire on the campus and into it every copy of that history was thrown." Rutherford commended their action and added that "the authorities were taught a lesson."[30]

As this incident suggests, while Confederate organizations had won the victory for true history in Southern public schools by the 1910s, private schools and colleges might still harbor Yankee textbooks. Therefore the UCV and UDC could not rest on their oars. Rutherford made this point explicit in her address to the first UDC convention held outside the South, in San Francisco in 1916. She claimed that 81 percent of Southern private schools "use histories which misrepresent the south."[31]

What this meant is unclear, for Rutherford's definition of "misrepresentation" was singular and her use of facts was loose. Nevertheless, as historian general of the UDC she led a crusade to expand the surveillance by historical committees to shape up private institutions and prevent backsliding by public ones. In 1919 Rutherford published *A Measuring Rod to Test Text Books and Reference Books in Schools, Colleges, and Libraries.* The UCV adopted this measuring rod as a set of criteria for "all authorities charged with the selection of text-books for colleges, schools, and all scholastic institutions" and requested "all library authorities in the southern States" to "mark all books in their collections which do not come up to the same measure, on the title page thereof, 'Unjust to the South.' "[32]

Here are some of Rutherford's instructions to teachers and librarians:

> Reject a book that speaks of the Constitution other than [as] a compact between Sovereign States.
>
> Reject a text-book that . . . does not clearly outline the interferences with the rights guaranteed to the South by the Constitution, and which caused secession. . . .
>
> Reject a book that says the South fought to hold her slaves.
>
> Reject a book that speaks of the slaveholder of the South as cruel and unjust to his slaves.
>
> Reject a text-book that glorifies Abraham Lincoln and vilifies Jefferson Davis.
>
> Reject a text-book that omits to tell of the South's heroes and their deeds.[33]

The UDC and the UCV also tirelessly promoted what Rutherford called the "Truths of History" in another of her pamphlets, in which she promised to present "a fair, unbiased, impartial, unprejudiced and Conscientious Study of History." Above all, she insisted, the historian must get her facts right, for the South had suffered from false history. Here are some examples of her facts, culled from many of similar purport:

> "Southern men were anxious for the slaves to be free. They were studying earnestly the problems of freedom, when Northern fanatical Abolitionists took matters in their own hands."

More slaveholders and sons of slaveholders fought for the Union
than for the Confederacy (this fit awkwardly with assertions elsewhere that the Yankees got immigrants and blacks to do most of
their fighting).

"Gen. Lee freed his slaves before the war began and Gen. Ulysses S.
Grant did not free his until the war ended."

"The war did not begin with the firing on Fort Sumter. It began
when Lincoln ordered 2,400 men and 285 guns to the defense of
Sumter."

Union forces outnumbered Confederate forces five to one, not sur-
prising when the Union population was thirty-one million while
the Confederate population was only five million whites and four
million slaves.[34]

Finally, Rutherford took great pains to describe Lincoln as a crude, vulgar,
cynical tyrant who violated the Constitution at every opportunity. To support
her portrait of Lincoln, she quoted James Ford Rhodes, perhaps the most influential Civil War historian of the time: Lincoln's "Emancipation Proclamation was not issued from a humane standpoint. He hoped it would incite the
negroes to rise against the women and children. His Emancipation Proclamation was intended only as a punishment for the seceding States."[35]

It mattered little to Rutherford's avid readers that this supposed Rhodes
quotation was a total fabrication, or that every one of her "facts" and "truths"
cited above was false. She was enormously influential in Southern education as
well as in the UDC. Many of her "truths" found their way into approved Southern history textbooks, at least those below the college level.[36]

The discipline of history in Southern colleges partook to some degree in the
professionalization occurring at the national level in the early twentieth century. Higher education, therefore, proved a tougher nut for neo-Confederates
to crack, but crack it they did. As early as 1902 Professor William E. Dodd of
Randolph-Macon College, who was a native of North Carolina and one of the
few Southern liberals of his time, complained that Confederate veterans had
imposed a straitjacket of censorship by requiring courses in American history
to teach that "the South was altogether right in seceding from the Union" and
"that the war was not waged about the negro." No serious scholarship was possible, wrote Dodd, "when such a confession of faith is made a *sine qua non* of
fitness for teaching or writing history."[37]

Some professional historians who gave lip service to academic freedom, however, were not above taking advantage of this climate of opinion. Professor Franklin L. Riley of the University of Mississippi, author of a U.S. history textbook, publicly championed what the profession in those days called "scientific history." But he privately told his agent to "hammer" a competing textbook in an Arkansas adoption struggle because the competitor gave more attention to Lincoln than to Davis and "devotes nearly 27 pages to 'the heroes who saved the Union' and only 7 pages . . . to only one Southern hero of the War—General Robert E. Lee."[38]

The cause célèbre in the college textbook wars began at Virginia's Roanoke College in 1910. A professor of history there, Herman J. Thorstenberg, a Northern-born son of Swedish immigrants, assigned Henry W. Elson's popular *History of the United States* as a textbook. A student whose father happened to be Confederate veteran as well as a local judge and a member of the college's board of trustees protested the book's treatment of the South and refused to attend class. Her father backed her up, brought the situation before the board, and publicized it in the local newspaper. From there it spread all over the South as the press and Confederate organizations seized upon the issue.

Not only was Elson a Yankee (from Ohio); he also had the temerity to suggest that Lincoln was a better man than Davis. Far worse was his treatment of the antebellum South, slavery, and the sectional conflict. Although he appeared to be evenhanded, holding Northern extremists like Charles Sumner and John Brown equally responsible with Southern fire-eaters for polarizing the sections, this apportionment of blame was unacceptable. Even more so was Elson's conclusion that the slavery issue was the main factor in provoking secession and war, which he called the "slaveholders' rebellion." Worst of all were two passages in which Elson quoted a sister of President James Madison, who had said that although "Southern ladies were complimented with the name of wife, they were only the mistresses of seraglios," and quoted another Southern woman who told Harriet Martineau that "the wife of many a planter was but the chief slave of his harem."[39]

The uproar over this affair went on for almost two years. Citizens in Roanoke and in the nearby town of Salem, where the college was located, threatened mob violence against Thorstenberg and the college. The *Roanoke Times* thundered: "We would like to see a fire kindled on the campus and every copy of the book formally and carefully committed to the flames." The same newspaper later declared that "we had better have poison put into the food of our sons [and daughters] than to have them taught that their forefathers were heads of harems . . . and that the soldiers of the Confederacy fought to maintain human slavery."[40] The editor of *Confederate Veteran Magazine* endorsed the determination of local citizens to "abolish their most cherished institution rather than tolerate such a book." UCV and UDC chapters all over the South took a position similar to the one expressed by the president of the Maryland UDC: "No history should be admitted into any school of the South until every sentence and word has been carefully scrutinized by competent and faithful Southern men, and the teacher who would commend such a book should be dismissed and advised that another climate would be conducive to his health."[41]

Although the faculty and president of Roanoke College offered a weak defense of academic freedom, the matter became moot when Thorstenberg caved in to pressure from the board of trustees to stop using Elson's text. Meanwhile, UDC and UCV chapters discovered that the book was also used in several other Southern colleges, including the state universities of North Carolina, South Carolina, and Texas. But UDC leaders in those states soon reported "with great pleasure" that the book had been "discontinued" at these and other institutions. The following year a UCV officer in Tennessee gave the book a careful reading and discovered another problem: Although it was "tinged with some make-believe of affection for the whites of the South, yet [it has] an uncontrollable love for the colored race and a desire upon the author's part, though unexpressed, to place them in every particular upon terms of equality with the better class of whites of the South."[42]

The UCV need not have worried that this unexpressed desire would continue to corrupt Southern youth. By the time Woodrow Wilson entered the White House in 1913, Elson's text had disappeared from Southern schools, along with any others that departed from the line laid down by the UCV and the UDC. The Lost Cause triumphed in the curriculum, if not on the battlefield. A North Carolinian educated in that state during the 1920s who later left the South and eventually became dean of Yale Divinity School looked back on the books he had read in school: "I never could understand how our Confederate troops could have won every battle in the War so decisively and then have lost the war itself!"[43]

Neo-Confederate historical committees had done their work well. Nevertheless, the crusade could not end. Eternal vigilance was still the price of true history. Few members of the UCV remained by 1932, the last year of publication of *Confederate Veteran Magazine*.[44] But the UDC and the Sons of Confederate Veterans remained vigilant. The Virginia chapter of the UDC expressed "shock" that year at the news that David Muzzey's all-time best seller among high school American history textbooks, described by the UDC as "atrocious" in its treatment of the South, had somehow been adopted by the Virginia textbook commission to replace a book by a native Virginian. The Sons of Confederate Veterans issued a "Call to Arms" to overturn this decision and return to "the purity of our history."[45] That quest for purity remains vital today, as any historian working in the field can testify.

# III
# Architects of Victory

# 9

## "We Stand by Each Other Always":
## Grant and Sherman

MANY PEOPLE WITH A CASUAL INTEREST in American history think they know four things about Ulysses S. Grant: He was a drunk; he failed at everything he tried before the Civil War; he managed to overcome Robert E. Lee's Army of Northern Virginia only by blunt, hammering tactics at enormous human cost; and his two presidential terms were riddled with corruption and cronyism. Though he was hailed in his own time as savior of the republic, Grant's reputation in the next half century sank more precipitously than that of any other major figure in our history. Countless historians have quoted Henry Adams's quip that "the progress of evolution from President Washington to President Grant was alone evidence enough to upset Darwin." As Brooks D. Simpson noted with wry understatement in his biography of the general: "Grant has not fared well as a biographical subject."[1]

There have been exceptions. In the 1930s the British military historian J.F.C. Fuller compared Grant favorably with Robert E. Lee and judged him the foremost general of the Civil War. The American historians T. Harry Williams and Kenneth P. Williams echoed these conclusions in the 1950s. Bruce Catton wrote two excellent and sympathetic volumes on Grant's wartime generalship in the 1960s.[2]

These books dented but did not overturn the popular impression of Grant as a mediocrity and a military "butcher." And William McFeely's *Grant*, which appeared in 1981 and won a Pulitzer Prize, left the reader with more negative than positive impressions. Since the 1980s, however, a Grant revival has taken place, fueled in part by the outstanding edition of Grant's papers produced by John Y. Simon and his colleagues at Southern Illinois University. New scholarship bids fair to restore Grant's reputation as one of the great captains of history, and even to elevate his presidency several notches in the historical rankings.[3]

Grant's early career gave little promise of future greatness. He graduated in the middle of his West Point class of 1843, did reasonably well as a junior officer in the Mexican War, but experienced loneliness for his wife and children when assigned to a remote army post in California in the 1850s. He did not get along with his commanding officer, who forced him to resign from the army in 1854 or face a court-martial for alleged drunkenness. Grant resigned and returned to his family in St. Louis but enjoyed little success in civilian occupations. The outbreak of the Civil War found him clerking in his father's leather store in Galena, Illinois. Three years later he was general in chief of the United States Army.

Almost everyone who knew Grant in the 1850s underestimated this impecunious ex-captain. In 1861 the governor of Illinois and the War Department shunted aside or ignored Grant's offer to train and command a regiment in the mobilization of the first Union troops. Only the influence of Illinois congressman Elihu Washburne, who had befriended Grant in Galena and remained his champion throughout the war, secured him an appointment as colonel of an Illinois regiment in June 1861 and as brigadier general later that year. Grant immediately exhibited the qualities of quiet authority, sangfroid, and control of men and of himself that became his hallmark as a commander. He turned the unruly farm boys of the 21st Illinois, whose lack of discipline had driven their first colonel from the service, into an effective fighting unit.

Grant's ascent thereafter was steady if not meteoric: command of a brigade, a division, an army (Army of the Tennessee), an army group, and all of the armies of the United States. Along the way, troops under his command forced the surrender of three enemy armies: at Fort Donelson on February 16, 1862; at Vicksburg on July 4, 1863; and at Appomattox on April 9, 1865. Grant did not win all of his battles, but he never suffered a decisive defeat. What is most important, he won all of his campaigns.

What explained Grant's success? Many contemporaries asked the same question. None could answer it, including Grant's closest wartime colleague, William Tecumseh Sherman. "I knew him as a cadet at West Point," wrote Sherman after the war, "as a lieutenant of the Fourth Infantry, as a citizen of St. Louis, and as a growing general all through the bloody Civil War. Yet to me he is a mystery, and I believe he is a mystery to himself."[4]

Shy with strangers, uncomfortable in the limelight, notoriously taciturn, Grant earned a reputation as "the American Sphinx." Yet wherever he went, things got done—quietly, efficiently, quickly, with no wasted motion. In crisis situations during combat, Grant remained calm. He did not panic. He persevered, and he never accepted defeat even when he appeared to be beaten. In his first battle, at Belmont, Missouri, on November 7, 1861, Grant's brigade initially broke the enemy line, but Confederate reinforcements then threatened to surround them and capture the lot. Harried subordinates counseled surrender, but Grant simply remarked: "We had cut our way in and could cut our way out just as well."[5] They proceeded to do just that.

At Fort Donelson on February 15, 1862, a Confederate breakout attack broke the Union right during Grant's temporary absence to consult the Union naval commander three miles downriver. Grant returned to find his division commander in that sector shocked and confused, the troops on the edge of panic. Where others perceived disaster, Grant saw opportunity. "Some of our men are pretty badly demoralized," he said to a staff officer, "but the enemy must be more so, for he has attempted to force his way out, but has fallen back: the one who attacks first now will be victorious and the enemy will have to be in a hurry if he gets ahead of me."[6] Grant promptly ordered his left division to make a diversionary counterattack, reorganized the right, repaired the breach, penned up the Confederates in their defenses, and compelled their surrender.

Seven weeks later at the battle of Shiloh in southwest Tennessee, after his army had been roughly handled and driven back two miles on April 6, one of Grant's staff officers asked about preparations for retreat. Surprised, Grant replied: "Retreat? No! I propose to attack at daylight, and whip them."[7] With the help of reinforcements that joined his army overnight, he did so.

This pattern persisted through the war. When Grant went east in the spring of 1864 to become general in chief, he made his headquarters in the field with the Army of the Potomac to oversee its campaign against Robert E. Lee's Army of Northern Virginia. Union officers who had faced Lee for two years warned repeatedly that he was up against the enemy's first team now. When the Army of the Potomac experienced a tactical reverse in its first battle under Grant, in the "Wilderness" of Virginia, a distraught brigadier rode up to Grant and blurted out a panicked warning that Lee would get in the Union rear and cut them off from their retreat route over the Rappahannock River. Grant fixed him with a glare and declared: "Oh, I am heartily tired of hearing what Lee is going to do. Some of you always think he is about to turn a double somersault, and land in our rear and on both of our flanks at the same time. Go back to your command, and try to think what we are going to do ourselves, instead of what Lee is going to do."[8] Grant suited action to words, and maintained the initiative to the end at Appomattox eleven months later.

It is one thing to describe Grant's calmness under pressure, his ability to size up a situation quickly, and his decisiveness in action. It is quite another to explain the inner sources of these strengths. Ultimately, as Sherman noted, the explanation must remain a mystery. But some things are clear. Grant possessed that most uncommon quality, common sense. He had the capacity—like Harry Truman, whom Grant resembled in many ways—to make a decision and stick with it. Union general John Schofield noted that the most extraordinary quality of Grant's "extraordinary character" was "its extreme simplicity—so extreme that many have entirely overlooked it in their search for some deeply hidden secret to account for so great a character, unmindful that simplicity is one of the most prominent attributes of greatness."[9] Grant made it look easy.

Grant modeled himself, consciously or subconsciously, on Zachary Taylor, his old commander in the Mexican War. "General Taylor," Grant wrote, "never made any great show or parade, either of uniform or retinue." Neither did Grant. "But he was known to every soldier in his army, and was respected by all." So was Grant. "Taylor was not a great conversationalist." Nor was Grant. "But on paper he could put his meaning so plainly that there could be no mistaking it." So could Grant; one of his virtues as a commander was the clarity of his orders and dispatches. "No soldier could face either danger or responsibility more calmly than Taylor. These are qualities more rarely found than genius or physical courage."[10]

Grant proved his physical courage under fire many times in the Mexican War as well as in the Civil War. So did many others. But as Grant noted, the willingness to take responsibility and to make decisions—which Grant called "moral courage"—was much rarer. It embraces a readiness to take risks and to accept the possibility of failure, for without the risk of failure there is little chance of success. Fear of failure caused paralysis of will and evasion of action by several Civil War generals—most notably George B. McClellan. Grant and Lee were the preeminent Civil War commanders because, more than any others, they were the ones willing to take the largest risks. Grant had known failure. He started the war with a lowly position and no reputation. As his biographer Brooks Simpson notes, "perhaps he was not afraid of failure because he had encountered setbacks so many times."[11]

Grant also possessed what Simpson calls a "sense of self." Even when others did not believe in him, he believed in himself. A passage in Grant's memoirs portrays a revelatory experience early in the war that gave him a sense of self thereafter. His first field operation as colonel of the 21st Illinois, in July 1861, was intended to find and break up a Confederate guerrilla band in Missouri commanded by one Tom Harris. "My sensations as we approached what I supposed might be 'a field of battle' were anything but agreeable," Grant recalled. "I had been in all the engagements in Mexico that it was possible for one person to be in; but not in command. If some one else had been colonel and I had been lieutenant-colonel I do not think I would have felt any trepidation." When they reached the enemy camp they found it abandoned. Grant's anxieties dissolved. "It occurred to me at once that Harris had been as much afraid of me as I had been of him. . . . From that event to the close of the war . . . I never forgot that the enemy had as much reason to fear my forces as I had his. The lesson was valuable."[12] It was a lesson that several other commanders never learned.

Grant needed every bit of that self-confidence when he came up against Lee in the final year of the war. This campaign, and especially the first six weeks of it, from May 5 to June 18, 1864, witnessed the most relentless fighting and the cruelest carnage of the war, culminating in a prolonged stalemate in the trenches before Petersburg and Richmond that anticipated the Western Front in World War I. Historians have often described these events as Grant's "campaign of attrition" to grind down the Confederates with superior numbers and resources. Union frontal assaults at Spotsylvania, Cold Harbor, and Petersburg gave Grant a reputation as a "butcher."

This description is distorted. The campaign turned out to be one of attrition, but that was more Lee's doing than Grant's. The Union commander intended to maneuver Lee into a position for open-field combat; Lee parried these efforts from elaborate entrenchments with the hope of holding out long enough to discourage the Northern people and force their leaders to make peace—a strategy of psychological attrition. It almost worked, but Lincoln's reelection and Grant's determination to stay the course brought victory in the end. And if any general deserved the label "butcher," it was Lee. Although the Confederates had the advantage of fighting on the defensive most of the time, they suffered almost as high a percentage of casualties as the Union forces in this campaign. For the war as a whole, Lee's army had a higher casualty rate than the armies commanded by Grant. The romantic glorification of the Army of Northern Virginia by generations of Lost Cause writers has obscured this truth.

If any one facet of Grant's popular image stands out above others, it is Grant the drunk. Brooks Simpson's biography offers the most balanced and informed analysis of this matter. Grant's reputation as a heavy drinker is based very little on evidence and a great deal on gossip, envy, and vengefulness. The truth seems to be that heavy drinking was the norm among officers in the antebellum army, to assuage the boredom of peacetime routine at remote outposts. Grant probably drank less than his peers, but he could not hold his liquor well. In 1854, two years and two thousand miles away from his family, including an infant son he had never seen, Grant probably drank to excess and may have resigned to escape a court-martial for drunkenness. Whatever happened, the story of his drinking became a staple of gossip in the old army. Grant "never shook the stories," writes Simpson; "they would haunt him for the rest of his life."[13]

During the war such stories proliferated, usually circulated by dishonest war contractors, corrupt subordinates, or jealous rivals whom Grant had reprimanded, dismissed, or supplanted. "Any time he offended someone," notes Simpson, "that someone was sure to whisper that the general was a drunkard."[14] The two most notorious incidents of Grant's alleged drunkenness during the war—during the Vicksburg campaign and soon after it—never happened, according to Simpson. Although Grant sometimes took a drink during the war, and may on occasion have taken two, his colleagues who knew him best and were in the best position to observe him were unanimous in their testimony that he was rarely if ever drunk. Simpson's findings should lay to rest the image of Grant the drunk—but given the power of myth over reality, they probably will not.

Grant's personal friend and comrade in arms General William T. Sherman suffered from his own image problem. Nervous, voluble, prone to overstatement, Sherman had suffered something of a nervous breakdown under the pressure of commanding the Department of the Cumberland in the fall of 1861. After a few months of rest and recuperation, he recovered to perform in outstanding fashion as a division commander under Grant at the battle of Shiloh in April 1862. But Sherman could never entirely escape the reputation of madness—especially when he made enemies of newspaper reporters, whom he despised. In a masterpiece of ironic satire, Sherman described his friendship with Grant: "He stood by me when I was crazy and I stood by him when he was drunk, and now, sir, we stand by each other always."[15]

Two recent books have portrayed the personal rapport and professional partnership between Grant and Sherman as, in the slightly overstated subtitle of one, "the friendship that won the Civil War." Their principal instrument in achieving this victory was the Army of the Tennessee, which Grant commanded from its origins in 1861 to October 1863 and Sherman commanded for the rest of the war. This army, according to Steven Woodworth, was "the most effective fighting force on the continent" by 1864. It "won the decisive battles in the decisive theater of the war" while other Union armies were losing battles or barely holding their own.[16]

Like most Union armies, the Army of the Tennessee was named after the river that flowed through its initial area of operations. It grew from a core of several brigades commanded by Grant that occupied the vital strategic region where four navigable rivers come together along the Illinois-Kentucky border: the Cumberland, Tennessee, Ohio, and Mississippi rivers. This army increased to its maximum size of about 60,000 men during the Vicksburg campaign in 1863. Soldiers in the Army of the Tennessee came almost entirely from the states of what we now call the Midwest: Ohio, Indiana, Illinois, Michigan, Wisconsin, Iowa, Missouri, and Minnesota. The Midwesterners Grant and Sherman (both born in Ohio) created this army in their own image, writes Woodworth: "It partook . . . of [Grant's] matter-of-fact steadiness and his hard-driving aggressiveness" as well as of Sherman's genius for strategic mobility.[17]

When Grant came east in 1864 to become general in chief, his efforts to instill into the Army of the Potomac the aggressive, can-do attitude that he brought with him enjoyed limited success. He was never able to turn that army into the supple, quick-striking instrument of his will that he had made of the smaller Army of the Tennessee. Woodworth implies a geographical explanation for this contrast. Most soldiers in the Army of the Potomac came from the longer-settled and more urban states of the Northeast, while "Grant's qualities tended to be those of that up-and-coming region" of the Midwest that furnished the soldiers in the Army of the Tennessee. They "were quick to adopt Grant's approach to war, because it was the way their own fathers had approached the challenges of carving farms out of the wilderness."[18] This interpretation may have some validity, but a more likely explanation for the Army of the Potomac's relative inertia is the legacy of General George B. McClellan, who created that army and stamped it with his trademark defensive-mindedness and lack of initiative.

Perhaps, too, the Army of the Tennessee was not quite so all-conquering as suggested by the title of Woodworth's book, *Nothing but Victory*. This title comes from a letter by Captain Jacob Ritner of the 25th Iowa Infantry to his wife just before the attack against Confederate defenses on Missionary Ridge at Chattanooga in November 1863. "We all expect a hot fight before long," wrote Ritner, "but we expect nothing but victory."[19] On this occasion, however, the three divisions of the Army of the Tennessee (commanded by Sherman) failed to carry their objective, while troops from the Army of the Cumberland and Army of the Potomac, in the first battle in which parts of all three principal Union armies fought together, attacked successfully and won the battle.

Nor were all the other actions fought by the Army of the Tennessee victorious. In December 1862 four divisions of that army attacked a strong Confederate position at Chickasaw Bluffs just north of Vicksburg and were repulsed with heavy casualties. And at the culmination of a successful campaign to drive Vicksburg's defenders back into their trenches in May 1863, the Army of the Tennessee's first two assaults against these formidable works suffered bloody setbacks.

Nevertheless, it is quite true that this army penetrated farther into Confederate territory, destroyed more enemy resources, and experienced more consistent success than any other Union army. Its capture of two Confederate strongholds in Tennessee, Fort Henry and Fort Donelson (with the help of river gunboats), in February 1862 enabled Union forces to drive deeply into the enemy heartland by way of the Tennessee and Cumberland rivers. Two months later Grant's snatching of victory from the jaws of defeat at Shiloh paved the way for the capture of Memphis and the breaking of the Confederacy's major east-west railroad. Despite the repulse of the first two assaults at Vicksburg, the Army of the Tennessee won five other battles leading up to those attacks and eventually captured this Confederate bastion along with its 30,000 defenders. Then, having cut the Confederacy in twain at Vicksburg, the Army of the Tennessee constituted the "maneuvering and striking force" of Sherman's army group in the campaign that captured Atlanta in September 1864 and half of his army as it marched from Atlanta to the sea and from Savannah to Raleigh by the war's end.[20]

The Army of the Tennessee's role as the *maneuvering* force in the Atlanta campaign was particularly significant. Despite Sherman's reputation in the South as a ferocious ogre of vengeance and spoliation, he was actually sparing of the lives of his own soldiers, of the enemy's soldiers, and of civilians. He preferred to accomplish his strategic goals by maneuver rather than by all-out combat. After the battle of Shiloh in 1862 he wrote to his wife: "The scenes on this field would have cured anybody of war. Mangled bodies, dead, dying, in every conceivable shape, without heads [or] legs."[21] Sherman tried to conduct his campaigns to avoid another Shiloh. Of seventeen Civil War army commanders on both sides, Sherman had the second-lowest percentage of casualties in his armies (Robert E. Lee's army had the highest).[22]

Although many historians have written about Sherman and the Atlanta campaign, the best study of Sherman's strategy remains Basil H. Liddell Hart's biography, published three-quarters of a century ago and strangely neglected by modern scholars.[23] There is a whiff of armchair generalship, or Monday-morning quarterbacking, in the writings of Civil War historians (myself included) who have never been in combat. Not so with Liddell Hart. A student at Cambridge when World War I began, he was commissioned in 1914 and fought on the Western Front until he was wounded and gassed at the Somme in 1916. After the war he became one of the foremost experts on military history and strategy in the English-speaking world. His main effort in the 1920s was to develop alternatives to the devastating trench warfare and frontal assaults that he had experienced on the Western Front. He found his alternative in the restoration of mobility and surprise, which he termed a "strategy of the indirect approach."[24]

Searching military history for examples to illustrate this strategy, Liddell Hart discovered Sherman's Georgia campaign of 1864. So impressed was he with Sherman that he not only drew upon this example in many articles and books but also wrote his 450-page biography of Sherman in 1929. Liddell Hart's ideas on mobility, deception, and the indirect approach shaped the new doctrine of armored warfare, which envisaged the employment of tanks and motorized infantry for deep penetration behind enemy lines. Liddell Hart helped create the British Mechanized Force in 1927. His writings were translated into German and had an impact on the ideas of Heinz Guderian, the chief architect of the Wehrmacht's Panzer strategy. In this indirect fashion, Sherman's Atlanta campaign may have influenced the development of Germany's blitzkrieg strategy in 1940.[25]

The Civil War as well as World War I offered many examples of a strategy of *direct* approach—an advance against the enemy by the most obvious route and an attack on the enemy's chosen defensive position. An indirect approach involved feints and turning movements to confuse the enemy and get on his flank or into his rear, forcing him out of position and compelling him to retreat or fight at a disadvantage. Liddell Hart's (and Sherman's) indirect approach also included two other maneuvers: first, "organized dispersion," an advance in wide, loosely grouped formations on separate roads within supporting distance of each other "like the waving tentacles of an octopus" to confuse the enemy and conceal the actual objective until the last moment; second, the use of a "baited gambit" (Liddell Hart was a chess player) to tempt an enemy force to attack an apparently isolated unit of one's own army, only to discover that this gambit was a trap that brought the enemy's flank or rear under attack once he was committed.[26]

In Sherman's Georgia campaign, Liddell Hart found numerous examples of deep turning movements, organized dispersion, and the baited gambit. Five times from May to July 1864 Sherman flanked the Confederate army commanded by General Joseph E. Johnston out of strong defensive positions with deep turning movements. Four were carried out by the Army of the Tennessee. After General John Bell Hood replaced Johnston as the Confederate commander, Sherman's baited gambits caused Hood to batter his army to pieces in four attacks that resulted in 18,000 Confederate casualties and the loss of Atlanta. Three of the four battles involved mainly the Army of the Tennessee on the Union side.

These events broke the spirit of many in the South. But not of Jefferson Davis, who insisted that the Confederacy remained "as erect and defiant as ever. Nothing [has] changed in the purpose of its Government, in the indomitable valor of its troops, or in the unquenchable spirit of its people. . . . There is no military success of the enemy which can accomplish its destruction." As for Sherman, said Davis, Southern guerrillas and cavalry would swarm in his rear and chop his army off at the knees. "The fate that befell the army of the French Empire in its retreat from Moscow will be reenacted. Our cavalry and our people will harass and destroy his army as did the Cossacks that of Napoleon, and the Yankee General, like him, will escape with only a bodyguard."[27]

When Grant read Davis's speech, he scoffed: "Mr. Davis has not made it quite plain who is to furnish the snow for this Moscow retreat."[28] A clever riposte; but Sherman proposed to break Davis's last-ditch defiance with more than words. One week after Lincoln's reelection, Sherman's army set forth from Atlanta on its famous march to the sea. This operation gave Sherman an opportunity to spread his octopus tentacles by sending each of his four corps on separate roads covering a swath of Georgia sixty miles wide, using baited gambits to keep the enemy in the dark about his objective. "Sherman had sought and found a solution in variability, or elasticity," wrote Liddell Hart, "the choice of a line leading to alternative objectives with the power to vary his course to gain whichever the enemy left open."[29]

Sherman's march from Atlanta to Savannah in November–December 1864 has become the stuff of legend, but the campaign of his army northward from Savannah to North Carolina in February–March 1865 was an even more stunning achievement. In both campaigns Sherman's 60,000 men lived off the land they marched through. But the Georgia march covered 285 miles in a direction parallel to the principal rivers in relatively dry fall weather against token enemy opposition. The march through the Carolinas covered a distance 50 percent greater and crossed many rain-swollen rivers and swamps in an unusually wet winter against increasing opposition as the Confederates scraped together a small army in a futile effort to stop Sherman. General Joseph E. Johnston, whom Jefferson Davis reluctantly restored to command in February 1865, believed that it would be "absolutely impossible for an army to march across lower portions of [South Carolina] in winter." But, he later wrote, "when I learned that Sherman's army was marching through the Salk swamps, making its own corduroy roads at the rate of a dozen miles a day and more, and bringing its artillery and wagons with it, I made up my mind that there had been no such army in existence since the days of Julius Caesar."[30]

The mobility and logistics of these marches were part of Sherman's strategy of the indirect approach. Without any large battles, they devastated Confederate resources and undermined the will of the Southern people to continue fighting. The Army of the Tennessee was the cutting edge of these marches. Their achievements added to a cocky conviction that they were better than other Union armies, especially the Army of the Potomac. "The war would never end were it left to the fighting of the band box army in the east," wrote an Indiana private in 1863. "They have been in but one Confederate state [Virginia] while we have been through five." An Illinois soldier thought that "the Potomac Army is only good to draw greenbacks and occupy winter quarters." For their part, Eastern Union soldiers sometimes derided the less-disciplined Westerners as "nothing but an armed mob, and [their adversaries] are not anything near so hard to whip as Lee's well disciplined soldiers."[31]

When soldiers from the Army of the Tennessee and the Army of the Potomac first came together, as did parts of both armies in October 1863 to reinforce the hard-pressed Army of the Cumberland at Chattanooga after its defeat in the battle of Chickamauga, they traded insults and sometimes blows. "The eastern men have always been defeated while the western men have been victorious," wrote an Iowa soldier, "yet these yankees [i.e., Northeasterners] pretend to look down on the western men & officers with contempt. . . . It will cause a rumpus yet & get some of these yankees an all fired thrashing."[32]

The experience of fighting together against a common foe diminished this enmity during Sherman's 1864 Georgia campaign, when transfers from the Army of the Potomac made up a significant part of his army. But the Westerners still considered themselves superior to the "Yankees" back in Virginia. And it is certainly true that while the Army of the Potomac and the Confederate Army of Northern Virginia fought each other to a bloody stalemate across a narrow front of two hundred miles for almost four years, Union armies in the West—especially the Army of the Tennessee—marched victoriously through twelve hundred miles of enemy territory. The Southern resources and railroads and other infrastructure they destroyed did much to bring about ultimate Union victory. Yet that victory could not be achieved until Confederate armies were eliminated, especially Robert E. Lee's Army of Northern Virginia. So long as that army existed, so did the Confederate nation. And it was the much-maligned Army of the Potomac that finally brought Lee's army to bay at Appomattox.

The war was won only by hard fighting, and the Army of the Potomac did most of that fighting. Of the ten largest battles in the war (each with combined Union and Confederate casualties of 23,000 or more), seven were fought between the Army of the Potomac and the Army of Northern Virginia. Of the fifty Union regiments with the largest percentage of battle casualties, forty-one fought in the Eastern theater. Of course, in the grim calculus of war, sustaining casualties is less important than inflicting them, but there too the Army of the Potomac did far more than other Union armies. Of the fifty Confederate regiments with the highest percentage of combat casualties, forty were in the Army of Northern Virginia.[33] In terms of fighting prowess, therefore, the "band box" soldiers in the Army of the Potomac more than held their own.

In other respects also the Western soldiers were perhaps not quite so tough as they—and some historians—have portrayed them. In all wars before the twentieth century, microbes were more lethal than bullets. Nearly twice as many soldiers died from disease as from combat in the Civil War. Recruits from rural areas were more vulnerable to microbes than those from cities and towns who had previously been exposed to diseases like measles and mumps that farm boys had not encountered while growing up. Virtual epidemics of these childhood diseases swept the camps of Midwestern soldiers, weakening their resistance to the killer diseases of the Civil War: diarrhea/dysentery, typhoid, pneumonia, and malaria. Soldiers from Midwestern states in Union armies suffered a disease mortality rate 43 percent higher than those from the more urban states of the Northeast—while the latter had a combat mortality rate 23 percent greater than Midwesterners.[34]

In any event, by the fall of 1864 Grant and Sherman had forged a winning strategy that combined the relentless hammering by the Army of the Potomac to cripple and eventually destroy the Army of Northern Virginia with the march through the Deep South by Sherman's army group, spearheaded by the Army of the Tennessee, to wreck the Southern infrastructure. Neither part of this strategy would have alone won the war; in combination they proved triumphant. It was not pretty, but it was effective. As Sherman famously expressed it in a speech fifteen years later to an audience too young to have fought in the war but already beginning to romanticize it, war is not a glorious adventure; when "you come down to the practical realities, boys, war is all hell."

# 10

# The Hard Hand of War

I N 1994, ONE HUNDRED AND THIRTY YEARS after General William T. Sherman's army set forth on its march from Atlanta to the sea, Sherman's legacy remained vivid and bitter in the South. A proposed monument to Sherman's soldiers at Bentonville, North Carolina, where one of the last battles of the Civil War took place, ran into a firestorm of local opposition. Sherman was "more evil than Ivan the Terrible or Genghis Khan," declared the secretary of cultural resources for North Carolina. His soldiers deserved no monument, agreed the state commander of the Sons of Confederate Veterans. "Monuments should be erected to heroes. These were no heroes. They were thieves, murderers, rapists, arsonists, trespassers."[1]

These words are a fair sample of opinion among guardians of the Lost Cause legend in the South. The Sons of Confederate Veterans celebrated their defeat of the plan for a monument (Bentonville Battlefield is a state park) as a glorious victory by the heirs of those who should have won the war. The American Civil War is a highly visible exception to the adage that victors write the history of wars. No other defeated nation has had more numerous and ardent champions than the Confederacy. And no other victorious general since Genghis Khan has had a worse historiographical reputation than Sherman. In recent years, however, his devil image has undergone considerable transformation outside the ranks of neo-Confederate partisans.[2]

Mark Grimsley's *The Hard Hand of War* strips away the myths and explores the reality of Sherman's attack on the Southern civilian economy and population as a means of winning the war. Grimsley maintains that the actions of Sherman and other Union commanders were "seldom the wanton, wholesale fury of legend" but rather struck a "balance between severity and restraint" and were "indeed discriminate and roughly proportional to legitimate needs."[3] Compared with the policies of Philip II of Spain against the Dutch in the sixteenth century, with those of the British in Ireland and of all armies in Germany

during the Thirty Years War in the seventeenth century, or with the murder
and bombing of civilians by both Axis and Allies in World War II, "the restraint of Union armies in the Civil War acquires fresh salience."[4] This argument will not change the minds of the Sons of Confederate Veterans. But it will
impress fair-minded readers.

Several historians have portrayed Sherman as the progenitor of modern
"total war," which reached its climax in World War II.[5] By 1864 Union military
leaders, especially Sherman, concentrated on the destruction of Southern railroads, factories, farms, and anything else that sustained the Confederate war
effort. The emancipation of slaves was part of this "total war" against Southern
resources, for the slaves made up most of the South's labor force and their liberation would cripple the Confederate economy. Sherman's recognition that
the civilian population can be as important in war as armies themselves is regarded as a harbinger of the future. "We are not only fighting hostile armies,"
he said, "but a hostile people, and must make old and young, rich and poor,
feel the hard hand of war."[6]

Sherman also practiced psychological warfare against enemy civilians in a
manner that supposedly anticipated total war in the twentieth century. The
terror that his soldiers provoked among Southern whites "was a power," he
wrote, "and I intended to utilize it . . . to humble their pride, to follow them to
their inmost recesses, and to make them fear and dread us. . . . We cannot
change the hearts and minds of those people of the South, but we can make
war so terrible" and "make them so sick of war that generations would pass
away before they would again appeal to it."[7]

These words make Sherman sound like an advocate of total war. But Grimsley
challenges this notion. He accepts the thesis of Mark Neely that true total war is
war "without any scruples or limitations" that "breaks down the distinction between soldiers and civilians, combatants and noncombatants," war in which soldiers give no quarter, take no prisoners, and make no discrimination between
the lives of enemy soldiers and enemy civilians, "and this no one in the Civil War
did systematically."[8] As Grimsley makes clear, the killing or even rape of white
civilians in the South by Union soldiers was extremely rare, in contrast to most
invading and conquering armies through history. Sherman's soldiers destroyed a
great deal of property, to be sure. But Axis and Allied bombers in World War II
destroyed hundreds of thousands of civilian lives as well. *That* was total war.

Grimsley searches for a different label to describe the kind of conflict the
American Civil War became by 1864. His solution is "hard war," characterized

by a military policy of "directed severity."[9] These phrases, however, are less important than the story that gives them meaning, and Grimsley tells that story more clearly than anyone else has done. In lucid, straightforward prose grounded in thorough research he analyzes the evolution of Union strategy through three main phases. The first was a policy of "conciliation," premised on a belief in the essential loyalty to the Union of a silent majority of Southern people. The passions of the moment, so the argument went, had stampeded them into the secessionist camp. If the Union government and its armies pursued a policy of firmness tempered by restraint, that silent majority would gradually be won back to loyalty. The deluded fire-eaters who had taken the South into rebellion and the armies they had raised were the enemy, but the mass of Southern people were not. Thus Northern commanders invading the Confederacy in the first year of the war issued strict orders against pillaging and placed guards around Southern civilian property to enforce these orders. Above all, the Lincoln administration and Congress pledged in 1861 not to touch the most sensitive property of all—the slaves.

None other than William T. Sherman was initially an outspoken advocate of the conciliation policy. In the summer of 1861 he deplored the marauding tendencies of Union soldiers in Virginia: "No goths or vandals ever had less respect for the lives and property of friends and foes, and henceforth we ought never to hope for any friends in Virginia."[10] As late as July 1862, when Sherman commanded Union occupation forces in the Memphis area, he punished some of his men who took mules and horses from farmers. Such "petty thieving and pillaging," he wrote, "does us infinite harm." He authorized military police to shoot soldiers who stole or vandalized private property. "This demoralizing and disgraceful practice of pillage must cease," he declared, "else the country will rise on us and justly shoot us down like dogs and wild beasts."[11] Sherman's brother John, a powerful senator from Ohio, even went so far in August 1862 as to rebuke the general for "your leniency to the rebels" who were "bitter enemies to be . . . conquered by confiscation . . . by terror, energy, audacity, rather than by conciliation."[12]

John Sherman's words foreshadowed a new policy—one that his brother soon embraced wholeheartedly. Several factors produced this turn toward "hard war." The first was loss of faith in those presumed legions of Southern Unionists ready to reassert their control once Northern armies conquered Southern territory and defeated Confederate armies. Northern forces *did* conquer thousands of square miles of territory and win several battles in the first half of 1862, but few Unionists came forward. Instead, guerrilla raids behind Union lines burned railroad bridges and ripped up tracks, fired into Northern supply boats on the Western rivers, attacked Union picket outposts, and ambushed Northern soldiers unless they moved in large groups. These activities convinced William T. Sherman as well as other Union officers that, in Sherman's words, they must act henceforth "on the proper rule that all in the South *are* enemies of all in the North. . . . The whole country is full of guerrilla bands. . . . The entire South, man, woman, and child, is against us, armed and determined."[13]

By 1862, also, the rank and file of Union soldiers had grown tired of the "kid glove" policy of leaving untouched the property of civilians whom they suspected of having rebel sympathies and of harboring guerrillas and snipers. Like soldiers in all wars who find themselves hungry, cold, and hated in enemy territory at the end of long and precarious supply lines, they helped themselves to crops and livestock owned by enemy civilians and to fence rails for fires to cook this booty and to keep warm. As one Union soldier in western Tennessee put it in August 1862, "This thing of guarding rebels' property has about 'played out.' " In the same month orders went out from General in Chief Henry W. Halleck in Washington to General Ulysses Grant in Mississippi: "Take up all active [rebel] sympathizers and either hold them as prisoners or put them beyond our lines. Handle that class without gloves, and take their property for public use. . . . It is time that they should begin to feel the presence of the war."[14]

As commander in chief, Lincoln played an active part in this movement toward hard war. He approved a War Department executive order on July 22, based on the Confiscation Act passed five days earlier, that authorized Union military commanders anywhere in the South to "seize and use any property, real or personal, which may be necessary or convenient . . . for supplies or other military purposes."[15] When complaints about this policy reached Lincoln from Northern Democrats and professed Southern Unionists, the president responded with a hard line. Did they expect him to prosecute the war "with elder-stalk squirts, charged with rose water? Would you deal lighter blows rather than heavier ones? . . . This government cannot much longer play a game in which it stakes all, and its enemies stake nothing. Those enemies must understand that they cannot experiment for ten years trying to destroy the government, and if they fail still come back into the Union unhurt."[16]

In the executive order of July 22, the reference to "personal" property could be construed to include slaves. Indeed, Lincoln had decided to issue an emancipation proclamation, and so informed his cabinet on that same day, July 22. Two months would pass before he actually issued the preliminary Emancipation Proclamation on September 22, after the Union military victory at Antietam. But the commitment to emancipation in July gave the coup de grace to the policy of conciliation. Lincoln had become convinced, as he told the cabinet, that "the slaves were undeniably an element of strength to those who had their service, and we must decide whether that element should be with us or against us. . . . Decisive and extensive measures must be adopted. We wanted the army to strike more vigorous blows. The Administration must set an example and strike at the heart of the rebellion"—slavery.[17]

In January 1863, after Lincoln had issued the final proclamation, General Halleck pronounced the epitaph of the conciliation policy: "The character of the war has very much changed within the last year," he wrote to Grant. "There is now no possible hope of reconciliation with the rebels. . . . We must conquer the rebels or be conquered by them. . . . Every slave withdrawn from the enemy is the equivalent of a white man put *hors de combat*."[18]

The end of conciliation did not lead immediately to the "hard war" of 1864–65. Grimsley describes an intermediate stage variously labeled "war in earnest" or "a vigorous war policy." Its chief characteristic was an expansion of foraging for supplies by Northern forces fighting deep in enemy territory. Union armies also practiced the age-old military policy of "area denial"— destruction of food and forage they did not consume in order to deny it to the enemy. Such legitimate and authorized activities often got out of hand; as with armies throughout history, the line between foraging and pillaging grew so thin that it sometimes disappeared altogether.[19]

These exercises became more frequent in the last year of the war as Union armies sliced through the Shenandoah Valley of Virginia, the interior of Georgia and South Carolina, and other regions that had previously escaped the hardest hand of war. With Grant now in command of all Union armies and Sherman in command of his most mobile field army, "the Union strategy of 1864–1865 aimed at both the destruction of rebel armies and the destruction of rebel war-making capability." This was not a policy of wanton devastation of all property. Rather it was "directed severity"—the targeting of resources capable of sustaining armies. This "combination of severity and restraint," Grimsley maintains, resulted from "a basic morality" that still prevailed among Union soldiers "even in 1864, after years of warfare. . . . Public and quasipublic property like railroads, warehouses, and factories received the rough ministrations of Federal troops more often than private property. Plantations—the lairs of the slaveholding aristocracy—were targeted far more often than small farms." Although "not averse to destruction," Union soldiers "wanted to see the hard hand of war descend on those who deserved it, and usually only in rough proportion to the extent of their sins."[20]

But what about all those houses that Yankee troops burned, leaving only their chimneys standing as "Sherman's sentinels" over hundreds of miles of ruined countryside? What about the burning of Atlanta, Columbia, and other towns? Grimsley concedes that Union soldiers did occasionally burn, loot, and pillage private property of no military value. But they burned far fewer houses in reality than they did in Southern memory—an interesting fact discovered by James Reston Jr. in 1982 when he retraced Sherman's route through Georgia. He encountered locals who said Sherman had burned everything in his path, but then proudly pointed out the fine examples of antebellum architecture in the neighborhood.[21]

In South Carolina, however, reality approached myth. "The truth is," Sherman wrote as he prepared to enter that state, "the whole army is burning with an insatiable desire to wreak vengeance on South Carolina. I almost tremble for her fate, but feel that she deserves all that seems in store for her." Union soldiers put hundreds of houses to the torch in South Carolina. They gleefully renamed the village of Barnwell "Burnwell." But to Grimsley this proves his thesis of directed severity. Northerners considered South Carolina the cockpit of secession, the home of the hottest fire-eaters, the state that started the war by firing on the American flag at Fort Sumter. A Union soldier was heard to say as he entered South Carolina: "Here is where treason began and, by God, here is where it shall end."[22] When the army crossed the border into North Carolina the "wanton destruction" ended, Grimsley notes, thus underscoring the "substantially directed nature of the severity that had preceded it" and furnishing "one of the strongest proofs of the sense of discriminating righteousness that animated the Federal rank and file."[23]

Grimsley has probably not converted many members of the Sons of Confederate Veterans to an appreciation of this sense of discriminating righteousness. They are not likely any time soon to support the building of a monument to Sherman and his soldiers. They will continue to revere Robert E. Lee as the greatest general of the Civil War—perhaps the greatest general in American history. But they probably will not appreciate Lee's role in the greatest irony of the Civil War—one that goes a long way toward explaining the evolution of

Union military policy into Mark Grimsley's "hard war." When Lee took command of the Army of Northern Virginia on June 1, 1862, the Confederacy was on the verge of defeat. Union conquests in the West had brought more than 50,000 square miles of Confederate territory under Northern control and had caused profound discouragement in the South. General George B. McClellan's large Army of the Potomac had approached to within six miles of Richmond. The Confederate government had packed its archives and treasury on trains to evacuate the capital. If the war had brought an end to the Confederacy in the summer of 1862, slavery and the antebellum Southern social order would have remained largely intact and the Southern infrastructure relatively undamaged. But Lee's counteroffensive in the Seven Days battles and other major victories during the next year ensured a prolongation of the war, opening the way to the emergence of Grant and Sherman to top Union commands, the abolition of slavery, the "directed severity" of Union policy in 1864–65, and the *Götterdämmerung* of the Old South. Here was the irony of Robert E. Lee: His success produced the destruction of everything he fought for.

# 11

# Unvexed to the Sea: Lincoln, Grant, and the Vicksburg Campaign

I N NOVEMBER 1861, ACCORDING TO ONE STORY, President Abraham Lincoln met with several of his military advisers to discuss strategy for gaining control of the Mississippi River. Lincoln pointed to a map of this great valley that stretched from Minnesota to the Gulf of Mexico and placed his finger on the town of Vicksburg, Mississippi. "See what a lot of land those fellows [Confederates] control of which Vicksburg is the key," he said. "The war can never be brought to a close until that key is in our pocket."[1]

This story appears in the memoirs of Admiral David Dixon Porter, written twenty years after the war. Porter was a good naval commander but an untrustworthy memoirist. He embellished many things and even constructed some things out of whole cloth—usually to make himself appear to better advantage. The meeting he described did take place, but its purpose was to plan a campaign to capture New Orleans, not Vicksburg. There is no confirmation from any other source that Lincoln mentioned Vicksburg at this meeting. At that time the Confederates controlled the whole Mississippi River from Belmont in Missouri and Columbus across the river in Kentucky to its mouth a hundred miles south of New Orleans, and Vicksburg was not then particularly more important than several other places along the river. In September 1861 Confederate general Leonidas Polk had seized Columbus, just twenty miles south of the confluence of the Ohio and Mississippi rivers at Cairo, Illinois, and fortified the bluffs there with dozens of big guns that could blow out of the water anything that tried to get past. Confederates called Columbus "the Gibraltar of the West."

If Vicksburg at this time had only marginal military importance, the river itself was a key to the strategy of both sides. The Confederates fortified several other points on the Mississippi, while Union general in chief Winfield Scott devised a strategy to snuff out the rebellion. His strategy was popularly labeled the Anaconda Plan, after the snake that wraps itself around its victims and squeezes them to death. Scott proposed to squeeze the Confederacy by a blockade of its seaports and a campaign by gunboats and troops down the Mississippi that would seal off the Confederacy from the world and slice it in two along the river. Although derided by some Northern newspapers that clamored instead for a campaign "On to Richmond," the Anaconda Plan remained a basic part of Northern strategy through the war. As the blockade tightened and Union forces eventually gained control of the whole Mississippi River, this strategy played an important part in ultimate Union victory. And Vicksburg did eventually become the key to that control.

But that did not happen until the war was more than a year old. In 1861 and the early months of 1862, Lincoln's main concern in the Western theater of the war was East Tennessee, where the majority of the population had voted against secession but Confederate troops were in control. Lincoln's focus on East Tennessee was part of his general strategy in 1861 to secure Union control of the border states and Upper South regions where Unionists were in the majority. By early 1862 that strategy had succeeded in western Virginia, which was on its way to becoming West Virginia, in Missouri except for continuing guerrilla warfare that plagued the state, and in northern Kentucky as well as Maryland. But to Lincoln's vexation, Union forces operating from Kentucky failed to come to the aid of East Tennessee Unionists when they rose in rebellion against Confederate occupation in November 1861. The Confederate army caught and hanged several of these Unionists.

Lincoln redoubled his efforts to get General Don Carlos Buell, Union commander in Kentucky, to invade East Tennessee. General in Chief George B. McClellan added his weight to the pressure on Buell. Both Lincoln and McClellan sent repeated orders to Buell to capture Knoxville with the dual purpose of liberating East Tennessee and severing the main east-west Confederate railroad, which ran through Knoxville and Chattanooga. This would aid McClellan's planned campaign against Richmond by preventing Confederate reinforcements from the West being transferred to the Virginia theater, and would disrupt the west-to-east movement of supplies for Confederate forces.

Buell just as frequently replied that central and western Tennessee were the true routes of Union advance, because the navigable Cumberland and Tennessee rivers would facilitate invasion and supply, while the rugged mountains and poor roads of East Tennessee prevented an advance in that direction. To one of these dispatches from Buell, Lincoln replied in January 1862: "It disappoints and distresses me." Knoxville was a more important strategic objective

than Nashville, Lincoln insisted, "first, because it cuts a great artery of the enemies' communication, which Nashville does not, and secondly because it is in
the midst of loyal people, who would rally around it, while Nashville is not. . . .
My distress is that our friends in East Tennessee are being hanged and driven to
despair, and even now I fear, are thinking of taking rebel arms for the sake of
personal protection. In this we lose the most valuable stake we have in the
South." At the same time, McClellan wrote to Buell: "I was extremely sorry to
learn from your telegram to the President that you had *from the beginning at-
tached little or no importance* to a movement in East Tennessee."[2]

Buell finally responded to this pressure by sending a small force under General George Thomas toward East Tennessee, provoking the battle of Mill
Springs in eastern Kentucky on January 19, 1862. It was a Union victory, but
Thomas could advance no farther, and East Tennessee remained under Confederate control for almost two more years.

Meanwhile Buell was able to move against his preferred target of Nashville
because of events farther west, along the Tennessee River. General Henry W.
Halleck, Union commander in that theater since November 1861, considered
the best line of Union operations to be the Tennessee and Cumberland rivers
rather than the Mississippi, as Scott had contemplated in the Anaconda Plan.
The Confederate bastion at Columbus was too strong to attack directly, said
Halleck, and a Union penetration up the Tennessee River (southward) would
flank both Columbus and Nashville and force the Confederates to abandon
both. Halleck had two subordinates who agreed with him and were eager to
get started: General Ulysses S. Grant and Flag Officer Andrew H. Foote. At the
beginning of February 1862 Halleck turned them loose. Once started, this
combined army-navy force proved unstoppable for several months. Foote and
Grant captured Forts Henry and Donelson; Union gunboats ranged all the way
up the Tennessee River to Florence, Alabama; the Confederates evacuated
Nashville and Columbus; Grant and Buell turned back a Confederate counteroffensive at Shiloh.

In March 1862 the Union leadership finally turned its attention to the Mis-
sissippi River and began to implement that part of Winfield Scott's Anaconda
Plan. Another army-navy task force under General John Pope and Flag Officer
Foote—soon to be replaced by Captain Charles C. Davis because a wound that
Foote had suffered at Fort Donelson incapacitated him—captured New
Madrid, Missouri, and Island No. 10 on the Mississippi. The river flotilla fought
its way south to capture Memphis in early June. A month earlier Flag Officer

Daniel Glasgow Farragut's fleet had accomplished the most spectacular feat of the war so far by capturing New Orleans. Farragut's fleet steamed upriver while Davis's gunboats continued downriver to meet at Vicksburg in June 1862. That fortified city high on the bluffs then did indeed become the key to control of the Mississippi River and its valley.

During these months Lincoln was preoccupied with the Virginia theater of the war. He spent most of his time and energy trying to get McClellan to advance and to fight. In the few spare hours that Lincoln could devote to the Western theater, he remained more concerned about East Tennessee than about Vicksburg. The main Union effort in the West after capture of the rail junction at Corinth, Mississippi, in May 1862 was Buell's effort to drive General Braxton Bragg's Army of Tennessee out of Chattanooga and finally to liberate East Tennessee. Instead, Buell found himself scrambling to defend Nashville and Louisville—and even Cincinnati—as a Confederate counteroffensive led by Bragg and General Edmund Kirby Smith invaded Kentucky, threatening Union control of that border state until they were turned back at the battle of Perryville.

When a prominent judge in St. Louis accused Lincoln of neglecting the Mississippi Valley, the president responded that he was strongly committed to opening the river, but "the country will not allow us to send our whole Western force down the Mississippi, while the enemy sacks Louisville and Cincinnati."[3] Even though circumstances continued to compel Lincoln to focus mainly on the Virginia and Kentucky-Tennessee theaters through the end of 1862, he was well aware of the importance of the great river that he had twice descended on a flatboat in his youth. He hoped that the combined power of Farragut's and Davis's fleets could capture Vicksburg in the summer of 1862. But the reinforced strength of this new Confederate "Gibraltar of the West" and the falling level of the river that threatened to ground Farragut's deep-draft vessels ended that effort in August 1862. The military crises in Kentucky and Maryland as well as attempts by two smaller Confederate armies under Generals Earl Van Dorn and Sterling Price to drive Grant out of northern Mississippi prevented any renewed effort against Vicksburg until November. And when that effort finally began, it was initially plagued by a divided Union command for which Lincoln was partly responsible.

In November 1862 the president decided to replace the notorious Benjamin Butler with Nathaniel P. Banks as commander of Union army forces in New Orleans and southern Louisiana. Banks's record in the Virginia theater, where Stonewall Jackson had handled him roughly in the spring and summer of 1862, did not give great promise of success as a combat commander in Louisiana. Nevertheless, Lincoln and his new general in chief Henry W. Halleck gave Banks the mission of opening the Mississippi River—which would of course require the capture of Vicksburg and of Port Hudson, a second fortified bastion two hundred miles south of Vicksburg. Halleck instructed Banks on November 9 that "the President regards the opening of the Mississippi River as the first and most important of all our military and naval operations, and it is hoped that you will not lose a moment in accomplishing it." Banks outranked Grant, so Halleck told Banks that "as the ranking general in the Southwest, you are authorized to assume control of any military forces from the Upper Mississippi which may come within your command. The line of division between your department and that of Major-General Grant is therefore left undecided for the present, and you will exercise superior authority as far north as you may ascend the river."[4]

Lincoln overrated Banks's command capacity, as future events would show. At this time he also overrated the abilities of another general who would complicate the command situation in the Vicksburg campaign: Major General John A. McClernand, who did not outrank Grant but thought he should. The origins of the McClernand issue may have gone back to a cabinet meeting in August 1862. A month earlier Lincoln had issued a call for 300,000 new three-year volunteers for the army, and the War Department was about to issue a requisition for an additional 300,000 nine-month militia under authorization from the recent enactment of a new militia law. The cabinet discussed the idea of using some of these new troops to supplement old regiments in a campaign to capture Vicksburg and open the Mississippi. This may have been the germ of a later project to create an army for that purpose with McClernand as its commander.[5]

A brief discussion of this project is important for an understanding of Lincoln, Grant, and the Vicksburg campaign. McClernand had served under Grant at Belmont, Forts Henry and Donelson, and Shiloh. He was ambitious for an independent command; he was also eager to get out from under Grant, and the feeling was undoubtedly mutual with Grant. Like Banks, McClernand was one of the "political generals" who had been commissioned in 1861 as part of Lincoln's effort to mobilize various political and ethnic constituencies for the war effort. Lincoln would come to regret some of these appointments—including McClernand's—but in 1861 that appointment had seemed important in order to rally lukewarm Democrats in southern and central Illinois for the war. Mc-Clernand had done a good job in that effort, and despite Grant's doubts he had also shown some aptitude for military command.

In September 1862 McClernand had persuaded Governor Richard Yates of Illinois, and through him President Lincoln, to give him authority to organize new troops recruited in the Midwest for a campaign to open the Mississippi River. Halleck and perhaps Secretary of War Edwin M. Stanton were less than enthusiastic about this project—though Stanton, like Lincoln, had become frustrated with West Point professionals like McClellan and Buell who had fumbled opportunities to win more decisive victories against the invading Confederates in Maryland and Kentucky. Lincoln was about to remove both of those generals from command, so Stanton as well as the president may have been more open to giving an independent command to the nonprofessional McClernand, who at least promised an aggressive campaign.[6]

In any case, on October 21 Stanton ordered McClernand to take charge of the remaining new regiments in Illinois, Indiana, Wisconsin, and Iowa for a campaign to open the Mississippi. But there were two significant clauses in this order, perhaps drafted or influenced by Halleck. They instructed McClernand to begin his campaign as soon as "a sufficient force not required by the operations of General Grant's command shall be raised" and also specified that "the forces so organized will remain subject to the designation of the General-in-Chief [Halleck], and be employed according to such exigencies as the service in his judgment may require."[7]

These clauses would prove to be McClernand's undoing, though perhaps only Halleck realized that at the time. Lincoln added his personal endorsement to this October 21 order: "I feel deep interest in the success of the expedition and desire it to be pushed forward with all possible dispatch."

Within a week Grant heard rumors of the proposed McClernand expedition. On November 10 Grant sought clarification from Halleck of his authority in this theater, especially as he was planning a campaign of his own against Vicksburg. Halleck wired back: "You have command of all troops sent to your Department, and have permission to fight the enemy when you please." Grant immediately telegraphed General William T. Sherman to "move on the enemy so soon as you can leave Memphis with two full Divisions"—including the regiments that McClernand had organized and sent south with the expectation that he would soon follow and take command. On December 9 Grant informed Halleck that "a letter from General McClernand, just received states that he expects to go forward in a few days. Sherman has already gone."[8] The West Pointers Grant and Halleck had outwitted the politician McClernand and had hijacked the army he expected to command.

Lincoln's role in this hijacking is unclear. What *is* clear is that he had initially appointed Banks and McClernand to important commands in the expectation that they would converge on Port Hudson and Vicksburg from the south and north to capture these bastions and open the river. The historian T. Harry Williams found this difficult to understand. "Why Lincoln passed over Grant and selected two incompetents to accomplish one of the most important objectives of Union strategy," wrote Williams in *Lincoln and His Generals*, "is hard to explain."[9] Of course, the incompetence of Banks and McClernand is more clear in retrospect than it was to Lincoln when he made these appointments. And the president was aware of the telegraphic exchanges between Halleck and Grant in which Grant received authority over all of the troops in his theater and Sherman appropriated those that McClernand expected to command. Lincoln saw all important telegrams coming into and going out of the War Department telegraph office, and Halleck rarely issued important orders without Lincoln's knowledge and approval.

McClernand arrived in Memphis at the end of December to find that his supposed army had gone south with Sherman. Grant subsequently assigned McClernand to command only one of the four corps that now constituted the Army of the Tennessee. McClernand sent angry protests to Lincoln—at precisely the time when Lincoln was bedeviled by the infighting in the officer corps of the Army of the Potomac during the aftermath of the disaster at Fredericksburg. Lincoln was in no mood to countenance McClernand's efforts to provoke similar controversies in the Army of the Tennessee. He responded to McClernand's expostulations with a stern letter advising him for his own good to bow to the inevitable and become a loyal corps commander under Grant. "I have too many *family* controversies (so to speak), already on my hands," Lincoln wrote, "to voluntarily take up another. You are now doing well—well for the country, and well for yourself—much better than you could possibly be, if engaged in open war with General Halleck. Allow me to beg, that for your sake, for my sake, & for the country's sake, you give your whole attention to the better work."[10]

It is also worth remembering that if it had not been for Lincoln's steadfast support of Grant and resistance to pressures for his removal during the past year, Grant would not have been in command of the Vicksburg campaign and perhaps not even have been in the army at all. When Halleck—now Grant's ally—had earlier chastised him after Fort Donelson for failing to send in reports and going to Nashville without authorization, and hinted that Grant had "resumed his former bad habits"—a thinly veiled reference to rumors about Grant's drinking—Lincoln had instructed Halleck to provide solid evidence of any wrongdoing by Grant, and Halleck had backed down. When similar rumors surfaced after Shiloh, Lincoln again demanded evidence, of which there was none.[11]

The story of Lincoln saying he wanted to know what brand of whiskey Grant drank so he could send some to his other generals is probably apocryphal. Also probably apocrychal is a quotation attributed to Lincoln: "I can't spare this man; he fights." But the point these stories illustrated—Lincoln's support of Grant—is quite genuine. Lincoln *did* say, after Grant had proved his worth and become famous, that "I have had stronger influence brought against Grant, praying for his removal, since the battle of Pittsburg Landing [Shiloh], than for any other object, coming too from good men. . . . If I had done as my Washington friends, who fight battles with their tongues instead of swords far from the enemy, demanded of me, Grant, who has proved himself so great a military captain, would never have been heard of again."[12] Grant's main supporter in Congress, Elihu Washburne, wrote the general in 1864 that "when the torrent of obloquy and detraction was rolling over you, and your friends, after the battle of Shiloh, Mr. Lincoln stood like a wall of fire between you and it, uninfluenced by the threats of Congressmen and the demands of insolent cowardice."[13] Perhaps the greatest contribution Lincoln made to the successful strategy of Union forces in the Western theater, and eventually in the war as a whole, was to stick with Grant through thick and thin when others wanted to get rid of him.

For a time in the winter of 1863, however, Lincoln's faith in Grant was sorely tested. The general's initial two-pronged campaign against Vicksburg in December 1862 came to grief. Troops under Grant's direct command moved overland from La Grange, Tennessee, while Sherman led others down the river from Memphis. Confederate general Earl Van Dorn commanded a cavalry raid that destroyed Grant's supply base at Holly Springs. Then Pemberton's Confederate force north of Vicksburg repulsed Sherman's attack at Chickasaw Bluffs. Grant came personally downriver to take charge of the whole Army of the Tennessee in its futile efforts to get at Vicksburg in February and March 1863. These months were a low point of the war for the North, not least because of repeated frustrations at Vicksburg: the failure of the attempt to divert the river through a canal intended to bypass the city; the wasted energy of the Lake Providence route; the repulse of the Union river fleet in the efforts to get troops on dry land east and northeast of Vicksburg by the Yazoo Pass and Steele's Bayou routes. Exaggerated reports of these failures reached Washington and the North, along with similarly exaggerated reports of the demoralization of Grant's soldiers and the ravages of typhoid fever, diarrhea and dysentery, and pneumonia killing off thousands of them.

The old rumors about Grant's drinking began to circulate again. Politicians renewed their pressure on Lincoln to get rid of Grant. One of the sharpest criticisms—made privately, but it certainly reached Lincoln's ears—came in a letter on February 19 from Joseph Medill, editor of the *Chicago Tribune,* the most powerful Republican newspaper in the Midwest, to Elihu Washburne. "Your man Grant" is a miserable failure, Medill wrote. "His army now is almost in a state of insubordination [a gross exaggeration]. Is it any wonder the military affairs of the West have been so woefully managed. No man's career in the army is more open to destructive criticism than Grant's. We have kept off him on your account. We could have made him stink in the nostrils of the public like an old fish had we properly criticised his military blunders. Was there ever a more weak and imbecile campaign?" Even Elihu Washburne's brother Cadwalader Washburn, a major general, wrote to his brother in March: "I fear Grant won't do. The truth is, Grant has no plan for taking Vicksburg, & is frittering away time & strength to no purpose. The truth must be told even when it hurts. You cannot make a silk purse out of a sow's ear."[14]

Lincoln also expressed private frustration with the apparent lack of progress in Grant's campaign.[15] In March Secretary of War Stanton, with Lincoln's approval, sent the War Department troubleshooter Charles A. Dana west, ostensibly to investigate the paymaster service in that theater but in reality to determine whether Grant deserved the administration's continued support. Dana soon began sending back confidential reports by special cipher to Stanton, who shared them with Lincoln, that were favorable to Grant. These reports probably were a major factor in Lincoln's decision to stick with Grant.[16]

At the same time, however, both Halleck and Lincoln thought that Grant's best strategy would be to combine with Banks's Army of the Gulf in a joint campaign first against Port Hudson and then against Vicksburg, or vice versa.[17] In such a case, Banks would have outranked Grant and taken command. But the distance between the two armies and the logistical nightmare of trying to unite and supply them, plus Banks's late start against Port Hudson—and also, probably, Grant's disinclination to yield command of the whole enterprise to Banks—combined to prevent any joint effort by the two armies. Moreover, by April Grant had matured the plan that he carried out brilliantly during the next several weeks and that led eventually to the capture not only of Vicksburg but also of its 30,000 defenders.

On April 16 Acting Rear Admiral David Dixon Porter began to implement Grant's plan by running his gunboat fleet plus several transports carrying supplies past the Vicksburg batteries in order to ferry the troops across to the east bank somewhere downriver. The soldiers had built bridges and corduroyed roads through the swamps and across the bayous to march down the west bank to rendezvous with the gunboats and transports. They crossed at Bruinsburg, about forty miles south of Vicksburg, against virtually no opposition.

The lack of opposition was owing to a pair of diversions that Grant organized to deceive the Confederate commander, John C. Pemberton. He sent a cavalry brigade under Colonel Benjamin Grierson on what turned out to be one of the most dramatic raids of the war from Tennessee all the way through Mississippi in the last half of April. Grierson tore up railroads and bridges, won several skirmishes and captured or killed more than six hundred Confederates at the cost of only two dozen casualties, lured most of Pemberton's cavalry and an entire infantry division into a futile effort to catch him, and rode safely into Union lines at Baton Rouge after marauding for six hundred miles, most of it through enemy territory. For the second diversion, Grant had Sherman's corps feign an attack from the Yazoo River against the bluffs north of Vicksburg near the site of his bloody repulse four months earlier. This feint worked perfectly, convincing Pemberton that it was the main attack while Grant's other two corps crossed at Bruinsburg and began a three-week campaign that most military historians consider without parallel in the war.

It was also one of the riskiest campaigns in the war. Even though most of Porter's gunboats and transports had successfully run the Vicksburg batteries *down*river with the aid of a four-knot current, they would be sitting ducks if they tried to go back up against the current to Grant's main supply base above Vicksburg. Thus, once they crossed the river deep in enemy territory, Grant's 44,000 men would be mostly on their own until they could fight their way back to some kind of base above Vicksburg. This problem worried Sherman and most of Grant's other subordinates, who advised against the move.

But Grant was confident that with the supplies his men brought with them plus those they could seize from the Mississippi countryside, they could keep going for as long as it took. When reports of Grant's success in crossing the river below Vicksburg on April 30 reached Washington, Halleck and Lincoln also worried about Grant's vulnerability deep in enemy territory where a larger enemy force might be concentrated against him. As late as May 11 Halleck sent a message to Grant urging him to combine with Banks, but such a move was out of date if not impossible by that time, and Grant demurred. If his campaign had failed he might have been in big trouble. Nothing succeeds like success, though, and Grant put his neck on the line to achieve that success.

During the three weeks after crossing the Mississippi, Grant's army marched 130 miles, fought and won five battles against enemy forces that, if combined, would have been almost as large as Grant's own, inflicted 7,200 casualties on the enemy at the cost of only 4,300 to themselves, and penned up an apparently demoralized army in the Vicksburg defenses. Union attacks on those defenses on May 19 and 22 proved that the Confederates were not as demoralized as Grant thought they were, so he reluctantly settled down to a siege. Reinforced to an eventual total of 70,000 men during the siege, Grant detached almost half of them under Sherman to guard against an attack on his rear by a force of almost 30,000 men that General Joseph E. Johnston built up east of the Big Black River. Johnston never attacked, however, and on the Fourth of July the starving Confederates surrendered. Five days later the similarly starving Confederates at Port Hudson also surrendered.

These combined captures of 37,000 men were the largest of the war, larger even than Appomattox. And Lincoln knew who deserved the credit. Even before definite news of Vicksburg's surrender reached Washington, Lincoln declared that "Grant is my man and I am his the rest of the war!" Two days later, when explicit word arrived, Lincoln told Secretary of the Navy Gideon Welles: "I cannot, in words, tell you my joy over this result. It is great, Mr. Welles, it is great!"[18]

Lincoln's joy contrasted with his disappointment at General George Meade's failure to inflict greater damage on the Army of Northern Virginia before it got back across the Potomac after Gettysburg. On July 13 Lincoln sat down and wrote a graceful letter to Grant expressing the president's "grateful acknowledgment for the almost inestimable service you have done the country." Lincoln added that "when you first reached the vicinity of Vicksburg, I thought you should do, what you finally did—march the troops across the neck, run the batteries with the transports, and thus go below; and I never had any faith, except a general hope that you knew better than I, that the Yazoo Pass expedition, and the like, could succeed. When you got below, and took Port Gibson,

Grand Gulf, and vicinity, I thought you should go down the river and join General Banks; and when you turned Northward East of the Big Black, I feared it was a mistake. I now wish to make the personal acknowledgment that you were right, and I was wrong."[19]

Grant was indeed Lincoln's man the rest of the war. In Lincoln's happy phrase, "the Father of Waters again goes unvexed to the sea."[20] The Confederacy was cut in twain. Grant's success at Vicksburg propelled his promotion to command of the entire Military Division of the Mississippi, including the Army of the Cumberland hunkered down in Chattanooga after its defeat at Chickamauga. Grant went personally to Chattanooga in October and orchestrated the Union counteroffensive in November that drove Braxton Bragg's Confederate Army of Tennessee back into Georgia, accomplished Lincoln's initial top priority for the Western theater by liberating East Tennessee, and set the stage for Sherman's campaign the next year that would slice the Confederacy into three parts. All of these triumphs stemmed primarily from two crucial factors that proved also to be the principal reasons why the North eventually won the war: Lincoln's faith in Grant through thick and thin, and Grant's vindication of that faith in the Vicksburg campaign.

# IV

# Home Front and Battle Front

# 12

# Brahmins at War

I N THE 1970S GENERAL JOHN A. WICKHAM of the U.S. Army, commander of the famed 101st Airborne Division, visited the Civil War battlefield of Antietam. There he gazed at Bloody Lane, where Union soldiers had attacked repeatedly before finally breaking through after suffering casualties greater than 50 percent in some regiments. "You couldn't get American soldiers today to make an attack like that," he said.[1]

Why not? Because neither the soldiers nor the American public would tolerate such losses. But that is probably the wrong question. The right question is: Why did Civil War soldiers do what they did? This percentage of casualties was far from unusual in Civil War battles. The 1st Texas Infantry lost 80 percent of its men killed, wounded, or missing at Antietam. Both the 1st Minnesota and 26th North Carolina similarly experienced close to 80 percent casualties at Gettysburg. Other units approached these figures in several battles. What motivated these men? How could they endure such losses and keep fighting?

I tried to answer these questions in my book *For Cause and Comrades: Why Men Fought in the Civil War*.[2] Drawing on soldiers' letters and diaries, I found that their motives included fervent patriotism, ideological convictions about the righteousness of their cause, the cohesion of community-based regimental companies, Victorian cultural values of duty, honor, courage, and manhood, in which cowardice and letting down one's comrades doomed one to eternal shame and dishonor, and religious beliefs that enabled many soldiers to face death with a composure that seems extraordinary today. I also discussed the importance of leadership by officers who could remain cool under fire, impose discipline without provoking corrosive resentment, command the confidence of their men, and not ask them to do anything or face any danger they were unwilling to do or face themselves. The best officers led from the front rather than giving orders from the rear. Among the most important factors that distinguished the best Civil War regiments from the mediocre ones were the quality and exemplary courage of their officers.

Two books published on the 140th anniversary of the war's end—one about the 20th Massachusetts Volunteer Infantry and the other a biography of Charles Russell Lowell, commander of the 2nd Massachusetts Volunteer Cavalry—have caused me to think that I may have underestimated the significance of leadership in the molding of an effective fighting unit.[3] Most of the original officers of the 20th Massachusetts Infantry and several of those in the 2nd Cavalry, including Lowell, were Harvard alumni, and an exceptional number of them were killed in battle leading their men from the front. For them the ideals of duty, honor, and sacrifice were not mere words; they were deep-rooted values for which they quite literally gave their lives. Of the 578 Harvard men who fought in the Civil War, ninety were killed—eight of them officers in the 20th Massachusetts.

Scores of additional non-Harvard sons of the Brahmin elite also served in the Union army. Massachusetts regiments—especially the 2nd and 20th Infantry and 2nd Cavalry—included such distinguished names as Abbott (two brothers, both killed), Adams, Barlow, Cabot, Crowninshield, Forbes, Higginson, Holmes (Oliver Wendell Holmes Jr., Harvard '61, wounded three times), James, Lee, Lowell (two brothers, both killed), Palfrey, Putnam, Quincy, Revere (two brothers, grandsons of Paul Revere, both killed), Russell, Sedgwick, Webster (Fletcher Webster, a son of Daniel Webster, killed at Second Bull Run as colonel of the 12th Massachusetts Infantry), and Whittier. Three nephews of the poet James Russell Lowell lost their lives in the war. Charles Russell Lowell, his brother, a brother-in-law, and six of his thirteen cousins who fought in the war were killed.

Most of these men served as officers, but a few Harvard alumni fought in the ranks. The most accomplished was Francis Balch, who enlisted in the 20th Massachusetts in 1862. Class of 1859 at Harvard, Balch had won the Detur Prize as a freshman and the Bowdoin Prize and Thayer Scholarship as a junior, graduated as valedictorian, and earned a law degree from Harvard in 1861. He survived the war and in 1867 fathered Emily Balch, who in 1946 won the Nobel Peace Prize for her work on behalf of the League of Nations and other international organizations.

What motivated these men, officers and privates alike, nearly all of whom enlisted before the Union draft went into effect in mid-1863—and who could have bought exemption in any case? First, many of them were descendants of the Revolutionary generation that had won independence from Britain and founded the nation now threatened with destruction. "The institutions of the country, indeed free institutions, hang on this moment," wrote Paul Revere—grandson of the Revolutionary War hero—two years before Abraham Lincoln made the same point at Gettysburg. "I should be ashamed of myself if I were to sit down in happy indulgence, and leave such a great matter as this to take its course."[4] Charles Russell Lowell's great-grandfather had roomed with James Madison when they were delegates to the Continental Congress. As Carol Bundy notes in *The Nature of Sacrifice*, "virtually all Lowell's friends could claim at least one ancestor who had been a Founding Father" or had "fought in the Revolutionary War." The same was true of most of the Brahmin elite in the Union army: "So the desire of these young men to preserve the Union, to defend the Constitution and its principles, was not an abstract or philosophical attitude but one imbued with almost hereditary, even proprietary feelings."[5]

Strong convictions of duty and honor grew from this heritage—the duty to serve, and the dishonor of failing to serve. Explaining his decision to enlist (against his father's wishes), Charles Francis Adams Jr. (the great-grandson of John Adams) declared that "it would have been an actual disgrace had [our] family, of all possible families American, been wholly unrepresented in the field." When Paul Revere, killed at Gettysburg, was buried next to his brother, killed at Antietam, in Mt. Auburn Cemetery, their mother wrote in her journal: "They knew the risk they ran. But the conflict must be met. It was their duty to aid it. The claim on them was as strong as on any and gallantly they answered it."[6]

Closely related to these values of duty and honor was an ethic of sacrifice, the noblesse-oblige conviction that the privileged classes had a greater obligation to defend the country precisely because of the privileged status they enjoyed. Captain Oliver Wendell Holmes Jr. praised the first colonel of the 20th Massachusetts, William Raymond Lee, for having "taught us more perfectly than we could learn elsewhere to strive not only to acquire the discipline of soldiers but [also] the high feelings and self-sacrifice of chivalrous gentlemen."[7]

Charles Russell Lowell shared this conviction with his brother-in-law and best friend, Robert Gould Shaw, a Harvard alumnus whose father was a prominent and well-to-do abolitionist. After serving as a captain in the 2nd Massachusetts Infantry, Shaw in January 1863 accepted a commission as colonel of the 54th Massachusetts Infantry, the first black regiment raised in the Northeast. He died at the head of his regiment in its attack on Fort Wagner in South

Carolina on July 18, 1863 (the subject of the movie *Glory*). Lowell wrote to his own grieving fiancée, Shaw's sister Josephine: "I see now that the best Colonel of the best black regiment had to die, it was a sacrifice we owed,—and how could it have been paid more gloriously?"[8] Fifteen months later Lowell made a similar sacrifice, leaving Josephine a widow six weeks before their child was born. She dedicated the remaining forty-one years of her life to working for the underprivileged in American society: freed slaves, exploited workers, women in poverty, the down-and-out of every ethnic group.

Like Robert Gould Shaw, many of these Massachusetts officers had been active in the antislavery movement. That was true of the whole Lowell clan. James Russell Lowell was one of the most prominent abolitionist writers, and his nephews Charles Russell Lowell and William Lowell Putnam echoed his sentiments. This was a war for freedom and human rights, wrote Charles Lowell in 1861, "in which decent men ought to engage for the sake of *humanity*." In William Putnam's last letter before he was killed at Ball's Bluff, he wrote: "He who said that 'A century of civil war is better than a day of slavery' was right. God grant that every river in this land of ours may run with blood, and every city be laid in ashes rather than this war should come to an end without the utter destruction of every vestige of this curse so monstrous."[9]

Not all Massachusetts officers shared these sentiments. A conservative strain infused part of the Brahmin class and turned them against abolitionism and the antislavery Republicans. This issue split the officers of the 20th Massachusetts into two camps. It became informally known as the "Democratic," or more conservative, Harvard regiment—in contrast with the "Republican" Harvard 2nd Massachusetts Infantry. The 20th became even more Democratic after many of its original antislavery officers were killed, badly wounded, or transferred to other regiments (two of them to become officers in the new 54th and 55th Massachusetts black regiments in 1863).

Disagreements about slavery and emancipation did not seem to affect the efficiency and fighting qualities of the 20th Massachusetts. General Andrew A. Humphreys, chief of staff for the Army of the Potomac in 1863–64, described the 20th as "one of the very best regiments in the service."[10] During the winter of 1862–63, inspecting officers rated the 20th among the top eleven of 330 Union infantry regiments in the Virginia theater. One consequence of such a reputation was the assignment of the regiment to the toughest, most dangerous combat missions. During the war the 20th had 795 men killed or wounded in action—40 percent of the total enrollment. The figure of 260 men killed or mortally wounded was greater than for any other Massachusetts regiment and fifth highest among the two thousand Union regiments.[11]

What explained the 20th's proficiency at fighting? Miller makes a persuasive case that it was the quality of its officers—especially their selfless willingness to share every danger with their men. In contrast to the practice in most volunteer regiments from other states, enlisted men in Massachusetts regiments did not elect their company officers. Governor John Andrew could therefore appoint officers for what he considered their ability (which he often equated with social standing) rather than for political popularity or expediency. Only a few of these officers had prior military training or experience, but they did have the prestige and status that provided Massachusetts regiments with a greater degree of discipline and order than those of most other states. Of no other regiment was this more true than of the 20th, owing in considerable part to Colonel William Raymond Lee, who had attended West Point as well as Harvard, and who shaped the character and ethos of the regiment during the year and a half he commanded it.

The social distance between officers and enlisted men in the 20th was greater than in most other regiments. Some of the original officers expressed a cliquish snobbery toward noncoms from middle- and working-class backgrounds who were commissioned from the ranks as the inevitable attrition of war whittled away the "gentlemen" officers. One of the qualities that make Miller's book among the best of the hundreds of Civil War regimental histories is his analysis of the dynamics of class in the 20th. The experience of combat gradually reduced the distance and tensions between Brahmin officers and the rank and file—an achievement all the more remarkable because of the ethnic and class heterogeneity of the regiment. Two of the ten companies were composed of German Americans, one of Irish, one of waterfront toughs of various ethnic backgrounds, and one mainly of whaling men from Nantucket.

Some of these recruits initially looked upon their officers as effete fops. They soon learned otherwise. These Harvard men had in them the steel of their ancestors who fought at Concord and Bunker Hill and Saratoga. They demonstrated their toughness at Antietam and Gettysburg and a dozen other battles. Even the disastrous defeat at Ball's Bluff on October 21, 1861, the regiment's first battle, helped to bind officers and men, who stuck together under the direst circumstances. One private later summed up an impression widely shared by the rank and file in the 20th: "We had a Grand Set of officers. . . . I hav often thought Since how brave the[y] ware the[y] Seamed to like to fight and Set the Men A Good Example."[12]

Loyalty to the regiment and to their men brought officers back again and again after recovering from wounds that could have sent them home with honorable discharges. Holmes was wounded once a year and returned all three times. (He not only survived the war; after serving for thirty years as a distinguished associate justice of the United States Supreme Court, he died two days before his ninety-fourth birthday in 1935.) Colonel Paul Revere, wounded at Antietam, came back after recovering in time to be killed at Gettysburg. His successor, George Macy, lost his left hand at Gettysburg, returned to take command just before the battle of the Wilderness, where he took bullets in both legs, and later came back to command the entire brigade to the end at Appomattox.

The examples of these "gentlemen" officers worked their way down to men promoted from the ranks. Captain John Kelliher, a former bootmaker who was commissioned in September 1863, was so badly wounded at Spotsylvania in May 1864 that the surgeon who removed his lower jaw, one arm, a shoulder blade, a clavicle, and two of his ribs had no hope for his recovery. But Kelliher not only confounded that diagnosis; he returned in November 1864 with the rank of major to command the surviving remnant of the regiment.

Charles Russell Lowell did not serve in the 20th Massachusetts—though his brother and several friends and cousins did. Valedictorian of the Harvard class of 1854, Lowell had a successful business career interrupted by two years in Europe to seek rest and treatment for tuberculosis. In 1861 he secured a commission in the 6th U.S. Cavalry and later served as a staff officer in the Army of the Potomac. In the winter of 1862–63 the governor of Massachusetts, John Andrew, commissioned him to recruit, organize, and command the 2nd Massachusetts Cavalry. Seven of the twelve companies in this unique regiment were composed of Massachusetts men; the other five were filled by Californians, most of them natives of New England who had gone west during the Gold Rush a decade or more earlier. These men represented California's principal military contribution to the Union war effort. They were older than the average Massachusetts recruit, more experienced as horsemen, and more accustomed to outdoor life. The California companies were the best in the regiment, especially adept at the counterguerrilla warfare that became the main activity of the 2nd Massachusetts in 1863 and 1864.

Although an excellent rider, the twenty-eight-year-old Colonel Lowell was slight in build and youthful in appearance. Several of the California company officers were older than Lowell. Yet he quickly gained their confidence and loyalty. Lowell's first challenge was to meld the disparate Massachusetts and California companies into a single fighting unit. One of the strengths of Carol Bundy's biography, as with Miller's history, is its analysis of the tensions within the regiment, which could be overcome only by strong qualities of leadership. Lowell possessed that elusive quality of personal magnetism known as charisma; as an early biographer put it, he had a natural "capacity of ruling men, which was the most remarkable of his gifts."[13] Cool under fire, Lowell found that men would follow him anywhere and obey his orders without hesitation. It helped their confidence that he seemed to lead a charmed life. In more than two years of combat he had thirteen horses shot from under him without suffering a scratch himself. Who would not follow this lucky colonel?

For more than a year the mission of Lowell's regiment was to disperse, capture, or destroy the Confederate guerrilla band known as Mosby's Rangers. John Singleton Mosby was the bold and apparently fearless leader of partisans who operated behind Union lines in occupied Confederate territory, attacking supply trains, burning bridges, cutting telegraph lines, robbing paymasters, and capturing or killing small Union forces separated from their units. Several counties in northern Virginia stretching from Washington to the Shenandoah Valley became known as Mosby's Confederacy. Mosby's raiders once captured a Union general in his bed only ten miles from Washington. Lowell's task was to eliminate this fishbone in the throat of the Union army. He came up with several new tactics in the deadly game of raids and counterraids. Despite setbacks and attrition from exhaustion and casualties during their continual patrols and ambushes, the 2nd Massachusetts gained several victories over Mosby and by mid-1864 had constricted his territory.

Even though successful, Lowell and his men grew weary of such inglorious duty and yearned for some "real cavalry fighting" in the field. In July 1864 they got their wish. Now part of a cavalry brigade with Lowell as brigade commander, the 2nd Massachusetts participated in the defense of Washington against the Confederate general Jubal Early's daring raid in July 1864. In the subsequent campaign to pursue Early's corps into the Shenandoah Valley and destroy it, Lowell's brigade was incorporated into the cavalry corps of the newly created Army of the Shenandoah commanded by General Philip Sheridan.

Lowell's experience in irregular warfare became invaluable to Sheridan in his quest for intelligence. Lowell led the 2nd Massachusetts in lightning raids on enemy units to capture prisoners for interrogation. Watching one of these attacks in which Lowell led his men over Confederate breastworks and brought away seventy-four prisoners including a lieutenant colonel and three captains, Sheridan commented that "Lowell is a brave man." That bravery earned Lowell command of a cavalry brigade of regulars (the 1st, 2nd, 5th, and 6th U.S. cavalries), a unique distinction for a volunteer officer from a civilian background.[14]

In command of this brigade, Lowell took part in a picture-book cavalry charge at the climax of the battle of Winchester in Virginia on September 19, 1864, one of the most decisive Union victories of the war. A month later, after more Northern victories, General Early struck back at dawn on October 19 with a surprise attack at Cedar Creek, fifteen miles south of Winchester, routing two Union infantry corps. In the absence of Sheridan, who was returning from consultations in Washington, Lowell helped form a new defensive position.

When Sheridan arrived at midday, knowing that "there was no cooler head or better brain in all the army," he ordered Lowell to form two brigades to hold the Union's left flank while Sheridan reorganized the army for a counterattack.[15] Lowell had just had his thirteenth horse shot under him, and this time it turned out to be an unlucky omen. Soon afterward he was hit in the chest by a ricocheted bullet that collapsed his right lung. Refusing to go to the rear, Lowell had himself lifted onto a borrowed horse, so weak that he had to be strapped in the saddle, and rode at the head of the 2nd Massachusetts as Sheridan launched what became a devastating counterattack. When the cavalry thundered forward, Lowell was again hit by a bullet, which severed his spine and left him paralyzed. "My poor wife," he whispered, "I am afraid it will kill her."[16] It did not. But it did kill him. A week after his death, Lowell's commission as brigadier general arrived from Washington.

Several dozen classmates attended Lowell's funeral in Appleton Chapel at Harvard on October 28. Some of them were on crutches or missing an arm or a leg, victims of the same war that claimed Lowell's life. They listened as the Reverend George Putnam, whose son had married Lowell's sister, delivered the eulogy. Putnam read aloud the names of Lowell's twelve relatives and close friends who had preceded him in death on the battlefield. Putnam then turned toward the coffin and asked: "Are we paying too heavy a price for our country's freedom?" After a long pause in the silent chapel, he continued: "Our full hearts answer—no—not too much—not too much."[17]

Today it is a moving experience to walk through Harvard's Memorial Hall, dedicated in 1878, where plaques and busts honor most of the ninety-three alumni who died in the war. Of them all the most affecting is the bust of Charles Russell Lowell by Daniel Chester French, the sculptor of the memorial in Washington to Abraham Lincoln, who, like Lowell, gave the nation the last full measure of devotion.

# 13

# "Spend Much Time in Reading the Daily Papers": The Press and Army Morale in the Civil War

WHETHER THEY WERE AT HOME OR AT THE FRONT, Southerners and Northerners passed through more intense experiences during the Civil War than any other generation of Americans. Time and consciousness seemed to take on new dimensions as apprehensive civilians gathered outside newspaper or telegraph offices waiting for news from the battlefields, and soldiers eagerly snatched the latest *New York Herald* or *Richmond Dispatch* from newsboys in army camps. "These are fearfully critical, anxious days," wrote a New Yorker waiting for news from the fighting in the Wilderness in May 1864, "in which the destinies of the continent for centuries will be decided." These words were echoed by Virginia's fire-eating secessionist Edmund Ruffin. "The excitement of the war, & interest in its incidents, have absorbed everything else," he wrote in his diary. "We think and talk of nothing else." From the American legation in London, Henry Adams wrote to his brother in the Army of the Potomac that the war might unfit them ever again "to live contented in times of peace and laziness. Our generation has been stirred up from its lowest layers and there is that in our history which will stamp every member of it until we are all in our graves. . . . One does every day and without a second thought, what would at another time be the event of a year, perhaps of a life."[1]

Some of this experience was direct and personal. Much of it, however, was lived vicariously through newspapers. "We must have something to eat, and the papers to read," declared Oliver Wendell Holmes in August 1861 as his son and namesake prepared to depart for Virginia as an officer in the 20th Massachusetts. "Everything else we can do without. . . . Only bread and the newspaper we must have." The same was true in the armies. Major daily papers from New York, Philadelphia, Washington, or Richmond were available to the armies in Virginia a day or two after publication, sometimes even during active campaigns. Elsewhere the papers might be delayed longer in reaching the armies, but reach them they did, and according to one contemporary, the soldiers "devour papers with a rapidity that astonished them that have less leisure time."[2]

Foreign observers expressed amazement at this phenomenon. When they reflected, however, that these soldiers were citizens in uniform, volunteers from civilian life in the world's most politicized society with the largest per capita newspaper circulation in the world, men who had joined the armies to resolve a national crisis but yielded none of their civilian concerns about that crisis, they understood better the soldiers' passion for newspapers. The comte de Paris, an exile from Napoleon's France—and a pretender to the French throne—came to the United States with his brother and their uncle and served on General George McClellan's staff for a time. The comte wrote that soldiers in the Army of the Potomac were "active citizens in their respective counties and States . . . fully acquainted with public affairs and could not dispense with newspapers. . . . In every tent the latest news brought by the *Herald* or *Tribune* was read in the evening and eagerly discussed, while the soldier on duty, if he thought himself unobserved, walked up and down with his musket in one hand and his newspaper in the other."[3]

Another French soldier of fortune was Gustave Paul Cluseret, a graduate of St. Cyr and a French army officer for two decades before he wangled a brigade command under General John C. Frémont in the Shenandoah Valley in 1862. Looking back on this Civil War adventure a few years later, Cluseret wrote that "if the American volunteers accomplished prodigies of patience, energy, and devotion it is because they fought with knowledge of the cause. In the midst of the messiest business one could hear the squeaking voice of the 'news boy' over the sound of the fusillade, crying 'New York Tribune, New York Herald.' The soldier paid up to 10 cents for the newspaper, stuffing it under the flap of his pack; and at the first break, he ran his eyes quickly over it."[4]

The leading historian of Civil War soldiers, Bell Irvin Wiley, found newspaper circulation to be greater among Union than Confederate soldiers. It is quite true that literacy rates were higher in the North than in the South and that the per capita antebellum circulation of newspapers had been three times as large in the free states as in the slave states. And during the Civil War there were four or five times as many reporters with Union armies as with Confederate armies.[5] Nevertheless, Johnny Reb was as avid a reader of newspapers—when he could get them—as Billy Yank. In January 1862 a private in the 17th Mississippi stationed near Leesburg, Virginia, wrote in his diary: "Spend much time in reading the daily papers & discussing the war question in general. We

allways close by coming to the conclusion that we will after much hard fighting
succeed in establishing our independence." Two years later a lieutenant in the
4th Virginia reported that "the boys" spent much of their time in winter quarters reading the papers. We "make comments on the news and express our
opinions quite freely about the blood and thunder editorials in the Richmond
papers, smoke again and go to bed." Even in the Petersburg trenches later that
summer, soldiers in the 43rd Alabama "have daily access to the Richmond
papers. . . . We spend much of our time in reading these journals and discussing the situation."[6]

As the war went on, however, the occupation of several Southern cities by
Union forces and growing shortages of paper and ink in the rest of the South
put an end to some Confederate newspapers and reduced the size of those that
remained. Few Confederate soldiers enjoyed the luxury noted by a lieutenant
in the 50th Ohio, which was not untypical in the Union army. "I receive the
'Chronicle' regularly," this lieutenant wrote to his brother back home in 1863.
"The boys all want to read it. . . . The officers subscribed $4.75 each for papers
for the benefit of the boys. [We] get *four daily* papers, all loyal and right on
politics"—that is, anti-Copperhead.[7]

Like most Americans today, Civil War soldiers had a kind of love-hate relationship with the media, which in their case consisted of newspapers and illustrated weeklies like *Harper's, Frank Leslie's,* and the *Southern Illustrated News.*
Soldiers often denounced the biases or inaccuracies of these journals but could
not stop reading them. In the Union armies, particularly, Republican and
Democratic soldiers argued over the editorial policies of the *New York Tribune*
vs. the *New York Herald,* the *Chicago Tribune* vs. the *Chicago Times,* and so on.
More than one fistfight, and sometimes a free-for-all melee, grew out of these
arguments.

Even more than the editorials or political news, soldiers read newspapers
for war news, especially stories about their own units or accounts of battles in
which they had fought. But they were by no means uncritical readers—quite
the contrary. The notoriously exaggerated, distorted, partisan, romanticized,
and in some cases fictionalized accounts of battles provoked increasing cynicism among soldiers. The tendency of Southern papers to report such battles as
Shiloh or Sharpsburg or Murfreesboro as "one of the most complete victories
that has yet immortalized the Confederate arms" became a byword. It probably
undermined Confederate morale in the long run because the truth, when it
eventually came out, was all the more dispiriting. "As to the newspapers, they

are perfectly absurd," wrote home a South Carolina officer after the first battle of Manassas. "I hope you don't believe one-tenth of what you read." In a letter to his fiancée in 1863, a Mississippi soldier declared that "I have been so often deceived by [newspaper reports] that I've lost confidence in our press and believe nothing coming through that channel, unless I know it is so."[8]

Northern newspapers were also no slouches in the business of distortion and exaggeration—or what one journalist conceded to be "the slam-bang, going-off-half-cocked style of reporting." A Union sergeant said that "we have learned not to swallow anything whole that we see in the papers. If half the victories we read of were true the Rebellion would not have a leg to stand on." A major in the Army of the Potomac recalled after the war that "we would read with amazement accounts of what our own troops were supposed to have done."[9]

Yet this cynicism did not prevent soldiers from devouring the newspapers and, almost in spite of themselves, believing or at least half-believing what they read. In that respect they were not much different from us today in our responses to what we read in the newspapers or see on television.

The counterparts to battle descriptions in daily newspapers were the drawings for illustrated weeklies. Some of these woodcuts were superb, such as Winslow Homer's drawings of life in camp, several of which became the basis for his earliest oil paintings. But the depictions of combat by many of the illustrators, especially in the war's early years, were so stylized and sentimentalized that soldiers ridiculed them. Next to Homer, one of the best illustrators was Alfred Waud. By the latter part of the war, Waud had learned how to draw realistic pictures of the chaotic, brutal, confusing reality of combat. But earlier, for example, in a drawing of a Union charge at the battle of Fair Oaks, Waud depicted nearly five hundred men in a perfect line, every man running with the same leg forward, every bayonet leveled at the same angle and height. When this issue of *Harper's Weekly* reached camp, veterans of the battle howled with derision. Cavalrymen alternately laughed and groaned at illustrations showing them riding straight at the enemy in perfect order at a gallop on fierce-looking horses while firing their carbines with one hand and waving their sabers with the other. Even as good an artist as Thomas Nast portrayed a trooper who had skewered his enemy with such force that the blade of his saber protruded six inches out of his adversary's back! Yet soldiers had the same love-hate complex toward the illustrated papers as toward print stories of battles. A British observer with the Army of the Potomac described the arrival of the mail boat with a shipment of *Harper's* and *Leslie's.* "A curious sight it was to me," he wrote, "a general rustle of opening leaves, and in a moment every man as if it had been part of his drill, was down upon the ground with the same big picture before him."[10]

Journalistic descriptions and pictorial depictions of combat never entirely caught up with reality. In another respect also, Civil War journalism diverged from the actual experience and mood of soldiers. At the beginning of the war, soldiers and reporters both declared that the men—Yankee and Rebel alike— were "spoiling for a fight," "anxious for the fray," eager to prove their manhood, to demonstrate their superiority, to smite the enemy. "Our boys are dieing for a fight," wrote a recruit in the 8th Georgia. An officer in the 37th North Carolina told his wife that "our Men are allmost Crazy to Meet the Enemy," while a private in the 13th North Carolina wrote to his father that "the Company is all anxious to get in to a battle and they cannot go home without a fite."[11]

Union soldiers were no less eager. "We are all impatient to get into Virginia and have a brush with the rebels," wrote a lieutenant in the 2nd Rhode Island in June 1861. A private in the 10th Wisconsin criticized "our *donothing* Generals" for "not leading us forward. . . . We came not for *the paltry pay* but to *Fight*. All we want is to be led to *Battle*." An Indiana private wrote that orders to move toward the enemy "filled me with an exciting feeling, & I took off my cap & gave one loud yell. We pushed off anxious for the fray."[12]

The first shock of combat cured most soldiers of this eagerness to "see the elephant." An Ohio soldier who had written home before his first battle that "wee ar all big for a fight" told his wife afterward: "Mary I went into the fight in good hart but I never want to get in another it was offal mary you cant form any idy how it was the bulets and cannon ball and shells flew thick as hail." A North Carolina private wrote his father after the first battle of Manassas: "Sutch a day the booming of the cannon the ratling of the muskets you have no idea how it was I have turned threw that old book of yours and looked at the pictures and read a little about war but I did not no anything what it was."[13] After similar experiences a Virginia soldier wrote that "I have seen enough of the glory of war. . . . I am sick of seeing dead men and men's limbs torn from their bodies." An Indiana teenager who had been eager to see action wrote after his first combat experience that he had "got to see the Elephant at last and to tell you the honest truth I dont care about seeing him very often any more, for if there was any fun in such work I couldent see it. . . . It is not the thing it is braged up to be."[14]

Long after reality had replaced romance in the soldiers' view of combat, the image conveyed by the press seemed unchanged. The "reports of newspaper correspondents that the troops are all 'eager for the fray,' " wrote a Minnesota sergeant to his wife in July 1862, are "simply all 'bosh.' I don't know any individual soldier who is at all anxious to be led, or driven for that matter, to another battle." A Massachusetts lieutenant who had seen plenty of action wrote that he hoped his regiment would be in reserve at the next battle. "You will call that a cowardly wish," he conceded, "but although we see a great many in print, we see very few in reality, of such desperate heroes that they had rather go into the heat of battle than not." Confederate veterans made the same point. "There are very few men really eager for a battle and 'spoiling for a fight,' at this stage of the war," wrote a private in the 3rd Georgia to his sweetheart in 1863. "Perhaps you will think this is a rather unchivalrous sentiment for a Southern soldier . . . but let me explain that we do not fear the foe with a cowardly fear, that would make us shrink from our duty to our country, but we have that undefinable dread which the knowledge of an unpleasant task before us always occasions."[15]

Many other veteran soldiers on both sides echoed this reference to duty rather than eagerness as their reason for continuing to risk their lives despite a personal preference for staying out of the path of bullets. An Illinois sergeant in Sherman's army reported in the spring of 1864 that "I dont particularly like fighting but if it has to be done we must try and do our duty." After six weeks of the campaign in north Georgia, he wrote to his family that "the boys are generally well & in good spirits but are not spoiling for a fight as some Reporters represent although we will try and doe our duty when we are called upon." A veteran officer in the 10th Massachusetts wrote in late 1863 that "we are expecting a hard time and plenty of fighting. We are not at all eager for the 'fray,' but we are all ready which is much better. Where ever you find a soldier 'eager for the fray' as the newspapers have it, you may be sure that he has never been in any fray, for being in one takes away all eagerness for it, I assure you."[16]

No matter how much they professed to disdain the press, Civil War soldiers and especially officers were aware of its power. One form of such awareness was exemplified by General William T. Sherman, who disliked reporters so much that he banned them from his army, or tried to. Such was Sherman's success and fame in the latter part of the war that he could get away with doing so. But when General George G. Meade in 1864 had a reporter who Meade thought had written lies about him drummed out of camp wearing a sign with the words "Libeler of the Press," reporters thereafter refused to mention Meade favorably in their dispatches. In truth, praise or criticism or silence in newspaper stories could go a long ways toward making or breaking an officer's reputation. Some officers therefore resorted to favoritism toward certain reporters, or even bribery, to win favorable treatment—which naturally caused bitter or sarcastic comments from other officers.

In one famous case such a contretemps almost led to a duel between Generals James Longstreet and A. P. Hill in the Army of Northern Virginia. The editor of the powerful *Richmond Examiner* was actually a member of Hill's staff during the Seven Days battles in June and July 1862. The *Examiner* extravagantly praised the performance of Hill's division, especially in the battle of Glendale, and obliquely criticized Longstreet, Hill's superior officer. Outraged, Longstreet wrote a reply that was published in the rival *Richmond Whig* over the signature of his adjutant G. Moxley Sorrel. Hill responded by requesting transfer from Longstreet's command. A bitter exchange of letters followed, and Longstreet finally ordered Hill placed under arrest and confined to camp. Hill then evidently challenged Longstreet to a duel—which would have done wonders for Confederate morale. But Lee finally stepped in and damped down the quarrel by transferring Hill's division to Stonewall Jackson's corps.[17]

The press sometimes exacerbated unit or state rivalries by allegedly exaggerating the fighting prowess of troops from one state or denigrating the cowardice of those from another. Because Southern brigades usually consisted of regiments all from the same state, and because the Richmond newspapers dominated the Confederate press, this was a more serious bone of contention in the South than the North. North Carolinians in particular complained of bias in the Richmond papers toward Virginia brigades at the expense of those from North Carolina. The longest-running controversy of this sort started after Gettysburg, when a bitter dispute arose over the performance of Virginia and North Carolina troops in the so-called Pickett's Charge, a controversy fought out in newspapers in 1863 and continued in various other media ever since.[18]

Union officers and units similarly complained about various kinds of distortion and favoritism in the press. Interservice rivalries between army and navy, not unknown in more recent wars, were sometimes reflected in Northern newspapers during the Civil War. One example will illustrate the point. During Longstreet's campaign against the Union position at Suffolk on the south side of the James River in April 1863, the main line of Union defenses was on the Nansemond River, a tributary of the James. Union army units dug in on the east bank of the Nansemond, while gunboat flotillas commanded by Lieutenants

Roswell H. Lamson and William B. Cushing, two of the best young officers in the U.S. Navy, patrolled the river. According to Lamson's letters to his fiancée, the gunboats did the only real fighting in the campaign, yet the kept reporters gave all the credit to the army. After one fight, Lamson wrote that "*everything* has been done by the Navy gunboats. . . . I have been complimented for the affair more than I should like to tell you. . . . It is well known who did it . . . but the reporters here are all under control of the army, so nothing is said about it." In another letter Lamson wrote that "I could tell you of some army movements that are so absurd you would hardly believe any 'General' would order them, but which have been ordered by 'Generals' who figure most conspicuously in the papers."[19]

At times it almost seemed that such internecine rivalries within and among the armies, navies, and press of one side or the other were bloodier than conflict with the enemy. For the most part, though, such rumblings and grumblings were the outlets for frustrations that have been typical of soldiers and sailors in all wars. The real battle was with the enemy, and the principal factors that shaped morale grew out of that conflict. These factors included the hardships, hunger, danger, shortages, and the like that were part of a soldier's lot. But the principal determinant of morale was victory or defeat. Victory pumped up morale; defeat deflated it.

On the home front the most immediate information about victory or defeat came from newspapers, followed later by soldiers' letters, which were uncensored during the Civil War. In the armies, of course, soldiers experienced victory or defeat directly. But the Civil War was fought over vast distances by several different armies on both sides. A victory or defeat in Mississippi could affect the morale of armies in Virginia, and vice versa. And soldiers learned of such distant victories or defeats mainly from the newspapers they read. In the summer of 1862, for example, the Confederate army that had been forced to evacuate Corinth, Mississippi, at the climax of an unbroken string of defeats in that theater suffered from low morale until they read about Lee's victories in the Seven Days battles in Virginia. That news "cheered our army a good deal," wrote a Mississippi artillery corporal, "and put all in much better spirits than they had been for some time. We fired a salute of 13 guns in honor of the victory." The same news from Virginia had the opposite effect on the morale of the victorious Union army in Mississippi. "There is a universal *depression* in camp at the bad news from Virginia," wrote a sergeant in the 15th Iowa. These reports "have a tremendous effect upon men as we gain or lose at distant points. So goes the thermometer of our hopes and fears in other places."[20]

In July 1863 the loss of Vicksburg and Port Hudson had a greater negative impact on the morale of many soldiers in the Army of Northern Virginia than their own retreat after the bloody carnage at Gettysburg. Two Georgia soldiers in Longstreet's corps commented that "the reverses in the West, have a bad effect. . . . Our army seems to be depressed. . . . It Don't look like that we will Ever whip the yankees." On the other side of the coin, reports of the Army of the Potomac's repulse of Lee at Gettysburg resonated loudly in the Western Union armies. A major in the 47th Ohio reported a few days after the capture of Vicksburg that "everybody is electrified" by the news from Pennsylvania. "We hardly know how to contain ourselves. . . . The army is on fire—as irresistible as an avalanch."[21]

News from home as well as from other theaters of war affected army morale. A soldier's conviction that he was risking his life for a worthwhile purpose, a Cause with a capital C, was rooted in the support of his family and community for that Cause. Some of that support, or the lack of it, was conveyed to soldiers by the letters they received from home. But much of it came via the press and the political process, which were intertwined institutions during the Civil War. In both North and South, antiwar movements arose and flourished at times when the war seemed to be going badly for one's own side. These movements advocated an armistice and a negotiated peace. The governments in both Washington and Richmond viewed such proposals as defeatist at best, treasonable at worst. So did most soldiers. They labeled the peace proponents in the Confederacy as "Tories" and in the North as "Copperheads." On both sides, opponents of the war—or more accurately, perhaps, opponents of their governments' war policies—made their case through the press as well as through the political process.

After the triple disasters to Confederate arms in the summer of 1863—Vicksburg, Gettysburg, and the Army of Tennessee's retreat from its namesake state—some Southern civilians began urging a compromise peace. A nineteen-year-old private in the 7th Alabama Cavalry denounced what he called this "miserable class of men that now infest the country," while another Alabamian, an infantry captain, deplored the lack of "patriotism of a great many of the people at home. The army cannot be sustained without the cooperation of the people." Even in South Carolina, a few Tories seemed to surface after Gettysburg and Vicksburg, causing a nineteen-year-old veteran from that state to cry out: "Shame for South Carolina! Go back into the union, degraded despised dishonorable. . . . This is the way we are rewarded—our own people forsake us in the trying hour—and after our all—honour—and everything else is at stake. . . . Degrading, wretched, unpatriotic, infamous thought!"[22]

In 1863 peace sentiment manifested itself most powerfully in North Carolina. The state's largest newspaper, the *North Carolina Standard,* edited in Raleigh by William W. Holden, became an outspoken advocate of peace negotiations. So incensed toward Holden were Confederate soldiers that on the night of September 9–10, 1863, several men of General Henry L. Benning's brigade of Georgia troops, passing through Raleigh on their way from Virginia to Georgia, where they would suffer heavy losses at Chickamauga ten days later, broke into the *Standard*'s office and wrecked it.[23]

Union soldiers did the same to so-called Copperhead papers in the North. And judging from the volume and bitterness of soldiers' denunciations of home-front "traitors," the Copperhead press in the North was far more extensive and outspoken than the Tory press in the South. Especially during the early months of 1863 and again in the summer of 1864, the drumbeat of defeatism and antiwar editorials in Copperhead newspapers caused morale problems in Union armies. A captain in the 8th Connecticut complained in January 1863 that "the papers (many of them) published at the North & letters rec[eive]d by the soldiers are doing the Army an immense amount of evil." From Grant's army in the Western theater came similar testimony from a captain in the 103rd Illinois: "You can't imagine how much harm these traitors are doing, not only with their papers, but they are writing letters to the boys which would discourage the most loyal of men." An enlisted man from Iowa believed that the Copperhead press not only discouraged the boys in blue but also encouraged the enemy. "The Rebels in the South well know how we are divided in the North," he wrote in March 1863. "It encourages them to hold out, with the hopes that we will get to fighting in the North, well knowing that 'a house divided against itself cannot stand.' "[24]

At the same time, however, a backlash against the Copperheads' antiwar rhetoric forged a bond of unity among Union soldiers that actually improved their morale. "Copperheadism has brought the soldiers here together more than anything else," wrote a corporal in the 101st Ohio in April 1863. "Some of the men that yoused to be almost willing to have the war settled in any way are now among the strongest Union soldiers we have got." Many Northern soldiers lumped the Rebels and Copperheads together as twin enemies who deserved the same treatment. "*My first* object is to crush this infernal Rebellion," wrote a Pennsylvania infantry captain in March 1863, "the *next* to come North and bayonet such fool miscreants as [Clement] Vallandigham," the foremost Copperhead political leader. A private in the 49th Ohio told his sister in June 1863 that "it would give me the greatest pleasure in the world to be one of a regiment that would march through Ohio and Indiana and hang every Copperhead in the two States."[25]

When Northern home-front morale plunged to perhaps its lowest point in the summer of 1864 because of horrendous casualties in the Army of the Potomac without much apparent progress toward victory, Union soldier morale remained higher than it had been in the spring of 1863 because of this bond of unity against the Copperheads. As a New York captain wrote to his wife, "It is the soldiers who have educated the people at home to a true knowledge . . . and to a just perception of our great duties in this contest."[26] That is one reason why many Union regiments established their own camp newspapers at various times and places during the war—at least one hundred such newspapers, most of them short-lived. (There seem to have been few counterparts in Confederate camps.) They bore such names as *Stars and Stripes, Whole Union, Banner of Freedom, New South, Free South, American Patriot,* and similar patriotic titles. Many Union soldiers (and some Confederates as well) also served as army correspondents for their hometown newspapers. Perhaps the most famous of these was Wilbur Fisk of the 2nd Vermont, whose dispatches have been published in book form in two modern editions. Fisk signed his letters with the pen name "Anti-Rebel," which pretty much sums up their dominant theme.[27]

That is why almost 80 percent of the Union soldiers who voted in 1864 cast their ballots for Lincoln on a platform of conquering a peace by military victory, compared with 53 percent of the civilian vote for Lincoln. As one Union officer put it in August 1864, at the low point of civilian morale: "*We must succeed.* If not this year, why then the next, or the next. And if it takes ten years, then ten years it must be, for we can never give up, and have a Country and Government left."[28]

Confederate army morale also remained higher than civilian morale until the final months of the war—at least in the Army of Northern Virginia, which by 1865 was the only institution that still propped up the Confederacy. In March 1865 an officer in the 61st Alabama still breathed defiance but conceded that civilians had become "craven hearted and weak kneed. . . . Our people are not the same as they were four years ago. Their courage, spirit and pride are gone. . . . I don't know what can be done to save us."[29]

At the same time, after Sherman's capture of Atlanta, Northern morale at home reversed its decline and rose toward the high level of army morale. The American correspondent of the *London Daily News* expressed astonishment in September 1864 at "the extent and depth of the[ir] determination to fight to the last. They are in earnest the like of which the world never saw before, silently, calmly, but desperately in earnest; they will fight on, in my opinion, as long as they have men, muskets, and powder," until they won an unconditional victory.[30] And so they did.

# 14

# No Peace Without Victory, 1861–1865

FOR AT LEAST THE PAST TWO CENTURIES, nations have usually found it harder to end a war than to start one. Americans relearned that bitter lesson in Vietnam and, having apparently forgotten it, were forced to learn it all over again in Iraq. The difficulties of achieving peace are compounded when the war aims of a belligerent include regime change in the enemy polity. In the Napoleonic Wars, the coalition forces finally managed to end the conflict when they forced Emperor Napoleon Bonaparte to abdicate—twice. In World War I, Woodrow Wilson insisted that the Allies would negotiate only with a democratic government in Germany, and the armistice did not go into effect until the kaiser abdicated. In World War II, the Allies demanded the unconditional surrender of Axis governments in order to destroy those governments and install new ones in their place.

Both sides in the American Civil War feared that regime change would be the result of losing the war. Defeat would blot the Confederate States of America from the face of the earth. Confederate victory would destroy the *United States* and create a precedent for further balkanization of the territory once governed under the Constitution of 1789. Both antagonists foresaw these potential consequences in 1861 and embraced war as the only alternative. By 1863, however, the death or wounding of half a million soldiers had replaced the *rage militaire* of 1861 with a longing for peace. This longing was expressed in music, especially the songs "Tenting on the Old Camp Ground" and "When This Cruel War Is Over." Both evinced a profound desire for an end to the killing and suffering. "Weeping, sad and lonely," begins the refrain of "When This Cruel War Is Over." "We are tired of war on the old camp ground," sang those at home and in the armies. "Many are the hearts that are weary tonight, Wishing for the war to cease."[1] Yet the war did not cease; many wondered whether this cruel war would ever be over.

The American Civil War could not end with a negotiated peace because the issues over which it was fought—Union vs. Disunion, Freedom vs. Slavery—proved to be nonnegotiable. This was a new experience for Americans. The American Revolution, the War of 1812, and the Mexican-American War had all been brought to an end by peace treaties. The Confederate government would have been happy to bring the Civil War to an end in the same way, because a negotiated treaty with the United States would have constituted de jure as well as de facto recognition of Confederate sovereignty as a separate nation. For that reason, the Lincoln administration refused to consider formal negotiations as a means to end the war.

This refusal did not prevent numerous efforts to achieve peace through negotiations, official or otherwise. These efforts proceeded through three stages: foreign mediation, unofficial contacts, quasi-official conversations. All failed.

Most civil wars tempt foreign powers to intervene either to end a conflict that threatens their own interests or to support one side or the other. The American Civil War was no exception. The French and British governments believed their nations had a large stake in the bloodbath occurring across the Atlantic. The American South had furnished three-quarters of the cotton for the textile industries that were leading sectors in the economies of both countries, especially Britain. By 1862 the cutoff of cotton imports from the South had caused widespread unemployment and social unrest in Britain and France. Emperor Napoleon III's intervention in Mexico's own civil war would go better if a Disunited States could not enforce the Monroe Doctrine. The Union naval blockade and Confederate contracts for the building of warships in British shipyards threatened to drag Britain into an unwanted war with the United States. And in any event, key officials in Britain and France believed that the North could never reestablish control over 750,000 square miles of territory defended by a determined and courageous people. For all of these reasons, in 1862 the world's two leading powers contemplated making an offer of mediation to bring an end to the American war. Such an offer would have been tantamount to recognition of Confederate independence. But the Union victory at Antietam in September 1862 and Lincoln's subsequent issuance of the Emancipation Proclamation caused the British to back off.[2]

Napoleon III did not give up the enterprise, however. Unrest among unemployed French textile workers inspired a new effort in January 1863 to bring the belligerents together for talks. France's foreign minister sent a note to the

U.S. State Department urging negotiations with the Confederates even as the fighting continued. Good precedents existed for such a procedure. The Americans and British had negotiated during the Revolution and the War of 1812; the United States and Mexico had done the same during the war of 1846–48. Horace Greeley, quixotic editor of the powerful *New York Tribune,* who fancied himself a peacemaker, threw his support to this effort and met personally with the French minister to the United States.

This was too much for Secretary of State William H. Seward. He urged Henry Raymond, editor of the *New York Times,* to stomp hard on Greeley for practicing diplomacy without a license. Raymond was a political ally of Seward, and the *Times* was a quasi-official spokesman for the Lincoln administration. Having no love for Greeley, Raymond was happy to oblige. In an editorial on January 29, he condemned Greeley as a fool and declared that no peace was possible except on the basis of the Confederacy's unconditional surrender. "*The war must go on until the Rebellion is conquered,*" he wrote. "There is no alternative. . . . Our people will . . . never sell or betray their national birthright, and above all they will never consent, under any circumstances, that any foreign Power shall dictate the destiny or decide the fate of this Republic."[3] For his part, Seward told a colleague that he would consent to hold discussions with Confederate representatives "when Louis Napoleon was prepared to consider the dismemberment of France, but not till then!" Seward made the same point in more diplomatic language to the French foreign minister.[4]

That ended the matter. Meanwhile, the British developed alternative sources of raw cotton from Egypt and India. A growing trickle of cotton from the South also made it through the blockade. Never again did the Confederacy come so close to foreign intervention and recognition as in the fall of 1862. Thereafter, the burden of peacemaking efforts shifted to the protagonists themselves. So long as the Lincoln administration insisted on the unconditional surrender of the Confederacy, however, and Jefferson Davis's administration insisted on unconditional recognition of Confederate independence, the chances for a negotiated peace appeared nil. And Lincoln's Emancipation Proclamation on January 1, 1863, raised the stakes of victory or defeat for both antagonists. Nevertheless, Union military triumphs at Gettysburg, Vicksburg, and Chattanooga and in Arkansas during the second half of 1863 encouraged a belief in the North that war-weary Southerners might be ready to throw in the towel and return to the Union. In December 1863 Lincoln issued a Proclamation of Amnesty and Reconstruction offering pardons to most Confederates who would take an oath of allegiance to the United States and agree to obey all laws and proclamations concerning emancipation.[5] In effect, this was a retail policy of unconditional surrender.

Because only a small percentage of Confederates took advantage of Lincoln's offer, however, it did not promise to bring this cruel war to an end anytime soon. More promising were the military campaigns planned for 1864. With Ulysses S. Grant now in Virginia as general in chief of Union armies and his principal subordinate William T. Sherman in command of an army group in Georgia, the Northern people expected these heavy hitters to crush the rebellion by the Fourth of July. The initial overoptimistic reports from the front seemed to confirm this confidence. "GLORIOUS NEWS . . . IMMENSE REBEL LOSSES," blazoned the headlines in the usually restrained *New York Times*. "The Virginia Campaign approaches a Glorious consummation," added the *New York Herald*. "Our long night of doubt and suspense is past." Horace Greeley's *New York Tribune* proclaimed that "Lee's Army as an effective force has practically ceased to exist" and "LIBERTY—UNION—PEACE" were nigh.[6] At the end of May 1864 Greeley remained confident that this "mortal" contest between "Truth and Error, between Absolute Right and Absolute Wrong," would soon end with "the unconditional surrender of the 'Confederacy.' "[7]

Within six weeks, however, the mood of the mercurial Greeley had swung by 180 degrees. And Greeley's growing despair reflected that of the Northern people. Instead of winning the war by the Fourth of July, the two principal Union armies were bogged down in front of Richmond and Atlanta after suffering a combined 95,000 casualties in the most concentrated carnage of the war. In the Army of the Potomac, the number of battle casualties during the two months from May 5 to July 4 was three-fifths of the total in *the previous three years*.

Northern despondency was all the greater because of the euphoric expectations at the beginning of these campaigns. "Who shall revive the withered hopes that bloomed at the opening of General Grant's campaign?" asked an editorial in the *New York World* on July 12. The stalemate had become "a national humiliation," declared the *World*. "This war, as now conducted, is a failure without hope of other issue than the success of the rebellion."[8] With unhappy timing, Lincoln on July 18 issued a call for 500,000 more volunteers, with the deficiencies in meeting quotas to be met by a new draft. This call was "a cry of distress," lamented the *World*. "Who is responsible for the terrible and unavailing waste of life which renders five hundred thousand new men necessary so soon after the opening of a campaign that promised to be triumphant?"[9]

The *World* was a Democratic newspaper, and with the presidential election approaching, it left readers with no doubt that Lincoln was responsible for this humiliating failure. But many Republicans were equally despondent. "The immense slaughter of our brave men chills and sickens us all," wrote Secretary of the Navy Gideon Welles. "It is impossible for the country to bear up under these monstrous errors and wrongs." A State Department translator visited Philadelphia in early August. "What a difference between now and last year!" he wrote in his diary. "No signs of any enthusiasm, no flags; most of the best men gloomy and almost despairing."[10] The staunch New York Republican George Templeton Strong could "see no bright spot anywhere." Even Sarah Butler, wife of General Benjamin Butler, a favorite of Radical Republicans, wondered "what is all this struggling and fighting for? This ruin and death to thousands of families? . . . What advancement of mankind to compensate for the present horrible calamities?"[11]

Sarah Butler's plaintive question has been asked in all wars, but it had special force in the terrible summer of 1864. As before in this war, the peace wing of the Democratic Party—the so-called Copperheads, who opposed the war as a means to restore the Union—came to the fore when events on the battlefield did not go well for Union arms. The plunge in Northern morale augured well for a Democratic victory on a peace platform in the presidential election. "Stop the War!" demanded editorials in Copperhead newspapers. "If nothing else would impress upon the people the absolute necessity of stopping this war, its utter failure to accomplish any results . . . would be sufficient." A Boston Peace Democrat believed Northerners were becoming convinced that "the Confederacy perhaps can never really be beaten, that the attempts to win might after all be too heavy a load to carry, and that perhaps it is time to agree to a peace without victory."[12]

Several Democratic district conventions passed resolutions calling for a ceasefire and peace negotiations. Confederate agents in Canada, who were subsidizing several Democratic newspapers and politicians across the border, encouraged the belief that such negotiations might pave the way for eventual reunion. First might come "a treaty of amity and commerce," suggested one of the Confederate agents, Clement C. Clay, followed "possibly" by "an alliance defensive, or even, for some purposes, both defensive and offensive." If Peace Democrats were taken in by such double-talk, wrote Clay to Confederate secretary of state

Judah Benjamin, who oversaw these Canadian operations, he was careful not to dispel their "fond delusion."[13]

By July 1864 the peace contagion had spread well beyond the Copperheads. The observation by the *Richmond Dispatch,* the Confederacy's largest newspaper, that a majority of Northern voters would support peace even at the price of Confederate independence may not have been far wrong. "They are sick at heart of the senseless waste of blood and treasure," declared the *Dispatch.* In New York, George Templeton Strong was "most seriously perturbed" by the "increasing prevalence" of "aspirations for 'peace at any price.' " The astute Republican politico Thurlow Weed wrote to Seward in August that Lincoln's reelection was "an impossibility" because "the people are wild for peace."[14]

Horace Greeley agreed with this assessment. In early July he launched a bizarre, failed peace initiative that nevertheless had large consequences. From a self-styled "intermediary" Greeley received word that two of the Confederate agents in Canada were accredited by Jefferson Davis to negotiate a peace settlement. The credulous editor enclosed this information in a letter to Lincoln on July 7. "Our bleeding, bankrupt, almost dying country," Greeley declaimed, "longs for peace—shudders at the prospect of fresh conscriptions, of further wholesale devastations, and of new rivers of human blood." Therefore "I entreat you to submit overtures for pacification to the Southern insurgents."[15]

Lincoln did not believe for a moment that the Confederate agents had genuine negotiating powers. And even if they did, the Union president knew that his Southern counterpart's inflexible condition for peace was Confederate independence. Yet, given the despondent Northern mood, Lincoln could not appear to rebuff any peace overture, however spurious. He also thought he saw a chance to rally Northern opinion by demonstrating that an acceptable peace was possible only through military victory. So Lincoln immediately sent Greeley a telegram authorizing him to bring to Washington under safe conduct "any person anywhere professing to have any proposition of Jefferson Davis in writing, for peace, embracing the restoration of the Union and abandonment of slavery."[16]

This put Greeley on the spot by making him a guarantor of the agents' credentials and a witness to Lincoln's good-faith willingness to negotiate. Greeley balked, but Lincoln prodded him into action by sending his private secretary John Hay to join Greeley at Niagara Falls, Canada, to meet with the Confederates. The president was willing to compromise his principle of refusing to acknowledge officially the existence of the Confederate government by insisting on restoration of the Union as a prerequisite for negotiations. Hay carried to Niagara Falls a letter from Lincoln addressed "To Whom It May Concern" stating that "any proposition which embraces the restoration of peace, the integrity of the whole Union, and the abandonment of slavery, and which comes by and with an authority that can control the armies now at war with the United States will be received and considered by the Executive government of the United States, and will be met by liberal terms on other substantial and collateral points."[17]

This was an immensely important document that framed all discussions of peace for the rest of the war. Lincoln intended it not only to lay out his own conditions but also to elicit and publicize the Confederacy's unacceptable counteroffer. But on this occasion the rebel agents outmaneuvered Lincoln. They admitted to Greeley and Hay that they had no authority to negotiate peace but then released to the press a letter to Greeley accusing Lincoln of sabotaging negotiations by prescribing conditions he knew to be unacceptable to the Confederacy. Shedding crocodile tears, they expressed "profound regret" that the Confederacy's genuine desire for a peace "mutually just, honorable, and advantageous to the North and South" had not been met with equal "moderation and equity" by President Lincoln. Instead, his "To Whom It May Concern" letter meant "no bargaining, no negotiations, no truces with rebels except to bury their dead. . . . If there be any citizen of the Confederate States who has clung to the hope that peace is possible," Lincoln's terms "will strip from their eyes the last film of such delusion." The Southern agents urged those "patriots and Christians" in the North "who shrink appalled from the illimitable vistas of private misery and public calamity" presented by Lincoln's policy of perpetual war to "recall the abused authority and vindicate the outraged civilization of their country" by voting Lincoln out of office in November.[18]

This letter was, as the New York Times noted editorially, "an electioneering dodge on a great scale" to damage Lincoln "by making him figure as an obstacle to peace." It worked. As Clement C. Clay reported with satisfaction to Judah Benjamin, Northern Democratic newspapers "denounce Mr. Lincoln's manifesto in strong terms, and many Republican presses (among them the New York Tribune) admit it was a blunder. . . . From all that I can see or hear, I am satisfied that this correspondence has tended strongly toward consolidating the Democracy and dividing the Republicans."[19]

Greeley did indeed criticize Lincoln both publicly and privately. The president, he wrote in an editorial, made "a very grave mistake" by announcing his own terms instead of asking the rebels to state their terms first.[20] In a remarkable letter to Lincoln on August 9, Greeley chastised the president for giving the impression that his policy was "No truce! No armistice! No negotiation! No mediation! Nothing but [Confederate] surrender at discretion! I never heard of such fatuity before." Greeley probably had in mind an editorial in the *New York Times* that clearly spoke for the administration. "Peace is a consummation devoutly to be wished," declared the *Times,* but not peace at the price of Union. "War alone can save the Republic. . . . If the Southern people will not give us peace as their fellow-countrymen, we shall secure it as their conquerors. We know this is not gracious language. But it is native fact." Greeley deplored such language, he told Lincoln, because "to the general eye, it now seems the rebels are anxious to negotiate and that we repulse their advances. . . . If this impression be not removed we shall be beaten out of sight next November."[21]

Greeley was right about the potential political consequences of this affair. The Confederates had scored a propaganda triumph and given the Copperheads a boost. Lincoln sought to neutralize the setback by sanctioning publication of the results of another and almost simultaneous peace contact. On July 17 two Northerners met under flag of truce with Jefferson Davis and Judah Benjamin in Richmond. They were James R. Gilmore, a journalist, and Colonel James Jaquess of the 73rd Illinois, on furlough and temporarily resuming his peacetime vocation as a Methodist clergyman who wished to stop fellow Christians from slaughtering each other. Lincoln had given them a pass through Union lines in Virginia with the understanding that their mission was strictly unofficial—though they were well acquainted with Lincoln's preconditions for peace. Davis decided to meet with them because, like Lincoln, he had to consider the desire for peace among his own people and could not appear to spurn any opportunity for negotiations.

Gilmore and Jaquess informally repeated the terms Lincoln had offered in his amnesty proclamation the previous December: reunion, emancipation, and amnesty. According to Gilmore's account, Davis responded angrily: "Amnesty, Sir, applies to criminals. We have committed no crime. At your door lies all the misery and crime of this war. . . . We are fighting for Independence—and that, or extermination, we *will* have. . . . You may emancipate every negro in the Confederacy, but *we will be free.* We will govern ourselves . . . if we have to see every Southern plantation sacked, and every Southern city in flames."[22]

Upon his return north, Gilmore published a brief account of the meeting in a Boston newspaper and a subsequent detailed narrative in the *Atlantic Monthly.* Lincoln approved these publications because they shifted part of the burden of refusing to negotiate from Lincoln's shoulders to Davis's.[23] The *New York Times* immediately grasped this point. The Gilmore-Jaquess mission, it declared, "proved of extreme service . . . because it established that Jeff. Davis will listen to no proposals of peace that do not embrace disunion. . . . In view of the efforts now being made by the Peace Party of the North to delude our people into a belief that peace is now practicable without disunion," Davis's words were "peculiarly timely and valuable."[24]

The *Richmond Enquirer* also recognized that Gilmore and Jaquess had "provoked" Davis into "expressions of hostility which might be represented as a refusal on our part to treat of peace" in order to "rally the war party" in the North. The *Enquirer* then proceeded to use this incident to fire up the Southern war party. To the Northern demand for unconditional surrender, declared this newspaper, the Southern people responded with the "sole and simple condition" of "unconditional recognition" of Confederate independence. "They will die with arms in their hands before they disgrace this demand by any qualification of their rights."[25]

The publicity surrounding these peace overtures should have put to rest the Copperhead argument that the North could have peace and reunion without military victory. But it did not. At the rock-bottom point of Northern morale in August 1864—when, as Thurlow Weed observed, "the people are wild for peace"—Democrats were able to slide around the awkward problem of Davis's conditions by pointing to Lincoln's second condition, "abandonment of slavery," as the real stumbling block to peace. Across the spectrum from Copperheads to War Democrats, and even beyond to conservative Republicans, came denunciations of the president for his "prostitution of the war for the Union into an abolition crusade."[26] Democratic newspapers proclaimed that "tens of thousands of white men must bite the dust to allay the negro mania of the President." For that purpose, "our soil is drenched in blood . . . the widows wail and the children hunger." Emancipation was now Lincoln's sole purpose; "the idea of restoring the Union no longer troubles the Executive brain."[27]

The most powerful Democratic newspaper was the *New York World*, which was closely affiliated with General George B. McClellan, whom the party was about to nominate for president. The *World* claimed that Lincoln "prefers to tear a half million more white men from their homes . . . to continue a war for the abolition of slavery rather than entertain a proposition for the return of the seceded states with their old rights." Never mind that no such proposition existed; Democratic newspapers convinced thousands of Northern voters that the South would have accepted such a proposition if Lincoln had not made abolition a condition of peace. The *New York Herald,* an independent but Democratic-leaning paper with the country's largest circulation, opined that Lincoln had signed his political death warrant by making abandonment of slavery "a *ne plus ultra* in the terms of peace."[28]

Even some Republican editors expressed "painful and perplexing surprise" that Lincoln had made "the abolition of slavery the principal object of prosecuting the war."[29] Horace Greeley, who two years earlier had criticized Lincoln for being slow to act against slavery, now condemned him for insisting on what Greeley had then demanded. "We do not contend," wrote Greeley in a widely reprinted *Tribune* editorial, "that reunion is possible or endurable only on the basis of Universal Freedom. . . . War has its exigencies which cannot be foreseen . . . and Peace is often desirable on other terms than those of our own choice." George Templeton Strong sadly concluded that Lincoln's emancipation condition was a "blunder" that "may cost him his election. [It has] given the disaffected and discontented a weapon that doubles their power of mischief."[30]

Henry J. Raymond of the *New York Times,* who doubled as Republican national chairman for this election campaign, thought he saw a way out of the dilemma. Lincoln "*did* say he *would* receive and consider propositions for peace . . . *if* they embraced the integrity of the Union *and* the abandonment of Slavery," wrote Raymond in an important editorial, "but he did *not* say he would not embrace them unless they embraced both conditions."[31] As a lawyer, Lincoln was no stranger to such hairsplitting. And the enormous pressure on him from all sides to drop his abandonment-of-slavery condition almost caused him to succumb. On August 17 Lincoln drafted a letter to a Wisconsin newspaper editor who had previously supported the administration but could no longer do so if the president intended the war to continue until slavery was abolished. "To me," Lincoln began his letter, "it seems plain that saying re-union and abandonment of slavery would be considered, if offered, is not saying that nothing *else* or *less* would be considered." Lincoln concluded the letter with these words: "If Jefferson Davis wishes . . . to know what I would do if he were to offer peace and re-union, saying nothing about slavery, let him try me."[32]

In the same draft, however, and in an interview two days later with a pair of Wisconsin Republicans, Lincoln explained forcefully and eloquently why he included abandonment of slavery as a precondition for peace. "No human power can subdue this rebellion without using the Emancipation lever as I have done," he insisted. Lincoln pointed out that 100,000 or more black soldiers and sailors were fighting for the Union. "If they stake their lives for us they must be prompted by the strongest motive—even the promise of freedom. And the promise being made, must be kept." To jettison emancipation would "ruin the Union cause itself," Lincoln continued. "All recruiting of colored men would instantly cease, and all colored men in our service would instantly desert us. And rightfully too. Why should they give their lives for us, with full notice of our purpose to betray them? . . . I should be damned in time and eternity for so doing. The world shall know that I will keep my faith to friends and enemies, come what will."[33]

Recognizing the inconsistency of these sentiments with his "let Jefferson Davis try me" challenge, Lincoln filed that letter away unsent. When he did so, he and everyone else believed that he would be defeated for reelection on the peace issue. "I am going to be beaten," he told a visitor, "and unless some great change takes place *badly* beaten." On August 23 Lincoln wrote his famous "blind memorandum" and asked cabinet members to endorse it sight unseen: "This morning, as for some days past, it seems exceedingly probable that this Administration will not be re-elected. Then it will be my duty to so co-operate with the President elect, as to save the Union between the election and the inauguration; as he will have secured his election on such ground that he can not possibly save it afterwards."[34]

This memorandum may have been prompted by a letter Lincoln received that day from Henry Raymond. "The tide is setting strongly against us," wrote the editor. "Two special causes are assigned to this great reaction in public sentiment—the want of military success, and the impression . . . that we *can* have peace with Union if we would . . . [but] that we are not to have peace *in any event* under this administration until Slavery is abandoned." To allay this impression, Raymond urged Lincoln to appoint a commissioner to *"make distinct proffers of peace to Davis . . . on the sole condition"* of reunion, leaving "all the other questions to be settled in a convention of all the people of all the States." Of course, Raymond added, Davis would reject such a proffer, and this rejection would "dispel all the delusions about peace that prevail in the North . . . [and] reconcile public sentiment to the War, the draft, & the tax as inevitable necessities."[35]

Once again Lincoln seemed to yield to such pressure. On August 24 he drafted instructions for Raymond himself to go to Richmond and "propose, on behalf [of] this government, that upon the restoration of the Union and

national authority, the war shall cease at once, all remaining questions to be
left for adjustment by peaceful modes." Lincoln's private secretaries and later
biographers, John G. Nicolay and John Hay, maintain that Lincoln had no intention of sending Raymond to Richmond. His purpose in drafting this document, they assert, was to make the editor a "witness of its absurdity."[36]

In any event, Raymond and the rest of the Republican National Committee
met with Lincoln and three cabinet members on August 25. The commit-
teemen, according to Nicolay, were "laboring under a severe fit of despondency
and discouragement . . . almost the condition of a disastrous panic." Lincoln
convinced them that the proposed mission to Richmond "would be utter
ruination . . . worse than losing the Presidential contest—it would be igno-
miniously surrendering it in advance."[37] To back away from emancipation
would not only betray a promise, it would also give the impression of an administration floundering in panic and would alienate the radical wing of the
Republican party.[38] After all, Lincoln had been renominated on a platform
pledging a constitutional amendment to abolish slavery and calling for the
"unconditional surrender" of the rebels. For weal or woe, Lincoln intended to
stand on that platform.[39]

For a week after that fateful meeting at the White House, woe seemed to be
the fate of Lincoln's reelection prospects. On August 31 the Democrats nominated McClellan for president and a Peace Democrat for vice president on a
platform that declared: "After four years of failure to restore the Union by the
experiment of war . . . [we] demand that immediate efforts be made for a cessation of hostilities, with a view to an ultimate convention of the states, or
other peaceable means, to the end that, at the earliest practicable moment,
peace may be restored on the basis of the Federal Union."[40] This last phrase
was little more than window dressing; almost everyone recognized that an appeal by the U.S. government for an armistice would be tantamount to confess-
ing defeat.[41] McClellan himself recognized this, and his letter accepting the
nomination made peace negotiations contingent on prior agreement to reunion as a basis for such negotiations.[42]

Whether these internal Democratic contradictions would be put to the test
suddenly became moot. On September 3 a telegram from General Sherman
arrived in Washington: "Atlanta is ours, and fairly won." This news turned
morale around 180 degrees in both North and South. "Glorious news this
morning," wrote George Templeton Strong in his diary. "Atlanta taken at
last!!! . . . It is (coming at this political crisis) the greatest event of the war."[43]

The *Richmond Examiner* reflected with despair that "the disaster at Atlanta" came "in the very nick of time" to "save the party of Lincoln from irretrievable ruin. . . . [It] obscures the prospect of peace, late so bright. It will diffuse gloom over the South." One of the North's foremost clergymen, Joseph T. Thompson, delivered a widely published sermon whose title summed up the meaning of Atlanta: "Peace Through Victory."[44]

Few others in the North urged this policy with more determination than Union soldiers themselves. Although many of them had a lingering affection for McClellan, most denounced the war-failure plank of the Democratic platform, and a remarkable 78 percent of them voted for Lincoln. "To ellect McClellan would be to undo all that we have don in the past four years," wrote a Michigan corporal. "Old Abe is slow but sure, he will accept nothing but an unconditional surrender." A New York lieutenant, a former Democrat, repudiated his party. "I had rather stay out here a lifetime (much as I dislike it)," he wrote, "than consent to a division of our country. . . . We all want peace, but none any but an honorable one."[45]

Prospects for that honorable peace—a peace through victory—continued to brighten through the fall and winter. General Philip Sheridan's Army of the Shenandoah won several important victories in September and October. Lincoln was triumphantly reelected in November. General George Thomas's Union Army of the Cumberland virtually destroyed the Confederate Army of Tennessee at the battle of Nashville in mid-December. A month later a combined assault by Union naval and army forces captured Fort Fisher in North Carolina, closing the port of Wilmington, which had been the principal remaining terminus for blockade runners. In his annual message to Congress in December, Lincoln promised no letup in the war. Northern determination to see the matter through "was never more firm, nor more nearly unanimous, than now," said the president. But this consummation could not be achieved by negotiations with "the insurgent leader," Jefferson Davis, who "does not attempt to deceive us. He affords us no excuse to deceive ourselves. He cannot voluntarily reaccept the Union; we cannot voluntarily yield it. Between him and us the issue is distinct, simple, and inflexible. It is an issue which can only be tried by war, and decided by victory."[46]

Nevertheless, one more bid to end the war by mutual agreement took place. This one was launched by Francis Preston Blair, the old Jacksonian Democrat whose powerful family had helped found the Republican Party in the mid-1850s. Blair had maintained his ties across party lines, however, and even across the bloody chasm of war. With Lincoln's tacit consent, Blair traveled to Richmond under flag of truce in January 1865 to visit his former friend and political associate Jefferson Davis. Although the content of their conversations remained secret, Blair's presence in Richmond gave rise to endless speculation in the press both North and South. Blair's purpose was to see if there might be some way to reunite Union and Confederacy in order to put an end to the internecine bloodletting.

Signs abounded that the Southern people, if not President Davis, were prepared to give up. Desertions from Confederate armies soared. The previously indefatigable chief of Confederate ordnance, Josiah Gorgas, made despairing entries in his diary during January: "Where is this to end? No money in the Treasury, no food to feed Gen. Lee's Army, no troops to oppose Gen. Sherman. . . . There is a strong disposition among members of congress to come to terms with the enemy, feeling that we cannot carry on the war any longer with hope of success. Wife & I sit talking of going to Mexico to live out the remnant of our days."[47]

Mexico was also on Blair's mind. That country experienced its own civil war in the 1860s, prompting Louis Napoleon to send 35,000 French troops and to install Austrian Archduke Ferdinand Maximilian as emperor of Mexico in 1864. Blair seemed obsessed with the idea that a joint campaign of Union and Confederate armies to throw the French out of Mexico would pave the way to reunion. Hints of Blair's suggestion to Davis of such a project leaked out and elicited cautious approval by Richmond newspapers and more enthusiastic endorsement by the jingo press in the North.[48] Davis returned a cool response to this Mexican scheme, but he did give Blair a letter for Lincoln's eyes offering to appoint commissioners to "enter into conference with a view to secure peace to the two countries."[49]

Lincoln wanted nothing to do with Blair's proposed Mexican adventure. But the president thought he saw an opportunity to end the war on his own terms without compromising his refusal to recognize the legitimacy of the Confederacy. He authorized Blair to return to Richmond with an offer to receive any commissioner that Davis "may *informally* send to me with the view of securing peace to the people of our *one common country*."[50]

Davis overlooked the discrepancy between "two countries" and "one common country." He appointed a commission composed of Vice President Alexander H. Stephens, President protem of the Senate Robert M. T. Hunter, and Assistant Secretary of War John A. Campbell, a former U.S. Supreme Court justice. Davis expected their efforts to fail because he knew Lincoln would stick to his terms of Union and Freedom. This was the outcome Davis wanted, for it would enable him to rally flagging Southern spirits to keep up the fight as the only alternative to degrading submission.[51]

This peace effort almost foundered before it was launched. Lincoln sent word to military commanders in Virginia that the Confederate commissioners should not be allowed through the lines for an "informal conference" with Secretary of State Seward, whom he had sent to Virginia, unless they agreed in advance to Lincoln's "one common country" phrase as a basis for talks. The commissioners instead showed to the army major Lincoln dispatched to meet them their "two countries" instructions from Davis. The major therefore barred them from crossing Union lines.

That would seem to have ended the matter. But this affair had generated huge coverage in the press—even more than the peace flurries of the previous summer—and had raised hopes that this cruel war might soon be over. On the morning of February 2, Lincoln read a telegram from General Grant: "I am convinced, upon conversation with Messrs Stevens & Hunter that their intentions are good and their desire sincere to restore peace and union. . . . I am sorry however that Mr. Lincoln cannot have an interview with [them]. . . . I fear now their going back without any expression from anyone in authority will have a bad influence."[52]

Grant's intervention was decisive. On the spur of the moment Lincoln decided to go to Virginia to join Seward for a personal meeting with the commissioners. This extraordinary "informal" four-hour meeting of the five men took place February 3 on the Union steamer *River Queen* anchored in Hampton Roads. No aides were present, and no formal record was kept, although Seward and Campbell wrote brief summaries and Stephens later penned a lengthy account, which must be used with care.[53] Despite an underlying tension, the mood was relaxed. Lincoln and Stephens had been friends and fellow Whigs in Congress nearly two decades earlier, providing a basis for a cordial atmosphere.

Lincoln nevertheless stuck to the terms he had written out for Seward before the president had decided to join him: "1 The restoration of the National authority throughout all the States. 2 No receding by the Executive of the United States, on the Slavery question. . . . 3 No cessation of hostilities short of an end of the war, and the disbanding of all forces hostile to the government."[54] Stephens tried to change the subject by alluding to Blair's Mexican project; Lincoln promptly disavowed it. What about an armistice while peace negotiations took place? asked the Confederates. No armistice, replied Lincoln, reiterating his third condition. Well, then, said Hunter, would it be possible to hold official negotiations while the war went on? After all, he noted, even King Charles I had entered into agreements with rebels in arms during the English civil war. "I do not profess to be posted in history," replied Lincoln—probably with a twinkle in his eye. "All I distinctly recollect about the case of Charles I, is, that he lost his head."[55]

On questions of punishing Confederate leaders and confiscating Southern property, Lincoln promised generous treatment based on his power of pardon. With respect to slavery, Lincoln even suggested that if Confederate states abolished it themselves as part of a peace settlement, he would ask Congress for partial compensation. In any event, the Union Congress had passed the Thirteenth Amendment three days earlier, and several states, including Lincoln's Illinois as the first, had already ratified it.[56] Slavery was dead, implied Lincoln, and to avoid further bloodshed the Confederate leaders should recognize that the Confederacy itself would soon be in the same condition.

Whatever their personal convictions, the commissioners had no authority to concede the death of their nation. They returned sadly to Richmond and admitted their failure to President Davis—who was neither surprised nor disappointed. Davis reported to the Confederate Congress that Lincoln's terms required "degrading submission" and "humiliating surrender." Richmond newspapers echoed the president's angry words. The *Examiner* paraphrased Lincoln in this fashion: "Down upon your knees, Confederates! . . . your mouths in the dust; kiss the rod, confess your sins." Davis addressed a rally in Richmond. He predicted that Seward and "His Majesty Abraham the First" would find "they had been speaking to their masters," for Southern armies would yet "compel the Yankees, in less than twelve months, to petition us for peace on our own terms."[57]

War fever in Richmond rose higher than at any other time since April 1861. "Every one thinks the Confederacy will at once gather up its military strength and strike such blows as will astonish the world," wrote the War Department clerk John Jones. One of the more moderate Richmond newspapers declared that "to talk now of any other arbitrament than that of the sword is to betray cowardice and treachery." We must "conquer or die," declared another. "There is no alternative. We must make good our independence, defend our institutions . . . or give up the . . . lands we have tilled, the slaves we have owned . . . all indeed that makes existence valuable."[58]

So be it, responded the Northern press. Davis had made it clear, conceded the onetime peace negotiator Horace Greeley, that there could only be "Peace through War." The *New York Times* pointed out that "we have always demanded 'unconditional surrender.' . . . We must fight it out."[59] Fight it out they did, for two more months, during which several thousand more young men died. In his second inaugural address, Lincoln acknowledged that in 1861 "neither party expected for the war, the magnitude, or the duration, which it has already attained" or "a result [so] fundamental and astounding." The same can be said of many wars. None of the nations that opened fire with the Guns of August 1914 foresaw the magnitude or duration of that war. The Germans who invaded Poland in 1939 and the Japanese who bombed Pearl Harbor two years later surely did not expect such a fundamental and astounding result of their actions. Nor, presumably, did the U.S. government when it sent American troops to South Vietnam in the 1960s. As historians we cannot know—though we can certainly speculate—that the leaders of these nations would have acted differently if they could have foreseen the consequences. It is also quite possible that Americans in 1861 would have chosen a different course if they had known that the war into which they plunged would last four years and cost 620,000 lives. In any event, when Lincoln was inaugurated for a second term on March 4, 1865, he remained committed to the fundamental and astounding results of a Union victory, no matter what it cost or how long it took. He served notice that, if necessary, the war would continue "until all the wealth piled by the bond-man's two hundred and fifty years of unrequited toil shall be sunk, and until every drop of blood drawn with the lash, shall be paid by another drawn with the sword."[60]

Mercifully, it did not take that long. Three months after Jefferson Davis had breathed defiance to "His Majesty Abraham the First," the ex–Confederate ordnance chief Josiah Gorgas pronounced his nation's epitaph: "The calamity which has fallen upon us in the total destruction of our government is of a character so overwhelming that I am as yet unable to comprehend it. . . . It is marvelous that a people that a month ago had money, armies, and the attributes of a nation should to-day be no more. . . . Will it be so when the Soul leaves the body behind it?"[61]

# V
# Lincoln

# 15

# To Remember That He Had Lived

O VER THE YEARS, I HAVE REVIEWED many books about Abraham Lincoln. Several of them contained new information, fresh insights, provocative interpretations, and sometimes distortions or errors. Reviewing these books gave me opportunities to offer my own views and amplifications of the authors' findings and interpretations. This essay constitutes an updated compendium of reviews of seven Lincoln books. It is designed to stand alone as an exploration of some critical elements in the Lincoln story.

Three books published within a few months of each other in 1997–98 provided a fuller portrait than previously existed of Lincoln during his formative years in New Salem and Springfield.[1] Two main themes emerge in these 1,400 pages: the rehabilitation of William H. Herndon as a researcher and biographer of Lincoln; and the crucial importance of the New Salem and early Springfield years in the shaping of Lincoln's character.

William Herndon was a Springfield lawyer when he joined Lincoln, nine years his elder, as a partner in 1844. From then until Lincoln went to Washington as president in 1861, Herndon was the nearest thing to a confidant that the notoriously "shut-mouthed" Lincoln had. After the president's assassination in 1865, Herndon anticipated the martyred Lincoln's elevation to secular sainthood and decided to write a biography that, unlike others, which portrayed a towering public figure of noble perfection who had saved the Union and freed the slaves, would reveal the "inner life" of Lincoln: "his passions—appetites—& affections—perceptions . . . just as he lived, breathed—ate & laughed in this world."[2] Herndon quickly discovered that information about the first thirty years of Lincoln's life was exceedingly sparse—in part because Lincoln had wanted it that way. When a campaign biographer in 1860 asked Lincoln for details of his youth and young manhood, the nominee replied: "It is a great piece of folly to attempt to make anything out of my early life. It can all be condensed into a single sentence, and that sentence you will find in Gray's elegy: 'The short and simple annals of the poor.' "[3]

For nearly two years after Lincoln's death, Herndon left his law practice in limbo and set himself the task of penetrating that veil of obscurity. With energy and ingenuity, he tracked down hundreds of people still living who had known Lincoln in Kentucky, Indiana, and Illinois. In what has been described as "one of the first extensive oral history projects in American history," Herndon interviewed many of these people and elicited written statements from others. In the 1880s Herndon returned to this enterprise and corresponded with or interviewed several more.[4]

The thousands of manuscript pages of correspondence and of interview notes written in Herndon's elliptical style and almost indecipherable handwriting have had a noteworthy history of their own. Herndon used the early material as the basis for a series of lectures in 1865–66, but his plans for a book fell victim to financial reverses and to his drinking habits and mercurial temperament. In 1869 Herndon sold transcriptions of his correspondence and notes to Ward Hill Lamon, a friend and political associate of Lincoln. Lamon turned Herndon's material over to a ghostwriter who fashioned a biography of Lincoln that appeared under Lamon's name in 1872. This book received a decidedly hostile reception because of its sensationalism about certain facets of Lincoln's life, particularly his possible illegitimacy and his troubled marriage to Mary Todd Lincoln.

Lamon's *Life of Abraham Lincoln* also fell far short of the kind of biography Herndon thought Lincoln deserved. When Herndon put his own life back together in the 1880s, he teamed up with a younger colleague, Jesse W. Weik, to do additional research and finally to produce *Herndon's Lincoln* in 1889. After Herndon's death in 1891, Weik retained ownership of Herndon's research materials and refused to give most other scholars access to them. Weik wrote *The Real Lincoln* and published it in 1922. He then turned the documents over to Albert J. Beveridge, who had written a favorable review of Weik's book. Beveridge's subsequent unfinished biography of Lincoln still stands today as the fullest treatment of Lincoln's early life.[5]

After the deaths of Beveridge and Weik in 1927 and 1929, a consortium of manuscript dealers bought what had become known as the Herndon-Weik Collection. The Library of Congress finally acquired the collection in 1941 and subsequently microfilmed it. Meanwhile the Huntington Library had acquired the transcriptions of the early material sold to Lamon in 1869. This material has been accessible to historians for decades. But the Library of Congress collection is another story. Herndon's handwriting was so bad, the arrangement and indexing of the material was so poorly done, and the quality of the microfilming was so poor that this collection remained almost as inaccessible to most historians as it had been before 1941.

Until 1998, that is. Douglas L. Wilson and his co-editor, Rodney O. Davis, along with a small army of research assistants and librarians, have done a service of inestimable value with the complete, accurately transcribed, indexed, and annotated edition of Herndon's interviews and correspondence with 274 people—a total of 634 documents. One can scarcely imagine the countless hours of eye-straining, nerve-agitating, mind-challenging labor necessary to produce *Herndon's Informants*. It is a monumental achievement of scholarship. That is true not simply because of the editorial skill and effort required to complete it but mainly because this material is the basis for most of what we know about the first half of Lincoln's life. Without Herndon's underappreciated efforts, Lincoln scholarship would be immensely poorer. And without the feat of Wilson and Davis, historians and biographers in the future would be much the poorer.

Yet there has been something of a catch-22 about the reputation of Herndon and of the source materials he assembled. On the one hand, Lincoln biographers have been dependent on his work, either directly or indirectly through *Herndon's Lincoln* and Beveridge's *Abraham Lincoln, 1809–1858*. On the other hand, many of these same biographers have challenged Herndon's credibility and questioned the authenticity of much of the evidence he collected—even as they used it. This is the anomalous state of affairs that Douglas Wilson undertook to revise in *Honor's Voice* and in several of the essays in *Lincoln Before Washington*. Co-director (with Rodney O. Davis) of the Lincoln Studies Center at Knox College in Galesburg, Illinois (site of one of the Lincoln-Douglas debates), Wilson has also written about Thomas Jefferson. He became fascinated by the contrasts between the education of Jefferson and that of Lincoln, who had barely a year of elementary school education a month or two at a time. Wilson wanted to understand how two of the greatest statesmen and writers in American history, whose Declaration of Independence and Gettysburg Address have shaped and defined the nation's ideals, emerged from such different backgrounds. "Any search for information on Lincoln's formative years," writes Wilson, "leads inevitably to the letters and interviews collected by his law partner," which are "unlike anything for the study of Jefferson or of virtually anyone else before the twentieth century."[6]

Once he started on this project, Wilson was hooked. Seven of the nine essays in *Lincoln Before Washington* chronicle work on the Herndon materials and offer important insights on a number of controversial issues in Lincoln scholarship. Foremost among these is what might be termed the Ann Rutledge Question. When Herndon began his research, he was startled to hear from several informants who had known Lincoln in New Salem that he had fallen in love with the prettiest young woman in town and had become engaged to her in 1835. When Ann Rutledge died of "brain fever" (probably typhoid) in August of that year, Lincoln sank into such a deep depression that friends feared he might take his own life.

Herndon had not previously heard of Ann Rutledge, but once he learned about her he avidly pursued additional reminiscences from informants. In 1866 Herndon devoted one of his lectures to the Ann Rutledge story. He harmed his own credibility, however, and gravely offended Lincoln's widow and their son Robert by speculating well beyond the evidence he had gathered from his informants. Ann Rutledge was Lincoln's only true love, said Herndon; his depression following her death was the origin of Lincoln's recurrent bouts of "melancholia" or "hypo" (for hypochondria, a contemporary medical term for depression); Lincoln later married Mary Todd, after breaking their initial engagement, only because he felt bound to honor that engagement, which trapped him in a loveless and joyless marriage.

Herndon had a hidden purpose in the interpretation he gave the Ann Rutledge story. He had never liked Mary Lincoln, who reciprocated the sentiment. Herndon's portrait of the Lincolns' marriage has echoed down the years, despite challenges by Mary Lincoln's biographers, and it still influences serious scholarship as well as popular images of Abraham and Mary Lincoln.[7] The Ann Rutledge story caught the popular fancy and took on so many layers of myth that the truth is difficult to determine. It did not help matters that Carl Sandburg's widely read biography of Lincoln invented "mawkish scenes and trembling soliloquies" in its treatment of Lincoln and Rutledge, or that the *Atlantic Monthly* published in 1928–29 a series of supposed love letters from Abraham to Ann (whose authenticity Sandburg endorsed), which turned out to be forgeries.[8]

The scholarly backlash against this sentimentalized love affair caused serious Lincoln biographers to doubt or deny the Ann Rutledge story in its entirety. This skepticism dominated Lincoln studies from the 1930s to the 1990s. Herndon's reputation suffered from the backlash, for if he and his informants were wrong about Ann Rutledge, how could their recollections about other aspects of Lincoln's early life be trusted?

Herndon's critics perhaps had concealed motives of their own. The principal challenge to Herndon's credibility came from James G. Randall, the leading Lincoln scholar from the 1930s to the 1950s. Randall's wife, Ruth Painter Randall, wrote a sympathetic biography of Mary Todd Lincoln suggesting that the Lincolns had a loving and fulfilling marriage. Randall's brightest student, David Donald, wrote a biography of Herndon that portrayed him in an unflattering light. And one of Donald's students, Jean H. Baker, has written a biography of Mary Lincoln that likewise has little good to say of Herndon.[9]

When it comes to such controversies, the scholarly pendulum has a way of swinging from one side to the other. During the 1990s it swung back partway in Herndon's favor, in large part owing to the scrupulous and careful analysis of the Herndon materials by Douglas Wilson. His precise prose should convince fair-minded readers of his two books, as Wilson's research gradually convinced him, "that in some important respects the great Lincoln scholars of this century have been wrong about Herndon and his informant testimony, that this judgment has prejudiced their constituency unduly against Herndon, and that Herndon's neglected materials still have new and unexpected things to tell us about Lincoln's prepresidential life."[10]

Because the Ann Rutledge Question became a touchstone of Herndon's reliability, Wilson devotes a great deal of attention to it. His main target of criticism is James G. Randall. In a famous appendix to his magisterial *Lincoln the President*, "Sifting the Ann Rutledge Evidence," Randall cited what he considered to be conflicting stories, faulty memory, and distortions by Herndon's informants plus leading questions from Herndon to discredit the story of Lincoln's love for Ann and his depression after her death. For Randall, these defects called all of Herndon's evidence into question. "The historian must use reminiscence, but he must do so critically," wrote Randall. "A careful writer will check it with known facts. . . . Unsupported memories are in themselves insufficient as proof; statements induced under suggestion, or psychological stimulus, as were some of the stories about Lincoln and Ann, call especially for careful appraisal. . . . When faulty memories are admitted the resulting product becomes something other than history."[11]

This is sound advice for historians and biographers. Wilson endorses every one of its tenets. But he then proceeds, in a tour de force of textual analysis, to convict Randall of violating his own rules and to defend Herndon from Randall's charges. Herndon, Wilson writes, was careful to avoid imposing his views on his correspondents and interviewees. Herndon was surprised and skeptical about the Ann Rutledge stories at first but was finally convinced by overwhelming testimony. He did in fact sift and balance contradictory or dubious testimony and ask probing questions to try to reconcile conflicting evidence. And for many important details of Lincoln's early life, there are no "known facts"—that is, contemporary documentary evidence—against which to test the admittedly fallible memories of informants. Herndon's evidence is all we have, and Wilson deftly demonstrates that Randall himself, as well as other historians critical of Herndon, "draws extensively on Herndon's informants and depends on them for the documentation of Lincoln's personal and political background. There he does not confine himself to testimony that can be checked with contemporary sources or 'known facts,' nor does he balk at accepting as historical incidents about which evidence is conflicting."[12]

Of twenty-four informants who offered testimony on Lincoln and Ann Rutledge—most of whom knew both of them—twenty-two said that Lincoln loved or courted Ann, two offered no opinion, and none disputed the existence of the relationship. Seventeen of the twenty-four stated that Lincoln grieved at her death, and most of these testified to his serious, almost suicidal depression; the other seven offered no opinion. Those informants who knew Lincoln and Rutledge best, and who had good reputations for truthfulness and lack of bias, testified most strongly to the reality of the relationship. According to the critical criteria that Wilson establishes for judging the reliability of long-after-the-fact oral history evidence, Lincoln did love Ann Rutledge and did grieve excessively at her death. That does not mean, however, that the extreme conclusions Herndon drew from the story were right—that Lincoln never loved another woman, that his marriage was a constant hell, or that Rutledge's death was the source of his subsequent tendency toward melancholia.

Why is all of this important? From his close examination of the Ann Rutledge evidence, Wilson derived a set of criteria for evaluating the accuracy and value of Herndon's research for an understanding of key events in Lincoln's life from 1831 to 1842, which helped to form his character. Wilson managed to unravel the tangled evidence about several puzzling or controversial events in Lincoln's life in a manner similar to that of a shrewd detective. *Honor's Voice* offers new insights on Lincoln's famous wrestling match with Jack Armstrong in 1831, in which Lincoln established his masculine credentials of physical courage, strength, good humor, and self-assurance—qualities that won him friends and influence in his new home at New Salem. Wilson analyzes Lincoln's awkward relations with women, which were punctuated by a clumsy and ill-fated courtship of Mary Owens and a brief unrequited infatuation with Matilda Edwards as well as Lincoln's love for Ann Rutledge and his eventual marriage to Mary Todd. Wilson also contributes new information about the youthful Lincoln's fondness for the freethinking doctrines of Thomas Paine and his skepticism about many tenets of the Christian faith.

In *Honor's Voice*, Wilson also discusses Lincoln's authorship of anonymous or pseudonymous newspaper articles that slashed his political opponents, his fondness for William Shakespeare and Robert Burns, and what really happened on "that fatal first of Jany. '41"—or more precisely what did not happen, for the available evidence does not definitively tell us what Lincoln meant by these words written in a letter to his best friend, Joshua Speed, in March 1842. Herndon's conclusion that they referred to Lincoln's failure to show up for his scheduled wedding to Mary Todd on that date has long since been discredited. Nor can these words refer to the date of breaking the engagement to Mary, which had occurred a month or more earlier and contributed to Lincoln's prolonged bout of "hypo" during the winter of 1840–41. In a dazzling analysis of probabilities, Wilson speculates that the phrase may have referred to some important event not in Lincoln's life but in Speed's—perhaps his decision to move from Springfield back to Kentucky—or to Speed's and Lincoln's rivalry for the affection of the apparently bewitching Matilda Edwards.

These incidents are all relevant to the two main themes of *Honor's Voice*, which can be summarized in two words: Ambition and Honor. From his teenage years onward, Lincoln pursued his own program of reading, study, and self-improvement in a relentless quest for upward mobility from farm laborer to successful lawyer. His ambition, as Herndon later said, "was a little engine that knew no rest." It was not an ambition for wealth; Lincoln was indifferent, almost careless, about money. It was an ambition for success, for distinction in his profession and in politics. During the depths of his depression in early 1841, Lincoln told Joshua Speed that he would be "more than willing to die" except "that he had done nothing to make any human being remember that he had lived."[13]

The most illuminating sections of *Honor's Voice* consist of the intricate analyses of the relationships among Lincoln's courtship of Mary Todd, the broken engagement, his depression, a near-duel with James Shields, and his marriage in

1842. Lincoln's practice of writing pseudonymous newspaper articles attacking political opponents was not unusual for the time. But his well-honed talent for ridicule and satire gave his articles a special power to "skin" their victims. In 1842 Lincoln, by then a prominent Whig, wrote such an article satirizing the Democratic state auditor, James Shields. The incensed Shields discovered Lincoln's authorship and challenged him to a duel. Lincoln could not refuse and maintain his honor, but just before the duel was to take place, friends of both men interceded and persuaded Shields to accept the following statement by Lincoln in lieu of an apology: "I wrote that, wholly for political effect. I had no intention of injuring your personal or private character, or standing as a man or a gentleman . . . and had I anticipated such an effect I would have foreborne to write it."[14]

This statement represented a transformation in Lincoln's sense of manliness and honor: He recognized that an honorable man could not hide behind anonymity or politics in an attack on the integrity or character of another; he must accept responsibility for his words and actions. As a result of this experience, wrote Wilson, "Lincoln may, for the first time, have understood 'honor' and honorable behavior as all-important, as necessary, as a matter of life and death."[15]

What made this event even more important was its relation to Lincoln's marriage. Lincoln's "hypo" during the winter of 1840–41 was probably the result of profound guilt feelings about the wounds he had inflicted on Mary Todd when he sought release from their initial engagement (which she granted). For more than a year, as Lincoln later wrote to Joshua Speed, he could have no happiness because of "the never-absent idea, that there is *one* still unhappy whom I have contributed to make so. That still kills my soul. I can not but reproach myself, for even wishing to be happy while she is otherwise." Lincoln felt dishonored by what he came to see as a betrayal of trust toward Mary. He also believed that he had lost the "ability to keep my resolves when they are made," a defect he regarded as fatal to his hopes for success and distinction.[16]

The Shields imbroglio proved to be a catalyst for resolution of these doubts and convictions of dishonor. Lincoln's article ridiculing Shields was one of three published in the Illinois press; Mary Todd probably wrote one of the others (far gentler in its satire than Lincoln's). This affair brought them together again, and Lincoln's new conception of honor in the settlement of the quarrel with Shields seems to have prompted a similar determination to dissolve his crippling guilt toward Mary by marrying her. In so doing, he regained his confidence in "my ability to keep my resolves" and, in Wilson's words, "affirmed something important in his identity."[17]

The married life of the Lincolns—its happiness and unhappiness, and whether Mary was a shrew who made Lincoln's life a hell—remains a matter of dispute among biographers. But the marriage did produce four sons, the first one born precisely nine months after the wedding. And as Wilson notes, "the debilitating episodes of the 'hypo' did not recur." Most important, perhaps, "Lincoln became known for his resolution."[18] Once he made a decision he stuck with it—a matter of no small importance when the issues became Union or Disunion, Victory or Defeat, Slavery or Freedom. Lincoln once said to prominent political leaders who urged him to back away from the Emancipation Proclamation or face possible defeat for reelection in 1864: "The promise, being made, must be kept."[19] The man who had contemplated suicide at the age of thirty-one but drew back because he "had done nothing to make any human being remember that he had lived" eventually caused the whole world to remember that he had lived.

## II

THREE MONTHS BEFORE the Republican national convention in May 1860, Abraham Lincoln of Illinois did not make anyone's list of potential presidential nominees. At best he could hope to receive his state's first-ballot support as a favorite son. Newspaper editors in the East knew so little about him that they spelled his first name "Abram." Lincoln had won favorable notices for his Senate campaign against the incumbent Stephen A. Douglas in 1858—but he lost that election. Except for a single term in Congress more than a decade earlier, Lincoln was a stranger to the national political scene. The presumptive favorite for the Republican nomination was Senator William H. Seward of New York. And if his candidacy faltered, several other prominent Republicans were waiting in the wings, headed by Governor Salmon P. Chase of Ohio.

In a long political career, however, Seward had made enemies, including some in his own state. In October 1859 a committee of anti-Seward New York Republicans invited Lincoln to give one of a series of political "lectures" in Brooklyn (later changed to Cooper Union in New York City, of which Brooklyn was not then a part). The New Yorkers' purpose was to stop Seward's triumphant march to the nomination by providing a public forum to other Republicans, including Lincoln, who had never before spoken in the Empire State. The committee that invited him supported Chase for the nomination. Whether Lincoln was aware that he was being used as a stalking horse for Chase is uncertain. In any event, he eagerly accepted the invitation, and the date for his speech was finally set for February 27, 1860.

With this single speech the stalking horse became a serious contestant. Two books with identical titles and almost identical subtitles, published only a few months apart, make a persuasive case that Lincoln's Cooper Union address "made him president."[20] If that seems slightly exaggerated, there is nevertheless no doubt that this speech and a subsequent two-week speaking tour of New England, in response to invitations that poured in after the Cooper Union address, did indeed give a huge boost to Lincoln's national stature and made him a viable presidential candidate.

These books are not the first to maintain that a single Lincoln speech changed history. Garry Wills devoted an entire book to the Gettysburg Address, "the words that remade America." Ronald C. White made a powerful argument for the significance of Lincoln's second inaugural address in defining the meaning of the Civil War.[21] Other Lincoln speeches have also been the subject of special analyses—particularly his Peoria speech of 1854 and his debates with Douglas in 1858. But those antebellum speeches gave Lincoln regional prominence; it was the Cooper Union address that projected him onto the national scene.

How did this happen? Part of the answer lies in the contrast between expectations and performance. Apart from his unusual height (6'4"), Lincoln's personal appearance did not inspire confidence—especially before he grew a beard after his election as president. With his disheveled hair, craggy face with oversize projecting ears, arms and legs too long for his ill-fitting clothes, flat-footed gait, and nasal tenor voice, he made a negative first impression. Lincoln bought a new suit for his New York visit, but unfortunately it fit poorly and was wrinkled by travel as well. Dozens of people who saw and heard him for the first time in New York—then as now the nation's media capital—commented on their initial dismay when Lincoln uncurled himself from his chair and shambled to the lectern and began speaking in a Southern-Midwestern twang. "The first impression of the man from the West did nothing to contradict the expectation of something weird, rough, and uncultivated," later wrote one listener. "The long ungainly figure upon which hung clothes that . . . were evidently the work of an unskilled tailor, the large feet and clumsy hands . . . the long gaunt head, capped by a shock of hair that seemed not to have been thoroughly brushed out, made a picture which did not fit in with New York's

conception of a finished statesman." Another member of the audience also recalled that he initially felt "pity for so ungainly a man" and thought: "Old fellow, you won't do; it's all very well for the Wild West, but this will never go
down in New York!"[22]

But according to everybody who later commented on Lincoln's speech, as
soon as he warmed to his subject the audience forgot all of these things. Lincoln soon had them "in the hollow of his hand," recalled another listener. He
"was transformed before us. His eye kindled, his voice rang, his face shone and
seemed to light up the whole assembly as by an electric flash."[23] With few of
the oratorical flourishes or gestures common at the time, Lincoln held his audience enthralled for an hour and a half. "His manner was to a New York audience a very strange one, but it was captivating," later wrote a member of the
committee that had invited Lincoln. "He held the vast meeting spellbound,
and as one by one his oddly expressed but trenchant and convincing arguments confirmed the accuracy . . . of his political conclusions, the house broke
out in wild and prolonged enthusiasm. I think I never saw an audience more
carried away by an orator."[24]

That so many accounts agree on the contrast between negative first impressions and subsequent enthusiasm raises suspicions that such recollections
were filtered through memories of Lincoln as the great war president and murdered martyr who had sprung from humble frontier origins. Yet many contemporary comments testify to the impact that the speech made *at the time*.
The five major New York newspapers printed it in full. The Republican *New
York Tribune* praised it as one of the "most convincing political arguments ever
made in this City. . . . The vast assemblage frequently rang with cheers and
shouts of applause. . . . No man ever before made such an impression on his
first appeal to a New-York audience."[25] The son of a prominent New York Republican, a Harvard College graduate and student at Harvard Law School, told
his father next morning that "it was the best speech I ever heard." Even the un-
friendly *New York Herald* grudgingly acknowledged "the loud and uproarious
applause of his hearers—nearly every man rising spontaneously, and cheering
with the full power of their lungs."[26]

The content of the speech rather than its oratorical style was mainly responsible for such enthusiasm. Lincoln had prepared this address more thoroughly
than any of the estimated 175 speeches he had delivered since reentering politics in 1854. The Kansas-Nebraska Act sponsored by Douglas and passed by a
Democratic Congress that year had repealed the earlier restriction, legislated

in the Missouri Compromise, on slavery in territories north of 36°30'. This law had inspired a determined and violent effort by proslavery elements to force slavery into Kansas Territory. In response, an antislavery coalition founded the Republican Party, which carried most Northern states in the election of 1856 on a platform calling for exclusion of slavery from all territories. Every one of Lincoln's 175 speeches addressed this matter in some fashion. Douglas wanted to leave the question of whether to have slavery up to voters in each territory, a policy he called "popular sovereignty." In 1857 the Supreme Court ruled in the Dred Scott decision that neither Congress nor voters could exclude slavery from any territory.

This issue dominated and polarized American politics during the 1850s as no other issue has ever done. The central theme of Lincoln's Cooper Union address was a challenge to the reasoning of the Dred Scott decision as well as to Douglas's conception of popular sovereignty. Lincoln maintained that the Founding Fathers had given Congress the power to prohibit slavery in the territories as a means of limiting the growth of an institution so embarrassing to American rhetoric about liberty and equality. To Lincoln and his contemporaries, the Founding Fathers were the "greatest generation." If they could be enlisted for a cause, it would prevail. In his debates with Douglas, Lincoln had repeatedly insisted that the Founders were opposed to the expansion of slavery. Douglas denied it, citing the awkward fact that most of them owned slaves.

Lincoln intended to put this question to rest once and for all in his Cooper Union address. For weeks he pored over the debates at the Constitutional Convention of 1787, the legislation of early Congresses, and other historical evidence. Perhaps no other political speech has ever been so exhaustively researched. Lincoln discovered that of the thirty-nine signers of the Constitution, twenty-three either subsequently voted as members of Congress on the question of excluding slavery from the territories or had otherwise taken a position on this issue. Of these twenty-three, all but two had supported Congress's power to ban slavery. In addition, several of the remaining sixteen had expressed antislavery positions in principle. Anyone who today compares Lincoln's Cooper Union address with Chief Justice Taney's opinion in the Dred Scott case will agree that Lincoln vanquished Taney on this issue.

By 1860, however, Southern political leaders were threatening to take their states out of the Union if a Republican president was elected on a platform restricting slavery. "I would address a few words to the Southern people," said Lincoln, "if they would listen—as I suppose they will not." Republicans did not intend to attack slavery in the states where it existed. Like the Founders, they wanted to contain its expansion as the first step toward bringing it eventually to an end. "But you will not abide the election of a Republican president! In that supposed event, you say, you will destroy the Union; and then, you say, the great crime of having destroyed it will be upon us! [Laughter] That is cool. [Great laughter] A highwayman holds a pistol to my ear, and mutters through his teeth, 'Stand and deliver, or I shall kill you, and then you will be a murderer!' [Continued laughter]"[27]

Lincoln's peroration urged Republicans to remain true to their principles despite Southern threats. His concluding sentence brought the audience to their feet with an ovation that went on and on: "LET US HAVE FAITH THAT RIGHT MAKES MIGHT, AND IN THAT FAITH, LET US, TO THE END, DARE TO DO OUR DUTY AS WE UNDERSTAND IT."[28]

### III

IN ADDITION TO THE HUNDREDS OF THOUSANDS of newspaper copies in which Lincoln's speech was printed, several pamphlet editions appeared in 1860, and these reached hundreds of thousands more readers. The Cooper Union address transformed Lincoln from just another Western politician with a country-bumpkin image into an eloquent national leader with what modern political pundits term the "gravitas" to be president. If he had not come to New York, or if his speech there had been a failure, the Lincoln of history would not have existed.

Nor would the Lincoln of myth and folklore, who has been the subject of more apocryphal stories and who has been more quoted as saying things he never said than perhaps any other person in history—certainly in American history. Historians must be alert to the existence of this vast apocrypha, lest they fall into the trap that snared Ronald Reagan, who brought the delegates to the Republican national convention of 1992 to their feet by quoting supposed probusiness maxims uttered by Lincoln—maxims that were in fact written by an obscure Pennsylvania clergyman in 1916 and attributed to Lincoln.[29]

I have personally confronted this historical pitfall. In 1984 I delivered a paper at a conference on Abraham Lincoln and the American political tradition at Brown University. This occasion was my first public foray into the perilous arena of Lincoln scholarship, and I was a bit nervous. My presentation followed a paper by Don Fehrenbacher, then one of the foremost living Lincoln scholars (now deceased), titled "The Words of Lincoln." Fehrenbacher warned would-be quoters of Lincoln to beware of dubious statements attributed to him. He distinguished between "the canon"—the eleven-volume *Collected Works* (including a two-volume supplement to the original edition), consisting of Lincoln's letters and speeches and telegrams and memoranda that he wrote himself, or that newspaper "phonographers" (stenographers) took down on the spot—as contrasted with remarks supposedly uttered by Lincoln in the presence of auditors who wrote them down later. Many of these recollected words of Lincoln were undoubtedly genuine, in their gist if not verbatim, but others were questionable at best and counterfeit at worst. The words of Lincoln as recollected by others are a "rich resource," Fehrenbacher said, but to use this resource "is to walk on treacherous ground."[30]

As I listened to this paper, I grew increasingly apprehensive. During the ten-minute break before my presentation I feverishly searched my footnote citations to determine whether my quotations from Lincoln met Fehrenbacher's standards of authenticity. Soon I sighed with relief: Nearly all were from the canon, and the two exceptions were from the diary of John Hay, Lincoln's private secretary—which Fehrenbacher gave the highest grade of veracity, because Hay wrote down Lincoln's words shortly after his conversations with the president.[31]

The rewards as well as the perils of recollected utterance are greater with respect to Lincoln than to any other person in our history. Without reliance on such material we would know little about his early life or about the decision making behind some of his most important political and presidential actions. Yet a mythical aura of recollected words and deeds surrounds him as it does no other American.

So how does the student of Lincoln separate the gold from the dross? Fehrenbacher conceded that "there is no simple formula for judging the authenticity of recollected utterances." The historian "must call upon his professional experience, his knowledge of the particular historical context, and his common sense to make a judgment of probability." That is all very well for the seasoned historian, who is trained in critical evaluation of sources. But what of the novice, the journalist, the Rotary Club speaker, the politician, who wants to quote Lincoln? "What we need, and may never have," Fehrenbacher said in 1984, "is a systematic, critically evaluative compilation of all the utterances, whether quoted or merely summarized, that have been attributed to Lincoln in contemporary and recollective primary sources."[32]

No one was better qualified than Fehrenbacher himself to put together such a compilation. So with his wife, Virginia, he set out to do so. Twelve years later, in 1996, the *Recollected Words of Abraham Lincoln* was the splendid result.[33] The Fehrenbachers sifted through countless recollective writings to document, classify, and evaluate some 1,900 quotations of Lincoln by 531 people. This awe-inspiring task was well worth the effort, for we now have a comprehensive and trustworthy guide of incalculable value to all students of Lincoln.

A few familiar quotations are missing. When Harriet Beecher Stowe, author of *Uncle Tom's Cabin,* visited Lincoln at the White House in November 1862, the president reportedly greeted her as "the little woman who made this great war." Many historians and biographers of both Lincoln and Stowe have quoted these words, but because their only source was "unverified family tradition," the Fehrenbachers do not include the phrase.[34] Nor do they include many other quotations that can only be "vaguely linked" to Lincoln by "anonymous narrative, contemporary gossip, family tradition, and other tenuous connections." The criteria for inclusion require that quotations be "traceable to named *auditors*"—that is, "persons claiming to have heard the quoted words directly from Lincoln."[35] The editors make exceptions to this rule, however. Forty-seven quotations from contemporary anonymous newspaper correspondents are included, as are numerous secondhand quotations: X quoting Y who quoted Lincoln.

The Fehrenbachers assign each quotation a letter grade as a guide to its authenticity. Most direct quotations recorded within days of their utterance earn an A; similar indirect quotations (summaries or paraphrases of Lincoln's words) earn a B. Most direct or indirect quotations written down weeks or years later earn a C. These grades, the editors write, are "classificatory" but obviously have "evaluative implications." Common sense, along with scholarly research on memory, tells us that observations or quotations recorded soon after the fact are more reliable than those filtered through the haze of memory. Thus quotations assigned an A or B are, as a general rule, more authentic than those given a C.

There are exceptions, however, and some contemporary as well as many later quotations earn a D or an E owing to their implausibility, the known or suspected unreliability of the recorder, factual errors or inconsistencies in the quotation or its context, or the secondhand nature of the quotation. A quotation "about whose authenticity there is more than average doubt" gets a D; a quotation "that is probably not an authentic" one earns an E.[36] Like a teacher who gives a student a low grade, the Fehrenbachers accompany most D's and E's with brief explanations of their reasons for assigning them. These evaluations offer a trenchant cram course in the perils and pitfalls of Lincoln scholarship.

Why not omit the most dubious quotations altogether? Because, the Fehren-bachers answer, the legendary Lincoln has had almost as powerful an influence on American culture as the historical Lincoln. Moreover, "credibility is so dif-ficult to gauge that learned opinions would differ about which ones to ex-clude."[37] All honest historians would echo this confession of fallibility. But they would also probably agree with nearly all of the editors' E grades. No serious scholar, for example, accepts the authenticity of statements attributed to Lin-coln by the renegade Catholic priest Charles Chiniquy to the effect that Jesuits caused the Civil War and were plotting his (Lincoln's) assassination. Nor would anyone challenge the E assigned to Nettie Maynard, a spiritualist who quoted Lincoln, saying he had taken part in her seances.[38]

The greatest potential for disagreement lies in the D rankings. Consider, for example, a Lincoln statement about black soldiers during a presidential visit to the Petersburg front in June 1864, shortly after black brigades had captured part of the Confederate defenses. Horace Porter, an officer on Grant's staff, quoted Lincoln as telling Grant on that occasion: "I was opposed on nearly every side when I first favored the raising of colored regiments, but they have proved their efficiency, and I am glad they have kept pace with the white troops in the recent assaults." The Fehrenbachers assign this statement a D be-cause "many northerners were ahead of Lincoln in favoring the enlistment of blacks, and it would have been absurd to claim otherwise."[39] But does this quo-tation show Lincoln claiming otherwise? Surely not. He was quoted as saying that he was opposed on *nearly* every side when he first committed himself to recruiting black regiments. It is true that black leaders and Radical Republi-cans urged such a policy for months before Lincoln endorsed it at the begin-ning of 1863. But the policy did provoke a storm of controversy and opposi-tion when he adopted it. "Nearly every side" overstates the case, to be sure, but Lincoln may well have remembered it that way more than a year later.

Most of the D grades seem right on, however, as do the other grades. If a bi-ographer or historian could confine his research to the *Collected Works* plus recollected quotations ranked A and B, he would have few worries about the reliability of evidence. But he would also leave large gaps in the Lincoln story, both in Lincoln's early life and in his presidential years. On many significant matters those two classes of sources are virtually silent.

Consider one of the most important decisions of Lincoln's presidency. During the secession crisis of early 1861 Lincoln evidently twice offered to withdraw troops from Fort Sumter in return for a pledge by Virginians to adjourn their convention without seceding. "A state for a fort is no bad business" is the way one contemporary quoted Lincoln. Not a word appears in the *Collected Works* about this matter. Controversy surrounds the questions of whether Lincoln did in fact make such an offer and, if so, its precise terms. No fewer than seven men—including Hay in a conversation with Lincoln six months later—quoted the president directly or indirectly on the issue. Six of them report that an offer was made, yet only Hay's statement earns a B; two others get C's, and three get D's, while one person, a Virginian, who denied that Lincoln made such an offer also earns a D. The matter remains unresolved, but the weight of the evidence and of the Fehrenbachers' careful commentary indicates that Lincoln probably made such an offer and that the Virginians who received it had neither the power nor the will to act on it.[40] So the troops remained in Fort Sumter, Confederate guns fired on them, and the war came.

Contradictions between contemporary and recollected words or actions have sometimes muddled Lincoln scholarship. Lincoln's vice president during his first term was Hannibal Hamlin of Maine. The convention that renominated Lincoln in 1864 dumped Hamlin in favor of Andrew Johnson, a Tennessee Unionist and War Democrat who moderate Republicans thought would strengthen the ticket by reaching out to the two constituencies he represented. This action had profound and tragic consequences for postwar Reconstruction, when as a consequence of Lincoln's assassination Johnson became president and did his worst to frustrate Republican reconstruction policies.

Who was responsible for the decision to replace Hamlin with Johnson? The only references in the *Collected Works* are a letter from Hay to Nicolay stating that Lincoln "wishes not to interfere in the nomination even by a confidential suggestion" and Lincoln's own written statement: "Wish not to interfere about V.P. . . . Convention must judge for itself."[41] This would seem to be conclusive, but a good many historians do not accept Lincoln's disavowal at face value. Michael F. Holt, for example, writing in *Abraham Lincoln and the American Political Tradition*, asserts flatly that Lincoln "engineered the dumping of Hannibal Hamlin and the selection of the Tennessee Democrat Andrew Johnson."[42] The evidence for this assertion consists of later recollections by Alexander McClure, a Pennsylvania politician, and by Lincoln's friend and self-appointed bodyguard, Ward Hill Lamon. In the 1890s both men claimed to have worked with Lincoln in behind-the-scenes maneuvers to get the convention to nominate Johnson. The Fehrenbachers are not convinced. They give McClure's and Lamon's testimony two E's and a D.[43] They have convinced me, at least, that Lincoln meant what he said about not interfering in the convention's choice.

David Herbert Donald's majestic biography of Lincoln, published a year before the Fehrenbachers' book, does not take a definite position on this vice-presidential question—except to point out that if Lincoln had wanted Hamlin renominated, he could have made it happen.[44] Along with Don Fehrenbacher, Donald stood in the first rank of Lincoln scholars in the latter half of the twentieth century. Like Fehrenbacher, Donald writes with precision and elegance, and weighs the often ambiguous or even contradictory evidence with judicious impartiality. His biography moves between Lincoln's private and public lives with a clarity that illuminates the connections between them.

Donald negotiates the potential pitfalls for Lincoln biographers with sure-footed grace: Lincoln's relationship with his father; his romance with Ann Rutledge; his bouts of "hypo"; his marriage; his political ambition; his attitudes toward slavery and black people; his relations with Radical Republicans during the Civil War; the mistakes and successes of his wartime leadership. Lincoln had an uneasy relationship with his father, but it was not an oedipal rivalry. He probably loved Ann Rutledge, but the memory of this lost love did not poison his marriage to Mary Todd—a marriage that had its good and bad days but was neither as smooth and fulfilling as Mary's partisans have claimed nor as tempestuous and barren as her detractors charge. Lincoln was politically ambitious and knew how to manipulate the system, but he was more principled and less corruptible than most other politicians of his time. He believed slavery to be a moral evil but was cautious in his approach to eradicating it. He shared the almost universal white-supremacy convictions of his age but rose above them during the Civil War to promote the cause of freedom and take the first tentative steps toward equal rights.

Using a wealth of new material uncovered by the Lincoln Legal Papers project from Illinois county courthouses, Donald offers a fuller account of Lincoln's legal career than previous biographers have done. Although largely self-taught, Lincoln was far more than the folksy country lawyer of legend. By the 1850s he had become one of the leaders of the Illinois bar. But Donald does not share the mistaken notion of some writers that Lincoln was a "corporation lawyer." To be sure, he represented corporations (mainly railroads) in several cases, but he opposed corporations about as often as he defended them. The bulk of his practice continued to concern small-scale property disputes, debts, damage to crops by marauding livestock, and other staples of county courts in rural Illinois. This might seem to make for dull reading, but Donald brings it alive.

Donald is at his best in discussing Lincoln's politics. From the time Lincoln first announced his candidacy for the Illinois legislature at the age of twenty-three until the cabinet meeting on the day of his assassination, politics was rarely absent from his consciousness. He was a Whig, a devotee of Henry Clay, whose "American System," with its emphasis on government support for education, internal improvements, banking, and economic development to promote growth and opportunity, attracted the upwardly mobile young lawyer. This philosophy undergirded Lincoln's commitment to what the historian Eric Foner has defined as the free-labor ideology. Social mobility was central to this ideology. Free men who practiced the virtues of hard work, self-discipline, and sobriety could climb the ladder of success. "I am not ashamed to confess," Lincoln said in 1860, "that twenty-five years ago I was a hired laborer, mauling rails, at work on a flat-boat—just what might happen to any poor man's son." But in the free states an ambitious youth knew that "he can better his condition" because "there is no such thing as a freeman being fatally fixed for life, in the condition of a hired laborer." The free-labor system "opens the way for all—gives hope to all, and consequent energy, and progress, and improvement of condition to all."[45]

It was the lack of hope, energy, and progress in the slave states, where most laborers were indeed "fatally fixed" in the condition of slavery, that made the United States a house divided. When the Whig Party died in the mid-1850s, Lincoln helped found the Republican Party in Illinois. The Republicans were determined to keep slavery out of the territories as the first step, in Lincoln's words, toward placing it "in course of ultimate extinction." "I want every man to have the chance," Lincoln said, "and I believe a black man is entitled to it—in which he *can* better his condition."[46]

On this platform Lincoln was elected president in 1860, provoking the secession of seven slave states (and later four more), which led the country down the slippery slope to civil war. More than half of Donald's *Lincoln* is devoted to the four years of war—the last four years of Lincoln's life. With a genius for pulling factions together, a sure sense of timing, and a determination to prevail despite defeats and despair, Lincoln led the Union to triumph and a new birth of freedom. Donald tells this story superbly. His analysis of the complex interplay of factions, parties, and personalities in the political conduct of the Union war effort is unexcelled. Donald's grasp of military events is less sure. The reader comes away with a better understanding of Lincoln's role as president and as head of his party than of his actions as commander in chief.

In a frontispiece quotation and in his preface, Donald sets forth what he intends to be the central theme of the biography. The quotation comes from an April 1864 letter of Lincoln to Albert Hodges, a Kentucky Unionist, in which the president wrote: "I claim not to have controlled events, but confess plainly that events have controlled me."[47] This statement, Donald writes, illustrates "a basic trait of character evident throughout Lincoln's life: the essential passivity of his nature." Elsewhere Donald speaks of Lincoln's "fatalism," his "reluctance to take the initiative and make bold plans," adding that "he preferred to respond to the actions of others." One of Lincoln's favorite Shakespeare passages was from Hamlet:[48]

> THERE'S A DIVINITY THAT SHAPES OUR ENDS,
> ROUGH-HEW THEM HOW WE WILL.

As the suffering and death of the war grew to monstrous proportions, Lincoln came to believe that man was helpless to alter the course of events predestined by God. In the same letter to Hodges, the president suggested that the war had not taken the course that either North or South had intended or expected three years earlier. A greater power had shaped the conflict, and "if God now wills the removal of a great wrong," slavery, we should "find therein new cause to attest and revere the justice and goodness of God."[49]

It is one thing to recognize that the stress and pain of a terrible war would cause Lincoln, or anyone else in a like position, to search for the meaning of such trauma in the divine will. It is quite another to construct an interpretation around the theme of passivity. To begin with, one might ask how it squares with Lincoln's "unquenchable ambition"—another theme in Donald's biography.[50] Lincoln's letter to Hodges must be understood in its context. Hodges and other Kentucky Unionists felt betrayed by Lincoln's emancipation policy and by the large-scale recruitment of slaves from Kentucky for the Union army—which of course freed those slaves and eventually their families. Many Kentuckians considered these actions a violation of Lincoln's original pledge to fight only to restore the Union and his exemption of Kentucky from the Emancipation Proclamation. This was not my doing, Lincoln told them in an effort to divert their anger; it was God's will that has reshaped this war from a war for Union to a war for Union and freedom.[51]

Lincoln undoubtedly believed that it was God's will, but he also believed in the adage that God helps those who help themselves. In both North and South the clergy consistently preached that God was on their side in this war. Both could not be right, said Lincoln in his second inaugural address; in fact neither was right, for "the Almighty has His own purposes," and Lincoln was telling them that it was time to recognize His purposes and to get themselves on God's side. Lincoln's decision to issue the Emancipation Proclamation was not a sign of passivity. Nor was his insistence that the Republican platform on which he ran for reelection in 1864 contain a plank calling for a constitutional amendment to abolish slavery. Nor were his decisions to sack failing generals but to stick with Ulysses S. Grant despite enormous pressures to sack *him* in early 1863.

At the very outset of his presidency Lincoln demonstrated traits that were the opposite of what Donald calls "his essentially passive personality." When some Republicans flirted with the idea of endorsing the Crittenden Compromise, which contravened the Republican platform on which Lincoln had been elected, the president-elect stiffened their backbones. "Entertain no proposition for a compromise in regard to the *extension* of slavery," he wrote to them. The very notion of such a compromise "acknowledges that slavery has equal right with liberty, and surrenders all we have contended for. . . . We have just carried an election on principles fairly stated to the people. Now we are told in advance, the government shall be broken up, unless we surrender to those we have beaten. . . . If we surrender, it is the end of us. . . . They will repeat the experiment upon us *ad libitum*."[52]

Having defeated compromise in January 1861, Lincoln two months later faced a decision whether to yield to Confederate demands for the withdrawal of U.S. troops from Fort Sumter. It was a decision for peace or war. It was also, in Lincoln's mind, a decision whether to give up the Union or fight for it. He made the lonely decision, opposed initially by most of his cabinet and by other advisers, to fight for it if necessary. But in a brilliant move he offered only to resupply the Sumter garrison without reinforcing it, thus placing the burden of deciding for peace or war on Jefferson Davis's shoulders. If Davis allowed the supplies to go in, Lincoln would score an important point asserting national sovereignty. If Davis ordered the firing on the supply ships or on Fort Sumter, the responsibility for starting a war would be his.

Donald somehow manages to find in Lincoln's handling of the Sumter crisis evidence of his "essential passivity." Lincoln was "temperamentally averse to making bold moves," Donald writes. "It was his style to react to decisions made by others rather than to take the initiative himself."[53] More convincing is the conclusion of Lincoln's private secretaries John Nicolay and John Hay: With his plan to resupply the fort Lincoln made himself "master of the situation . . . master if the rebels hesitated or repented, because they would thereby forfeit their prestige with the South; master if they persisted, for he would then command a united North."[54] And so it turned out.

Donald is too good a historian to ride the passivity thesis roughshod over the evidence in most cases. As he lays out the story of Lincoln's leadership during the war, with all its ups and downs, its successes and failures, the reader gains a clear impression of mastery rather than passivity. And Donald can quote with approval an entry from John Hay's diary in August 1863: The president "is managing this war, the draft, foreign relations, and planning a reconstruction of the Union, all at once. I never knew with what tyrannous authority he rules the Cabinet, till now. The most important things he decides and there is no cavil."[55] Recognizing that the facts mostly do not fit the passivity thesis, Donald wisely allows it to fade away as the book proceeds.

In one important respect, however, Lincoln was fatalistic about events he perceived as beyond his control. Despite a large number of death threats, the president refused to sanction elaborate security arrangements and philosophically accepted the possibility of assassination. "It would never do," he said, "for a President to have guards with drawn sabres at his door, as if he fancied he were an . . . emperor." Such precautions were useless anyway: "A conspiracy to assassinate, if such there were, could easily obtain a pass to see me for any one or more of its instruments."[56] So when Lincoln attended Ford's Theater on April 14, 1865, the sole guard on duty moved away from the door of the box to see the play.

# 16

# "As Commander-in-Chief I Have a Right to Take Any Measure Which May Best Subdue the Enemy"

O N THE FOURTH OF JULY 1864, Senator Zachariah Chandler of Michigan hovered anxiously near Abraham Lincoln as the president signed last-minute bills passed by the just-adjourned session of Congress. When Lincoln put aside the Wade-Davis bill that stipulated stringent terms for reconstruction of Confederate states—including the abolition of slavery therein—Chandler urged the president to sign it. The most important provision in the bill, said the senator, "is the one prohibiting slavery in the reconstructed states." Lincoln replied, "That is the point on which I doubt the authority of Congress to act." Chandler was indignant. Alluding to the Emancipation Proclamation, he said: "It is no more than you have done yourself." Quite true, responded Lincoln, but "I conceive that I may in an emergency do things on military grounds which cannot be done constitutionally by Congress."[1]

This breathtaking assertion of presidential prerogative left Chandler almost speechless. It should not have. From the outset of the Civil War, Lincoln had exercised unprecedented powers as commander in chief. Two years before this conversation with Chandler, the president had told a delegation of antislavery clergymen from Chicago that he could, if he judged it necessary, proclaim emancipation in Confederate states because, "as commander-in-chief of the army and navy, in time of war, I suppose I have a right to take any measure which may best subdue the enemy."[2] Whether the measures he took exceeded his constitutional authority was much debated at the time and is still controversial today.[3] What remains certain, however, is that Lincoln vastly expanded presidential war powers and established precedents invoked by several of his successors in later wars.

Article II, Section 2 of the Constitution states simply that "The President shall be Commander in Chief of the Army and Navy of the United States, and of the Militia of the several States, when called into the actual Service of the United States." But the Constitution does not define the functions and powers of the president as commander in chief. In *Federalist No. 69*, Alexander Hamilton tried to reassure opponents of the Constitution, who feared executive tyranny, that the commander-in-chief power "would amount to nothing more than the supreme command and direction of the military forces, as first General and Admiral" of the nation. Wartime presidents James Madison and James K. Polk did not go much beyond this limited function.

Nevertheless, the brevity and vagueness of the Constitution's specification of presidential powers, in contrast with its detailed listing of congressional powers and limitations thereon, bothered some observers. In 1840 a Virginia jurist and future secretary of state, Abel Upshur, deplored "the loose and unguarded terms in which the powers and duties of the President are pointed out" in the Constitution. "In regard to the Executive, the [constitutional] convention seems to have studiously selected such loose and general expressions as would enable the President, by implications and constructions either to neglect his duties or to enlarge his powers."[4] In a case growing out of the Mexican War, the Supreme Court ruled that the president as commander in chief was authorized to employ the army and navy "in the manner he may deem most effectual to harass and conquer and subdue the enemy," but added that this was a power limited to "purely military" matters.[5]

Whether Lincoln was familiar with this decision is unknown, but his actions as commander in chief certainly went beyond "purely military" matters. The Constitution restricts to Congress the power to declare war. Yet one of Lincoln's first acts after the firing on Fort Sumter was to proclaim a blockade of Confederate ports.[6] In effect this proclamation was a declaration of war, and both Congress and the Supreme Court subsequently endorsed it as such. During these hectic days in the spring of 1861, Lincoln preempted congressional authority to raise and support armies. His proclamation of April 15 calling on the states for 75,000 ninety-day militia to suppress the insurrection was, to be sure, based on the militia act of 1795. But on May 3 Lincoln issued an executive order calling for 43,034 three-year volunteers for the army and also increasing the size of the regular army and navy by 40,714 men.[7] Both actions were an apparent violation of the Constitution, which grants Congress exclusive authority to "raise and support armies" and to "provide and maintain a navy" (Article I, Section 7). And because Lincoln believed that the federal bureaucracy, in these early days of the war, was still infested with Confederate sympathizers, he ordered Secretary of the Treasury Salmon P. Chase to advance $2 million to three private citizens in New York to purchase arms and vessels.[8] This order directly contravened Article I, Section 9 of the Constitution, which stipulates that "No Money shall be drawn from the Treasury, but in Consequence of Appropriations made by Law."

Lincoln made no secret of these actions, which he justified on the grounds that "existing exigencies demand immediate and adequate measures for the protection of the National Constitution and the National Union." A year later, in response to charges of dictatorship, Lincoln insisted that "it became necessary for me to choose whether, using only the existing means, agencies, and processes which Congress had provided, I should let the government fall at once into ruin, or whether, availing myself of the broader powers conferred by the Constitution in cases of insurrection, I would make an effort to save it with all its blessings for the present age and for posterity."[9]

Lincoln did not define those "broader powers conferred by the Constitution." At other times, however, he cited the commander-in-chief clause and the constitutional mandate that the president "shall take Care that the Laws be faithfully executed" (Article II, Section 3). Later presidents also invoked these vague provisions to justify far-reaching executive actions—in some cases drawing on Lincolnian precedents. Lincoln believed that "by these and other similar measures taken in that crisis [of April–May 1861], some of which were without any authority of law, the government was saved from overthrow." Lincoln had taken an oath to "preserve, protect, and defend the Constitution of the United States." This larger duty overrode his obligation to heed a lesser specific provision in the Constitution—or, as a modern constitutional scholar expressed it, "*a part cannot be supreme over the whole, to the injury or destruction of the whole.*"[10]

Lincoln's proclamation of May 3 calling for three-year volunteers and increasing the regular army and navy stated that he would seek retroactive congressional approval of these measures when Congress met in the special session he had called for July 4, 1861. The special session of the new Congress could not meet earlier because of the timetable of elections and congressional sessions in that age. No federal law mandated a single date for congressional elections. Most states held such elections in the fall of even-numbered years, as today. But the first regular session of a new Congress did not meet until December of the following year—thirteen months later. Seven Northern states thus held congressional elections in the spring of odd-numbered years—in this case 1861—making it impossible for a special session to be scheduled before July. In the emergency precipitated by the attack on Fort Sumter, Lincoln therefore had to appropriate some legislative as well as executive functions.

When Congress did convene on July 4, Lincoln sent a message explaining what he had done and why. After summarizing the events leading up to the firing on Fort Sumter, the president explained that this attack left him with no choice "but to call out the war power of the Government; and so to resist force, employed for its destruction, by force, for its preservation." Lincoln had written "military power" in the first draft but changed it to "war power" in the final version. Whether he did so because "war power" seemed stronger is unclear. Later in the message he again used the phrase: He had employed the "war power" as the only alternative to yielding "the existence of the government."[11]

The Constitution makes no mention of war power—the closest it comes is the clause that authorizes Congress to declare war. Both the phrase and the idea of presidential war powers seem to have been Lincoln's own.[12] In effect, by invoking an executive war power Lincoln preempted the prerogative of Congress to declare war. Two years later the Supreme Court upheld Lincoln's position by the narrowest of margins (5–4) in the *Prize Cases.* These cases grew out of the navy's seizure of ships trying to evade the blockade declared by Lincoln in April 1861. Merchants whose ships and cargo were captured argued that because only Congress can declare war, the blockade was illegal before Congress in July declared the existence of hostilities. The majority of the Court ruled, however, that a state of war—especially a civil war—can exist without a formal declaration. The president has a duty to resist force with force; therefore the blockade and related war powers exercised by Lincoln were within his authority as commander in chief.[13]

The Court did not rule on the other measures Lincoln carried out before Congress met. But Congress had already taken care of that. In his message to the special session, Lincoln conceded that his executive orders calling for volunteers and increasing the size of the regular army and navy may not have been "strictly legal," but they were a "public necessity" that he trusted Congress would "readily ratify." Congress did so, passing almost unanimously a law that "approved and in all respects legalized and made valid . . . all the acts, proclamations, and orders of the President of the United States respecting the army and navy . . . as if they had been done under the previous express authority and direction of the Congress."[14]

Despite congressional and Court endorsements of Lincoln's actions, opposition to presidential "tyranny" was strong and grew stronger as the war escalated in scope and severity. The mildest of epithets provoked by Lincoln's most controversial uses of his war powers—suspension of habeas corpus and emancipation—were "despot," "tyrant," and "dictator."

After a mob in Baltimore attacked the 6th Massachusetts Infantry as it passed through the city on its way to defend Washington in April 1861, other Confederate sympathizers in Maryland tore down telegraph wires and burned railroad bridges linking the capital to the outside world. In response, Lincoln suspended the writ of habeas corpus between Philadelphia and Washington. Subsequent presidential orders expanded the areas where the writ was suspended until a proclamation of September 24, 1862, suspended it throughout the whole country—North as well as South—and for good measure authorized martial law and trials by military courts of "all Rebels and Insurgents, their aiders and abettors . . . and all persons discouraging volunteer enlistments, resisting militia drafts, or guilty of any disloyal practice, affording aid and comfort to Rebels against the authority of the United States."[15]

Under these orders an estimated 13,000 civilians were arrested and detained without trial for varying lengths of time, most of them in the border slave states where Confederates and guerrillas were numerous. But even in the North a number of antiwar Copperheads were arrested, and several were tried and convicted by military tribunals for draft resistance, trading with the enemy, sabotage, or other alleged pro-Confederate activities. No other actions by the Lincoln administration—except perhaps emancipation—generated greater hostility than these apparent violations of civil liberties. And one of the first arrests under the initial order to suspend the writ produced a confrontation between the president and the chief justice of the United States.

John Merryman was a wealthy Maryland landowner and lieutenant in a secessionist cavalry company that had torn down telegraph lines. Arrested and confined at Fort McHenry in Baltimore harbor, he petitioned the federal circuit court for a writ of habeas corpus. The senior judge in this circuit was none other than Chief Justice Roger B. Taney, who issued a writ ordering the commanding officer at the fort to bring Merryman before the court to show cause for his arrest. The officer refused, citing the president's suspension of the writ. Taney immediately delivered a ruling denying the president's right to do so. The Constitution states that "The Privilege of the Writ of Habeas Corpus shall not be suspended, unless when in cases of Rebellion or Invasion the public Safety may require it." At issue was not whether the writ could be suspended, but *who* could suspend it. Because this clause is placed in Article I of the Constitution, which deals with congressional powers, Taney insisted—citing precedents—that only Congress could do so.[16]

Taney had no power to enforce his ruling, which Lincoln refused to obey. Because he was the author of the notorious Dred Scott decision, Taney's opinions carried little weight in Republican circles. Lincoln had challenged the Dred Scott decision, and he challenged this ruling as well. In his message to the special session of Congress, the president included an elaborate defense of his suspension of the writ. He noted (without mentioning Taney's name or position) that he had been admonished "that one who is sworn to 'take care that the laws be faithfully executed,' should not himself violate them." But he had not violated the law, Lincoln insisted. Confederates in Virginia and secessionists in Maryland had surrounded and cut off the capital, whose capture would have brought the downfall of the government. Surely this met the constitutional criterion for suspending the writ. "Now it is insisted that Congress, not the Executive, is vested with this power," acknowledged Lincoln. "But the Constitution itself, is silent as to which, or who, is to exercise the power; and as the provision was plainly made for a dangerous emergency, it cannot be believed the framers of the government intended, that in every case, the danger should run its course, until Congress should be called together; the very assembling of which might be prevented, as was intended in this case, by the rebellion."[17]

But even if this were not true, Lincoln averred a higher constitutional duty to do whatever was necessary to preserve, protect, and defend the nation and to take care that the laws be faithfully executed. "The whole of the laws which were to be faithfully executed, were being resisted, and failing of execution, in nearly one-third of the States. Must they be allowed to finally fail of execution . . . [because] some single law . . . should, to a very limited extent, be violated? To state the question more directly, are all the laws, *but one* [the privilege of the writ of habeas corpus], to go unexecuted, and the government itself go to pieces, lest that one be violated?"[18]

Here we have the core of Lincoln's concept of his war powers as commander in chief: His supreme constitutional obligation was to preserve the nation by winning the war. Any measures necessary to achieve that purpose overrode lesser constitutional restrictions—or, to quote a modern scholar, *"A part cannot control the whole, to the destruction of the whole."*[19] A master of metaphors designed to make abstruse concepts clear to laymen, Lincoln used the analogy of a surgeon who amputates a limb to save a life. Looking back in 1864 to events three years earlier, Lincoln asked: "Was it possible to lose the nation, and yet preserve the constitution? By general law life *and* limb must be protected; yet often a limb must be amputated to save a life; but a life is never wisely given to save a limb. I felt that measures, otherwise unconstitutional, might become lawful, by becoming indispensable to the preservation of the constitution, through preservation of the nation."[20]

Most of those arrested and kept in "preventive detention" under suspension of habeas corpus were released after several weeks (including John Merryman) or months upon taking an oath of allegiance to the United States. Attorney General Edward Bates and two of the nation's foremost lawyers wrote treatises upholding the legality of Lincoln's action.[21] The Supreme Court never ruled on the constitutionality of Lincoln's suspension of the writ (Taney's ruling on Merryman was filed in circuit court). In March 1863 Congress finally enacted legislation giving the president explicit authority to do what he had been doing for almost two years. In the meantime, however, Lincoln's proclamation of September 24, 1862, declaring martial law and authorizing military trials of civilians generated a new uproar.

On May 5, 1863, Union soldiers arrested Clement L. Vallandigham at his home in Ohio. The leading Northern Copperhead, Vallandigham had repeatedly attacked the Lincoln administration and the war, calling for a cease-fire and negotiations with the enemy. Lincoln's Emancipation Proclamation and the recent passage by Congress of a conscription law had intensified Copperhead attacks. And reverses to Union arms in the winter and spring of 1863 had caused widespread demoralization in the North and in the army that imperiled the government's efforts to carry on the war. In this climate of opinion, Vallandigham's rhetoric seemed a genuine threat to the cause of Union. A military court convicted him of uttering "disloyal sentiments and opinions, with the object and purpose of weakening the power of the Government [to suppress] an unlawful rebellion." The tribunal sentenced him to a military prison for the rest of the war.[22]

These proceedings produced cries of outrage by Northern Democrats and expressions of anxiety even among Republicans. Governor Horatio Seymour of New York denounced the arrest and trial as "cowardly, brutal, infamous. . . . It is not merely a step toward revolution, it *is* revolution. . . . It establishes military despotism. . . . If it is upheld, our liberties are overthrown."[23] Lincoln had been surprised and embarrassed by Vallandigham's arrest. But he decided that he must uphold the military commission, which had been established under his own proclamation of the previous September. When Vallandigham's attorneys applied for a writ of habeas corpus, the circuit judge in Cincinnati denied it on the ground that the president had suspended the writ. In an effort to quell the uproar and tarnish Vallandigham's martyrdom, Lincoln commuted the sentence from imprisonment to banishment to the Confederacy. Federal troops escorted Vallandigham under flag of truce to Confederate lines in Tennessee. Ohio Democrats nominated him in absentia for governor. Vallandigham eventually slipped out of the Confederacy on a blockade runner and settled in Windsor, Ontario, from where he conducted his gubernatorial campaign. He went down to a decisive defeat in October 1863 after Union military fortunes had taken a turn for the better. Meanwhile Vallandigham's lawyers appealed his case to the Supreme Court, arguing that the trial of a civilian by a military court outside the war zone when civil courts were open was unconstitutional. The Supreme Court ducked the issue by claiming lack of jurisdiction over military courts![24]

Nevertheless, the Vallandigham case became a cause célèbre for Democrats. Party leaders in New York and Ohio addressed formal protests to the president in the form of resolutions charging him with "a palpable violation of the Constitution" that "abrogates the right of the people to assemble and discuss the affairs of government, the liberty of speech and of the press, the right of trial by jury and the privilege of habeas corpus . . . aimed at the rights of every citizen of the North."[25]

These resolutions gave Lincoln an opening to make his case to the Northern people. On several occasions during the war he used the medium of public letters for that purpose, as a modern president uses televised speeches and news conferences. On June 12 and 23 Lincoln addressed such letters to the New York and Ohio Democrats. He denied that Vallandigham had been arrested "for no other reason than words addressed to a public meeting." On the contrary, Vallandigham's antiwar activities were part of a broader effort by Confederate agents and their Copperhead allies to undermine the draft and encourage desertions from the army. Several enrollment officers had recently been murdered by draft resisters. Vallandigham "was damaging the army, upon the existence and vigor of which the life of the nation depends." Lincoln posed a rhetorical question that turned out to be the most powerful—and famous— illustration of his point. Noting that the official punishment for desertion was death (Lincoln spent many hours reviewing such cases and finding reasons to pardon deserters or commute their sentences), he asked: "Must I shoot a simple-minded soldier boy who deserts, while I must not touch the hair of a wily agitator who induces him to desert?"

This "clear, flagrant, and giant" rebellion, said Lincoln, was precisely the contingency anticipated by the framers of the Constitution when they wrote the clause permitting suspension of habeas corpus. To make the case that wartime suspension or military trials would not create a precedent for peacetime violations of civil liberties, Lincoln offered one of his piquant metaphors. He could no more believe this, he wrote, "than I am able to believe that a man could contract so strong an appetite for emetics during temporary illness, as to persist in feeding upon them through the remainder of his healthful life." As for the argument that military courts cannot try civilians outside the war zone, Lincoln insisted that the whole country was a war zone. Draft resistance and attacks on enrollment officers took place in the North, and in some places Copperhead influence was so strong that no jury would convict those who tried to sabotage the war effort.[26]

These letters were enormously effective. They were published in hundreds of Northern newspapers. Half a million copies of the letter to New York Democrats were also published as a pamphlet. The timing turned out to be fortuitous, for within a few days of their publication, Union victories at Gettysburg, Vicksburg, and Port Hudson and in Tennessee lifted the pall of Northern gloom and demoralization that had fueled antiwar protests against Lincoln's "despotism." These victories also helped convert many who had been skeptical or hostile toward Lincoln's other contentious exercise of war powers—the Emancipation Proclamation.

In contrast with his early suspension of habeas corpus, for a year Lincoln resisted pressures from his own party to move against slavery. Although he was personally and morally opposed to the institution, he feared that premature action for emancipation would alienate Northern Democratic supporters of the war effort and drive border slave states into the Confederacy.

Nor did Lincoln initially see any way in which he could constitutionally declare emancipation. The Constitution *did* authorize suspension of habeas corpus in case of rebellion, but it did *not* say anything similar about slavery. When General John C. Frémont issued an order declaring martial law and freeing the slaves of Confederate activists in Missouri on August 30, 1861, Lincoln rescinded the order because it would "alarm our Southern Union friends, and turn them against us—perhaps ruin our rather fair prospect for Kentucky."[27] When Lincoln's friend Orville Browning, a senator from Illinois, criticized the revocation of Frémont's order, the president responded that a military commander had no power to confiscate slave property. "If a commanding General finds a necessity to seize the farm of a private owner, for . . . an encampment, he has the right to do so . . . because within military necessity," Lincoln wrote. "But to say the farm shall no longer belong to the owner, or his heirs . . . when the farm is no longer needed for military purposes" is unconstitutional. "And the same is true of slaves. If the General needs them, he can seize them, and use them; but when the need is past, it is not for him to fix their permanent future condition. . . . Can it be pretended that it is any longer the government of the U.S.—any government of Constitution and laws,—wherein a General, or a President, may make permanent rules of property by proclamation?"[28]

The date of this letter is ironic: September 22, 1861, one year to the day before Lincoln did precisely what he said a general or president could not do— proclaim slaves in rebellious states "forever free" unless these states returned to the Union by January 1, 1863. They did not, so on that fateful day Lincoln proclaimed that "by virtue of the power in me vested as Commander-in-Chief . . . and as a fit and necessary war measure for suppressing said rebellion . . . [I] do order and declare that all persons held as slaves within said designated States, and parts of States, are, and henceforward shall be free."[29]

Lincoln's apparently radical change of mind about his war power to emancipate slaves was caused by the escalating scope of the war, which convinced him that any measure to weaken the Confederacy and strengthen the Union war effort was justifiable as a military necessity. Lincoln may also have been influenced by a long pamphlet titled *The War Powers of the President, and the Legislative Powers of Congress in Relation to Rebellion, Treason, and Slavery,* first published in the spring of 1862. Its author was William Whiting, a Boston abolitionist and one of the ablest lawyers in New England. Whiting's pamphlet went through seven editions in little more than a year. On the strength of it he was appointed solicitor of the War Department. Lincoln's own legal mind grasped Whiting's powerful argument that the laws of war, based on long precedent, "give the President full belligerent rights," including the right to confiscate permanently enemy property being used to wage war against the United States. Slaves were a majority of the labor force sustaining the Confederate war effort, and as property they were certainly liable to such confiscation. "This right of seizure and condemnation is harsh," wrote Whiting, "as all the proceedings of war are harsh, in the extreme, but is nevertheless lawful." And once the slaves were "confiscated," the government surely could not reenslave them.[30]

When General David Hunter, commander of Union occupation forces in the coastal regions of the South Atlantic, issued his emancipation edict in May

1862, Lincoln rescinded it. This time, however, his revocation order contained an ominous hint to anyone discerning enough to detect it. "Whether at any time, in any case, it shall have become a necessity indispensable to the maintenance of the government, to exercise such supposed power," declared the president, "are questions which, under my responsibility, I reserve to myself " and not to commanders in the field.[31]

By July 1862 the president had concluded that a blow against the Confederate war economy was indispensable to maintenance of the government. During a carriage ride to attend the funeral of Secretary of War Edwin M. Stanton's infant son, Lincoln startled his seatmates, Secretary of State William H. Seward and Secretary of the Navy Gideon Welles, with the announcement of his decision to issue an emancipation edict. As Welles later recorded the conversation, Lincoln said that an emancipation policy "was forced on him by the rebels themselves." They had "made war upon the government . . . and it was our duty to avail ourselves of every necessary measure to maintain the Union." Emancipation was "a military necessity, absolutely essential to the preservation of the Union. We must free the slaves or be ourselves subdued. The slaves were undeniably an element of strength to those who had their service, and we must decide whether that element should be for us or against us. . . . We wanted the army to strike more vigorous blows. The administration must set the army an example and strike at the heart of the rebellion."[32]

Eight days later Lincoln informed the full cabinet of his intention. On Seward's advice, however, he decided to withhold the proclamation until a Union military victory could give it legitimacy and force. Five days after the battle of Antietam, and exactly a year after his disavowal to Browning of any power to do so, Lincoln published his promise to declare the slaves in rebellious states "forever free." Eleven months later, in another of his expressive public letters, the president defended the constitutionality of his action in words that succinctly summarized William Whiting's treatise on war powers. "The constitution invests its commander-in-chief, with the law of war, in time of war," said Lincoln. "Is there—has there ever been—any question that by the law of war, property, both of enemies and friends, may be taken when needed? And is it not needed whenever taking it, helps us, or hurts the enemy? Armies, the world over, destroy enemies' property when they can not use it. . . . Civilized belligerents do all in their power to help themselves, or hurt the enemy."[33]

On another occasion Lincoln again used his favorite analogy—so graphically familiar in wartime—of a surgeon amputating a limb to save a life: "When the crisis comes, and the limb must be sacrificed as the only chance of saving the life, no honest man will hesitate." Likewise, Lincoln pointed out, "if any local institution threatened the existence of the Union, the Executive could not hesitate as to his duty. In our case, the moment came when I felt that slavery must die that the nation might live!"[34]

As a war measure, however, the Emancipation Proclamation would cease to have any legal or military force when the war ended. The institution of slavery would still live even if slaves freed by the war remained free. Only a constitutional amendment could abolish slavery and make all slaves "forever free." Lincoln ran for reelection in 1864 on a platform endorsing a Thirteenth Amendment to abolish slavery. "Such alone," wrote the president in his acceptance of the nomination, "can meet and cover all cavils."[35]

Ten days after the Senate passed the Thirteenth Amendment in April 1864, Lincoln went to Baltimore for the first time since he had passed incognito through the city three years earlier to avoid a suspected assassination plot. Now, in 1864, Maryland was about to abolish slavery by a state constitutional amendment. In one of his best—but least known—short speeches, Lincoln addressed residents of this border state, many of whom had condemned him as a tyrant who had robbed them of their liberties by "arbitrary arrests" and detentions of Confederate sympathizers.

Lincoln's speech demonstrated his genius for animal metaphors—in this case a parable, which is an extended metaphor—that illustrated an important point about human affairs. "The world has never had a good definition of the word liberty," said the president. "We all declare for liberty, but in using the same *word* we do not all mean the same *thing*." For some in his audience, liberty meant the right to own property in slaves and the freedom to support a rebellion to preserve that right. But for others, liberty meant freedom from being owned by another person. "The shepherd drives the wolf from the sheep's throat," Lincoln continued, "for which the sheep thanks the shepherd as a *liberator*, while the wolf denounces him for the same act as a destroyer of liberty, especially as the sheep is a black one. Plainly the sheep and the wolf are not agreed upon a definition of the word liberty; and precisely the same difference prevails to-day among us human creatures, even in the North, and all professing to love liberty. Hence we behold the processes by which thousands are daily passing from under the yoke of bondage, hailed by some as the advance of liberty, and bewailed by others as the destruction of all liberty."[36]

In this striking fable, the shepherd (commander in chief) wielded his staff (war powers) to liberate the sheep (slaves) from the predatory wolf (slave-owner). If many of these wolves were killed and others penned up for a time, that was the necessary price for the freedom of four million sheep and their descendants.

# Notes

PREFACE

1. John Morley, *Recollections* (London, 1917), p. 20.
2. Roy P. Basler, ed., *The Collected Works of Abraham Lincoln,* 9 vols. (New Brunswick, N.J., 1953–55), 8:332–33.


CHAPTER 1

1. Roy P. Basler, ed., *The Collected Works of Abraham Lincoln,* 9 vols. (New Brunswick, N.J., 1953–55), 8:332.
2. Dunbar Rowland, ed., *Jefferson Davis, Constitutionalist: His Letters, Papers, and Speeches,* 10 vols. (Jackson, Miss., 1923), 5:72.
3. *Augusta Daily Constitutionalist,* March 30, 1861.
4. Jefferson Davis, *The Rise and Fall of the Confederate Government,* 2 vols. (1881; New York, 1990), 1:vii, 67, 156; Alexander H. Stephens, *A Constitutional View of the Late War Between the States,* 2 vols. (Philadelphia, 1868–70), 1:10.
5. *Newsweek,* Oct. 8, 1990, pp. 62–63; *North & South* 4 (March 2001): 6.
6. Charles A. Beard and Mary R. Beard, *The Rise of American Civilization,* 2 vols. (New York, 1927), 2:53.
7. Frank Owsley, "The Irrepressible Conflict," in Twelve Southerners, *I'll Take My Stand* (New York, 1930), pp. 68–91.
8. Avery Craven, "Coming of the War Between the States: An Interpretation" (1936), in Craven, *An Historian and the Civil War* (Chicago, 1964), pp. 28–29; Arthur M. Schlesinger Jr., "The Causes of the American Civil War: A Note on Historical Sentimentalism," *Partisan Review* 16 (1949), rpt. in *The Causes of the Civil War,* ed. Hans L. Trefousse (New York, 1971), p. 83.
9. Cited by Schlesinger, "Causes of the American Civil War," p. 83.
10. Quoted in Norman K. Risjord, *The Old Republicans: Southern Conservatism in the Age of Jefferson* (New York, 1965), p. 242.
11. Leonard L. Richards, *The Slave Power: The Free North and Southern Domination, 1780–1860* (Baton Rouge, 2000).

12. Quoted in Eric Foner, *Free Soil, Free Labor, Free Men: The Ideology of the Republican Party Before the Civil War* (New York, 1970), p. 223, from Adams's diary entry of Nov. 7, 1860.

13. George E. Baker, ed., *The Works of William H. Seward,* 5 vols. (New York, 1853–84), 4:289–92.

14. Basler, *Collected Works of Lincoln* 2:461.

15. *Charleston Mercury,* Feb. 1, 1858; William Grimball to Elizabeth Grimball, Nov. 20, 1860, Berkley Grimball to Elizabeth Grimball, Dec. 8, 1860, John Berkley Grimball Papers, Perkins Library, Duke University.

16. "Declaration of Causes Which Induced the Secession of South Carolina," in Frank Moore, ed., *The Rebellion Record,* 12 vols. (1864–65; New York, 1977), vol. 1, *Documents,* p. 4; William Nugent to Eleanor Nugent, Sept. 7, 1863, in William M. Cash and Lucy Somerville Howarth, eds., *My Dear Nellie: The Civil War Letters of William L. Nugent* (Jackson, Miss., 1977), p. 132.

17. Charles B. Dew, *Apostles of Disunion: Southern Secession Commissioners and the Causes of the Civil War* (Charlottesville, Va., 2001), pp. 1–2.

18. Ibid., pp. 2, 81.

19. Ibid., pp. 70, 72, 33.

20. Ibid., pp. 29, 66, 54.

21. *Congressional Globe,* 25th Cong., 2nd Sess. (1838), Appendix, pp. 61–62; *Senate Documents,* 28th Cong., 1st Sess., no. 341 (1844).

22. Basler, *Collected Works of Lincoln* 2:255.

23. *New York Evening Post,* Nov. 8, 1847.

24. Quoted in William L. Barney, *The Road to Secession: A New Perspective on the Old South* (New York, 1972), pp. 105–6.

25. Quoted in Lacy K. Ford Jr., *Origins of Southern Radicalism: The South Carolina Upcountry, 1800–1860* (New York, 1988), p. 369.

26. Basler, *Collected Works of Lincoln* 2:255, 3:92; Bertram Wyatt-Brown, *Southern Honor: Ethics and Behavior in the Old South* (New York, 1982).

27. Quotations from Michael A. Morrison, *Slavery and the American West: The Eclipse of Manifest Destiny and the Coming of the Civil War* (Chapel Hill, N.C., 1997), p. 59.

28. Quoted in William C. Cooper, *The South and the Politics of Slavery, 1828–1856* (Baton Rouge, 1978), p. 239.

29. *New Orleans Crescent,* Nov. 9, 1860; *Congressional Globe,* 36th Cong., 1st Sess., p. 455.

30. *Cincinnati Daily Commercial,* May 6, 1861, in Howard C. Perkins, ed., *Northern Editorials on Secession* (New York, 1942), p. 183.

31. James D. Richardson, ed., *Compilation of the Messages and Papers of the Presidents,* 10 vols. (Washington, 1897), 5:628–37.

32. Basler, *Collected Works of Lincoln* 4:264–65; Michael Burlingame and John R. Turner Ettlinger, eds., *Inside Lincoln's White House: The Complete Civil War Diary of John Hay* (Carbondale, Ill., 1997), p. 20, diary entry of May 7, 1861.

CHAPTER 2

1. Michael Frisch, "American History and the Structures of Collective Memory: A Modest Exercise in Empirical Iconography," *Journal of American History* 75 (March 1989): 1130–55.
2. Quoted in Jean M. Humez, *Harriet Tubman: The Life and the Life Stories* (Madison, Wis., 2003), p. 153.
3. Ibid.; Kate Clifford Larson, *Bound for the Promised Land: Harriet Tubman, Portrait of an American Hero* (New York, 2003); Catherine Clinton, *Harriet Tubman: The Road to Freedom* (Boston, 2004).
4. Clinton, *Tubman*, pp. 219–22.
5. Ibid., p. 219.
6. Ibid., pp. 27, 34, 186–88; Larson, *Bound for Promised Land*, pp. 41–44, 136, 263, quotation from p. 43.
7. Clinton, *Tubman*, pp. 25, 28, 96; Larson, *Bound for Promised Land*, pp. 56, 64–65, 182–83.
8. Clinton, *Tubman*, p. 96.
9. Humez, *Tubman*, pp. 349–52; Larson, *Bound for Promised Land*, pp. xvii, 100.
10. Larson, *Bound for Promised Land*, p. 191.
11. Jean Fagan Yellin, *Harriet Jacobs: A Life* (Cambridge, Mass., 2004).
12. Humez, *Tubman*, p. 261.
13. Clinton, *Tubman*, p. 181.
14. Ibid., pp. 132, 136.
15. David S. Reynolds, *John Brown, Abolitionist: The Man Who Killed Slavery, Sparked the Civil War, and Seeded Civil Rights* (New York, 2005), p. 395.
16. Ibid., pp. 158–59.
17. Ibid., p. 292.
18. Ibid., p. 299.
19. Three of the most recent books are ibid.; Merrill D. Peterson, *John Brown: The Legend Revisited* (Charlottesville, Va., 2002); and Peggy A. Russo and Paul Finkelman, eds., *Terrible Swift Sword: The Legacy of John Brown* (Athens, Ohio, 2005). Among several novels, Russell Banks, *Cloudsplitter* (New York, 1998) is the most important.
20. Affidavit by A. H. Lewis, a newspaper editor in Akron, quoted in Kenneth R. Carroll, "A Psychological Examination of John Brown," in Russo and Finkelman, *Terrible Swift Sword*, p. 119.
21. Carroll, "Psychological Examination," pp. 118–37.

22. Brown quoted in Reynolds, *John Brown,* p. 351; Wise quoted in Carroll, "Psychological Examination," p. 120.

23. Reynolds, *John Brown,* pp. 381, 382, 387.

24. Ibid., p. 315.

25. Ibid., pp. 339–40.

26. Ibid., p. 366.

27. Ibid., p. 354.

28. Stephen B. Oates, *To Purge This Land with Blood: A Biography of John Brown* (New York, 1970), p. 310.

29. Roy P. Basler, ed., *The Collected Works of Abraham Lincoln,* 9 vols. (New Brunswick, N.J., 1953–55), 3:538.

30. Henry G. Pearson, *The Life of John A. Andrew,* 2 vols. (Boston, 1904), 1:100–101; Beecher quoted in Reynolds, *John Brown,* p. 382.

31. Allan Nevins, *The Emergence of Lincoln,* 2 vols. (New York, 1950), vol. 2, *Prologue to Civil War, 1859–1861,* p. 100.

32. *De Bow's Review* quoted in Oates, *To Purge This Land,* p. 323; newspaper editor quoted in Oswald Garrison Villard, *John Brown, 1800–1859: A Biography Fifty Years After* (Boston, 1910), p. 568.

33. North Carolinian quoted in Avery Craven, *The Growth of Southern Nationalism, 1848–1861* (Baton Rouge, 1953), p. 311; South Carolinian quoted in Mary Boykin Chesnut, *A Diary from Dixie,* ed. Isabella D. Martin and Myrta Lockett Avary (New York, 1905), p. 1.

34. Basler, *Collected Works of Lincoln* 8:333. For Brown's wartime image in the North, see Peterson, *John Brown,* pp. 33–49.

35. Quoted in Peterson, *John Brown,* p. 118.

36. Bruce Catton, *The Coming Fury* (New York, 1961), p. 20.

37. Quoted in Peterson, *John Brown,* p. 101.

38. Ibid., pp. 152–53.

39. Reynolds, *John Brown,* pp. 500–501.

40. James N. Gilbert, "A Behavioral Analysis of John Brown," in Russo and Finkelman, *Terrible Swift Sword,* pp. 107–17; Scott John Hammond, "John Brown as Founder," in ibid., pp. 61–76, quotations from pp. 115, 109, 74.

41. Reynolds, *John Brown,* pp. 11, 52, 56, 149.

42. Ibid., pp. 502, 166, 503.

43. Ibid., p. 504.

## CHAPTER 3

1. Some of the principal books published from 1960 to 1996 that analyzed these questions include David Donald, ed., *Why the North Won the Civil War* (Baton

Rouge, 1960); Paul D. Escott, *After Secession: Jefferson Davis and the Failure of Confederate Nationalism* (Baton Rouge, 1978); Herman Hattaway and Archer Jones, *How the North Won: A Military History of the Civil War* (Urbana, Ill., 1983); Richard E. Beringer, Herman Hattaway, Archer Jones, and William M. Still Jr., *Why the South Lost the Civil War* (Athens, Ga., 1986) and its abridged version *The Elements of Confederate Defeat* (Athens, Ga., 1988); Gabor S. Boritt, ed., *Why the Confederacy Lost* (New York, 1992); Drew Gilpin Faust, *Mothers of Invention: Women of the Slaveholding South in the American Civil War* (Chapel Hill, N.C., 1996). Armstead L. Robinson, *Bitter Fruits of Bondage: The Demise of Slavery and the Collapse of the Confederacy* (Charlottesville, Va., 2005), published posthumously, is a revised version of a doctoral dissertation completed in 1977.

2. Douglas Southall Freeman, *R. E. Lee: A Biography*, 4 vols. (New York, 1934–35), 4:154; Foote quoted in Geoffrey C. Ward with Ric Burns and Ken Burns, *The Civil War: An Illustrated History* (New York, 1990), p. 272.

3. Joseph E. Johnston, *Narrative of Military Operations* (New York, 1874), p. 421; P.G.T. Beauregard, "The First Battle of Bull Run," in *Battles and Leaders of the Civil War,* ed. Robert U. Johnson and Clarence C. Buel, 4 vols. (New York, 1888), 1:222.

4. In addition to works cited in subsequent notes, see the books by Escott, Beringer et al., Faust, and Robinson cited in note 1.

5. Charles W. Ramsdell, *Behind the Lines in the Southern Confederacy* (Baton Rouge, 1997), p. ix.

6. Drew Gilpin Faust, "Altars of Sacrifice: Confederate Women and the Narratives of War," *Journal of American History* 76 (March 1990): 1228.

7. William W. Freehling, *The South vs. the South* (New York, 2001), p. xii.

8. William C. Davis, *Look Away!* (New York, 2002), p. 396.

9. Gary W. Gallagher, *The Confederate War* (Cambridge, Mass., 1997) and *Lee and His Army in Confederate History* (Chapel Hill, N.C., 2001); quotation from *Confederate War*, p. 153.

10. "The Civil War Diary of Colonel John Henry Smith," ed. David M. Smith, *Iowa Journal of History* 47 (April 1949): 164.

11. Gallagher, *Confederate War*, p. 11.

12. John E. Clark Jr., *Railroads in the Civil War: The Impact of Management on Victory and Defeat* (Baton Rouge, 2001) lays out the story of these railroad transfers in fascinating detail.

13. Gallagher, *Confederate War*, p. 172.

14. Ernest B. Furgurson, *Ashes of Glory: Richmond at War* (New York, 1996); Daniel E. Sutherland, *Seasons of War: The Ordeal of a Confederate Community, 1861–1865* (New York, 1995), about Culpeper County; Steven Elliott Tripp, *Yankee Town, Southern City: Race and Class Relations in Civil War Lynchburg* (New York, 1997); William Blair, *Virginia's Private War: Feeding Body and Soul in the Confederacy,*

*1861–1865* (New York, 1998); Brian Steel Wills, *The War Hits Home: The Civil War in Southeastern Virginia* (Charlottesville, Va., 2001).

15. Wills, *War Hits Home,* p. 6.


CHAPTER 4

1. Jefferson Davis, *The Rise and Fall of the Confederate Government,* 2 vols. (1881; New York, 1990), 1:321.
2. Craig L. Symonds, "A Fatal Relationship: Davis and Johnston at War," in *Jefferson Davis's Generals,* ed. Gabor S. Boritt (New York, 1999), pp. 25–26; "powerful team" from Frank E. Vandiver, *Their Tattered Flags: The Epic of the Confederacy* (New York, 1970), p. 140.
3. J.F.C. Fuller, *The Generalship of Ulysses S. Grant* (London, 1929); John Keegan, "Grant and Unheroic Leadership," in Keegan, *The Mask of Command* (New York, 1987), pp. 164–234; Basil H. Liddell Hart, *Sherman: Soldier, Realist, American* (New York, 1929); Colin R. Ballard, *The Military Genius of Abraham Lincoln* (London, 1926); T. Harry Williams, *Lincoln and His Generals* (New York, 1952); Kenneth P. Williams, *Lincoln Finds a General,* 5 vols. (New York, 1949–59); Herman Hattaway and Archer Jones, *How the North Won: A Military History of the Civil War* (New York, 1983).
4. Quoted in Shelby Foote, *The Civil War: A Narrative, Fort Sumter to Perryville* (New York, 1958), p. 143.
5. Quoted in ibid., p. 65.
6. Dunbar Rowland, ed., *Jefferson Davis, Constitutionalist: His Letters, Papers, and Speeches,* 10 vols. (Jackson, Miss., 1923), 5:84.
7. Steven E. Woodworth, *Davis and Lee at War* (Lawrence, Kans., 1995), p. xii.
8. Rowland, *Jefferson Davis, Constitutionalist* 6:386.
9. Rpt. in Emory M. Thomas, *The Confederate Nation, 1861–1865* (New York, 1979), p. 307.
10. T. Harry Williams, "The Military Leadership of North and South," in *Why the North Won the Civil War,* ed. David Donald (Baton Rouge, 1960), p. 46; Symonds, "Fatal Relationship," p. 11.
11. Davis to William M. Brooks, March 15, 1862, in Lynda Lasswell Crist, Mary Seaton Dix, and Kenneth H. Williams, eds., *The Papers of Jefferson Davis,* 11 vols. so far (Baton Rouge, 1971–2004), 8:100.
12. Symonds, "Fatal Relationship," pp. 12–13.
13. Davis, *Rise and Fall* 1:314. For "offensive defense," see Emory M. Thomas, "Ambivalent Visions of Victory: Davis, Lee, and Confederate Grand Strategy," in Boritt, *Jefferson Davis's Generals,* p. 31; for "defensive-offensive," see William C. Davis, *Jefferson Davis: The Man and His Hour* (New York, 1991), p. 700.

14. Lee to James A. Seddon, June 8, 1863, and Lee to Davis, June 25, 1863, in Clifford Dowdey and Louis H. Manarin, eds., *The Wartime Papers of R. E. Lee* (New York, 1961), pp. 505, 532; Lee's comment to Early quoted in J. William Jones, *Personal Reminiscences of Gen. Robert E. Lee* (New York, 1875), p. 40.

15. Woodworth, *Davis and Lee at War,* p. 157; see also Emory M. Thomas, *Robert E. Lee: A Biography* (New York, 1995) and Thomas, "Ambivalent Visions of Victory."

16. Thomas, "Ambivalent Visions of Victory," pp. 35, 29.

17. Ibid., pp. 37, 39.

18. Ibid., p. 32.

19. Personal conversation.

20. See especially Thomas L. Connelly, "Robert E. Lee and the Western Confederacy: A Criticism of Lee's Strategic Ability," in *Battles Lost and Won,* ed. John T. Hubbell (Westport, Conn., 1975), pp. 197–214; Grady McWhiney and Perry D. Jamieson, *Attack and Die: Civil War Military Tactics and the Southern Heritage* (Tuscaloosa, Ala., 1982); J.F.C. Fuller, *Grant and Lee: A Study in Personality and Generalship* (Bloomington, Ind., 1957); Alan T. Nolan, *Lee Considered: General Robert E. Lee and Civil War History* (Chapel Hill, N.C., 1991); and John D. McKenzie, *Uncertain Glory: Lee's Generalship Re-Examined* (New York, 1997).

21. Sumner to John Bright, Feb. 13, 1865, in Beverly Wilson Palmer, ed., *The Selected Letters of Charles Sumner,* 2 vols. (Boston, 1990), 2:268.

CHAPTER 5

1. Quoted in Brian Jenkins, *Britain and the War for the Union,* 2 vols. (Montreal, 1974), 1:104.

2. *Richmond Enquirer,* June 6, 18, 1862; Judah P. Benjamin to James Mason, April 12, July 19, 1862, in Virginia Mason, ed., *The Public Life and Diplomatic Correspondence of James M. Mason* (New York, 1906), pp. 294, 303.

3. Quoted in Henry Donaldson Jordan and Edwin J. Pratt, *Europe and the American Civil War* (Boston, 1931), p. 17.

4. Henry Adams to Henry Raymond, Jan. 24, 1862, in J. C. Levenson, ed., *The Letters of Henry Adams,* vol. 1, *1858–1868* (Cambridge, Mass., 1982), p. 272; *New York Tribune,* Feb. 11, 1862.

5. James Mason to Robert M. T. Hunter, March 11, 1862, in V. Mason, *Public Life and Diplomatic Correspondence of Mason,* p. 266; Charles Francis Adams to William H. Seward, March 13, 1862, in *Papers Relating to the Foreign Affairs of the United States, 1862,* pt. 1 (Washington, 1863), p. 48; Henry Adams to Charles Francis Adams Jr., March 15, 1862, in Levenson, *Letters of Henry Adams,* pp. 284–85.

6. *Times,* March 31, 1862; William L. Dayton to William H. Seward, April 17, 1862, in *Papers Relating to Foreign Affairs, 1862,* pt. 1, p. 333.

7. Henry Adams to Charles Francis Adams Jr., May 16, 1862, in Levenson, *Letters of Henry Adams,* pp. 297–98; James Mason to Jefferson Davis, May 16, 1862, in V. Mason, *Public Life and Diplomatic Correspondence of Mason,* p. 276.

8. Mason to Lord John Russell, Aug. 2, 1862, and Russell to Mason, Aug. 2, 1862, in V. Mason, *Public Life and Diplomatic Correspondence of Mason,* pp. 327–29; Palmerston to Austen H. Layard, June 19, 1862, in Hubert Du Brulle, "'A War of Wonders': The Battle in Britain over Americanization and the American Civil War" (PhD dissertation, University of California at Santa Barbara, 1999), p. 210n.

9. Adams to Seward, June 26, March 13, 1862, in *Papers Relating to Foreign Affairs, 1862,* pt. 1, pp. 118, 48.

10. *Constitutionnel,* June 7, 1862; *Times,* June 23, 1862.

11. William L. Dayton to William H. Seward, June 12, 1862, in *Papers Relating to Foreign Affairs, 1862,* pt. 1, pp. 349–50.

12. *Richmond Dispatch,* June 16, 1862; *New York Times,* July 10, 11, 12, 1862.

13. *The Diary of Edmund Ruffin,* ed. William Kauffman Scarborough, 3 vols. (Baton Rouge, 1972–89), 2:360, entry of June 30, 1862; *Richmond Dispatch,* July 4, 1862.

14. *New York Herald,* July 9, 1862; *New York Evening Post,* quoted in *Richmond Dispatch,* July 15, 1862.

15. *Constitutionnel,* July 19, 1862; Lynn M. Case and Warren F. Spencer, *The United States and France: Civil War Diplomacy* (Philadelphia, 1970), pp. 300–307.

16. *Times,* July 17, Aug. 15, 1862; *Morning Post,* quoted in *New York Tribune,* July 30, 1862.

17. Bright to Sumner, July 12, 1862, Cobden to Sumner, July 11, 1862, Charles Sumner Papers, Houghton Library, Harvard University.

18. De Gasparin to Lincoln, July 18, 1862, Lincoln to de Gasparin, Aug. 4, 1862, in Roy P. Basler, ed., *The Collected Works of Abraham Lincoln,* 9 vols. (New Brunswick, N.J., 1953–55), 5:355–56.

19. Henry Adams to Charles Francis Adams Jr., July 19, 1862, in Worthington Chauncey Ford, ed., *A Cycle of Adams Letters, 1861–1865,* 2 vols. (Boston, 1920), 1:166.

20. Ephraim Douglass Adams, *Great Britain and the American Civil War,* 2 vols. (New York, 1925), 2:20–23; Howard Jones, *Union in Peril: The Crisis over British Intervention in the Civil War* (Chapel Hill, N.C., 1992), p. 135.

21. Mason to his wife, July 20, 1862, in V. Mason, *Public Life and Diplomatic Correspondence of Mason,* p. 281; Slidell to Judah P. Benjamin, July 25, 1862, quoted in Case and Spencer, *United States and France,* p. 310.

22. *The Journal of Benjamin Moran, 1857–1865,* 2 vols. (Chicago, 1949), 2:1071–73, entries of Sept. 13, 15, 17, 20, 1862.

23. William L. Dayton to William H. Seward, Sept. 17, 1862, quoted in Howard Jones, *Abraham Lincoln and the New Birth of Freedom* (Lincoln, Neb., 1999),

p. 98; Gladstone to Lord John Russell, Aug. 30, 1862, Gladstone to William Stuart, Sept. 8, 1862, Gladstone Letterbook, quoted in ibid., p. 93.

24. This exchange is conveniently reprinted in James V. Murfin, *The Gleam of Bayonets: The Battle of Antietam and Robert E. Lee's Maryland Campaign, September 1862* (Baton Rouge, 1965), pp. 394, 396–97, from the Russell Papers, Public Record Office, London.

25. Palmerston to Gladstone, Sept. 24, 1862, in Phillip Guedella, ed., *Gladstone and Palmerston, Being the Correspondence of Lord Palmerston with Mr. Gladstone, 1861–1865* (London, 1928), pp. 232–33.

26. Russell to Henry R. C. Wellesley, earl of Cowley (the British ambassador to France), Sept. 26, 1862, in Frank Merli and Theodore A. Wilson, "The British Cabinet and the Confederacy: Autumn, 1862," *Maryland Historical Magazine* 65 (1970): 247n.; Palmerston to Russell, Sept. 23, 1862, in Murfin, *Gleam of Bayonets*, p. 400; Palmerston to Gladstone, Sept. 24, 1862, in Guedella, *Gladstone and Palmerston*, p. 233.

27. *Journal of Moran* 2:1075, entry of Sept. 27, 1862. The reports referred to here were of the battles at South Mountain on September 14.

28. *Times*, Oct. 2, 1862.

29. Charles Francis Adams to Charles Francis Adams Jr., Oct. 17, 1862, in Ford, *Cycle of Adams Letters* 1:192; Charles Francis Adams to William H. Seward, Oct. 3, 1862, in *Papers Relating to Foreign Affairs, 1862*, pt. 1, p. 205.

30. These two letters are reprinted in E. Adams, *Great Britain and the American Civil War* 2:43–44, 54–55.

31. Palmerston to King Leopold, Nov. 18, 1862, quoted in Merli and Wilson, "British Cabinet and the Confederacy," p. 261.

32. John Slidell to James Mason, Oct. 2, 1862, enclosing parts of a letter from Shaftesbury, quoted in Charles M. Hubbard, *The Failure of Confederate Diplomacy* (Knoxville, Tenn., 1998), p. 117; Mason to Judah Benjamin, Sept. 18, 1862, Mason to his son, Oct. 1, 1862, Mason to Benjamin, Nov. 7, 1862, in V. Mason, *Public Life and Diplomatic Correspondence of Mason*, pp. 338, 342, 353–54.

33. Lincoln to Greeley, Aug. 22, 1862, in Basler, *Collected Works of Lincoln* 5:388–89; *Saturday Review*, Sept. 14, 1861, quoted in E. Adams, *Great Britain and the American Civil War* 2:181. See also *Economist*, Sept. 1861, quoted in Karl Marx and Friedrich Engels, *The Civil War in the United States*, ed. Richard Enmale (New York, 1937), p. 12; *Reynolds' Weekly Newspaper*, Summer 1861, quoted in G. D. Lillibridge, *Beacon of Freedom: The Impact of American Democracy upon Great Britain, 1830–1870* (Philadelphia, 1955), p. 115.

34. Basler, *Collected Works of Lincoln* 5:336–37; Francis B. Carpenter, *Six Months at the White House with Abraham Lincoln* (New York, 1866), pp. 20–22.

35. Basler, *Collected Works of Lincoln* 5:433–36.

36. Henry Adams to Charles Francis Adams Jr., Jan. 23, 1862, in Levenson, *Letters of Henry Adams*, p. 327; *Journal of Moran* 2:1107, 1110, 1115, 1161.

37. Cobden to Sumner, Feb. 13, 1863, in Belle Becker Sideman and Lillian Friedman, eds., *Europe Looks at the Civil War* (New York, 1960), p. 222; James Shepherd Pike to Seward, Dec. 31, 1862, quoted in Dean B. Mahin, *One War at a Time: The International Dimensions of the American Civil War* (Washington, 1999), p. 139.

CHAPTER 6

1. *War of the Rebellion . . . Official Records of the Union and Confederate Armies*, 128 vols. (Washington, 1880–1901), ser. 1, vol. 27, pt. 2, pp. 305–11, 313–25. Hereinafter *O. R.*

2. Kent Masterson Brown, *Retreat from Gettysburg: Lee, Logistics, and the Pennsylvania Campaign* (Chapel Hill, N.C., 2005); Gary W. Gallagher, "Lee's Army Has Not Lost Any of Its Prestige: The Impact of Gettysburg on the Army of Northern Virginia and the Confederate Home Front," in Gallagher, *Lee and His Army in Confederate History* (Chapel Hill, N.C., 2001), pp. 83–114; Richard McMurry, "The Pennsylvania Gambit and the Gettysburg Splash," in *The Gettysburg Nobody Knows*, ed. Gabor S. Boritt (New York, 1997), pp. 175–202; Archer Jones, *Civil War Command and Strategy: The Process of Victory and Defeat* (New York, 1992), pp. 167–71; Carol Reardon, "Gettysburg: a Turning Point in Memory," in *New Turning Points of the Civil War*, ed. Kenneth J. Winkle (Lincoln, Neb., forthcoming); Charles P. Roland, "Lee's Invasion Strategy," *North & South* 1 (Oct. 1998): 34–38; Robert Himmer, "What if Lee Had Been Victorious at the Battle of Gettysburg?" ibid. 8 (June 2005): 64–65.

3. Lee to Mary Lee (wife), July 9, 1862, in Clifford Dowdey and Louis H. Manarin, eds., *The Wartime Papers of R. E. Lee* (New York, 1961), p. 230; *O. R.*, ser. 1, vol. 11, pt. 2, p. 497 (from Lee's official report).

4. Lee to Davis, Sept. 3, 1862, in Dowdey and Manarin, *Wartime Papers of R. E. Lee*, p. 230; *O. R.*, ser. 1, vol. 19, pt. 2, p. 596.

5. Lee to Davis, Sept. 8, 1862, in Dowdey and Manarin, *Wartime Papers of R. E. Lee*, p. 301.

6. Jedediah Hotchkiss, *Make Me a Map of the Valley: The Civil War Journal of Stonewall Jackson's Topographer*, ed. Archie P. McDonald (Dallas, 1973), p. 116, entry of Feb. 23, 1863.

7. Stephen W. Sears, *Gettysburg* (Boston, 2003), pp. 13–14.

8. Lee to Davis, April 16, 1862, Lee to Mary Lee, April 19, 1862, in Dowdey and Manarin, *Wartime Papers of R. E. Lee*, pp. 435, 438.

9. Accounts of these discussions can be found in Sears, *Gettysburg*, pp. 1–6; Archer Jones, *Confederate Strategy from Shiloh to Vicksburg* (Baton Rouge, 1961), pp. 206–14; Edwin B. Coddington, *The Gettysburg Campaign: A Study in Command* (New York, 1968), pp. 5–7; and Douglas Southall Freeman, *R. E. Lee: A Biography*, 4 vols. (New York, 1934–35), 3:18–20. See also Lee to James A.

Seddon, May 10, 1863, in Dowdey and Manarin, *Wartime Papers of R. E. Lee,* p. 482.

10. Quoted in Sears, *Gettysburg,* p. 7. It should be noted, however, that Longstreet spoke of crossing the Potomac with 150,000 men—twice as many as actually invaded Pennsylvania.

11. Ibid., p. 8.

12. Dorsey Pender to Frances Pender (wife), June 23, 1863, in William W. Hassler, ed., *The General to His Lady: The Civil War Letters of William Dorsey Pender to Fanny Pender* (Chapel Hill, N.C., 1962), p. 251.

13. Lee to John Bell Hood, May 21, 1863, in Dowdey and Manarin, *Wartime Papers of R. E. Lee,* p. 490.

14. Freeman, *R. E. Lee* 3:58–59.

15. Lee to Davis, June 10, 1863, in Dowdey and Manarin, *Wartime Papers of R. E. Lee,* pp. 507–9.

16. Thomas E. Schott, "The Stephens 'Peace' Mission," *North & South* 1 (Oct. 1998): 39–40.

17. *Richmond Examiner,* July 7, 1863. Lee's army was not in telegraphic communication with Richmond, so this editorial was based on information almost a week old. Definite news of the battle of Gettysburg did not reach the Confederate capital until July 9.

18. Roy P. Basler, ed., *The Collected Works of Abraham Lincoln,* 9 vols. (New Brunswick, N.J., 1953–55), 6:315–17.

CHAPTER 7

1. E. J. Hobsbawm, *Primitive Rebels: Studies in Archaic Forms of Social Movement in the 19th and 20th Centuries* (New York, 1965), and *Bandits,* 2nd ed. (New York, 1985), p. 17; on pp. 41–57 of *Bandits,* Hobsbawm places the James brothers explicitly in this tradition.

2. Richard White, "Outlaw Gangs of the Middle Border: American Social Bandits," *Western Historical Quarterly* 12 (Oct. 1981): 394, 406.

3. David Thelen, *Paths of Resistance: Tradition and Dignity in Industrializing Missouri* (New York, 1985), pp. 35, 75, 58, 71.

4. T. J. Stiles, *Jesse James: Last Rebel of the Civil War* (New York, 2002), p. 238.

5. Ibid., p. 237.

6. Don R. Bowen, "Guerrilla War in Western Missouri, 1862–1865: Historical Extensions of the Relative Deprivation Hypothesis," *Comparative Studies in Society and History* 19 (Jan. 1977): 30–51.

7. Stiles, *Jesse James,* p. 392.

8. Ibid., p. 5.

9. Ibid., p. 191.

10. Quoted in ibid., p. 224.

11. Quoted in ibid., pp. 224–25.

12. Ibid., p. 394.


CHAPTER 8

1. Quoted in David W. Blight, *Race and Reunion: The Civil War in American Memory* (Cambridge, Mass., 2001), p. 11.

2. Quoted in Keith S. Bohannon, " 'These Few Gray-Haired, Battle-Scarred Veterans': Confederate Army Reunions in Georgia, 1885–1895," in *The Myth of the Lost Cause and Civil War History,* ed. Gary W. Gallagher and Alan T. Nolan (Bloomington, Ind., 2000), pp. 96–97.

3. Quoted in Lloyd A. Hunter, "The Immortal Confederacy: Another Look at Lost Cause Religion," in Gallagher and Nolan, *Myth of the Lost Cause,* p. 207.

4. *Confederate Veteran Magazine* (hereinafter *CVM*) 15 (1907): 199.

5. Katharine Du Pre Lumpkin, *The Making of a Southerner* (New York, 1947), p. 118.

6. Ibid.

7. Ibid., pp. 121–26.

8. *CVM* 17 (1909): 171.

9. *CVM* 16 (1908): 671.

10. *CVM* 6 (1898): 29.

11. *CVM* 11 (1903): 138.

12. *CVM* 15 (1907): 264.

13. Bessie Louise Pierce, *Public Opinion and the Teaching of History in the United States* (New York, 1926), chap. 2; Frances Fitzgerald, *America Revised: History Schoolbooks in the Twentieth Century* (Boston, 1979), pp. 47–50, 227–28.

14. *CVM* 20 (1912): 512, 7 (1899): 507, 6 (1898): 476.

15. *CVM* 20 (1912): 440.

16. *Minutes of the Third Annual Meeting and Reunion of the United Confederate Veterans* (1892), p. 99.

17. *Minutes of the Ninth Annual Meeting and Reunion of the United Confederate Veterans* (1898), p. 147; Basil Gildersleeve, "The Creed of the Old South," *Atlantic Monthly* 49 (Jan. 1892): 87; *CVM* 5 (1897): 345.

18. *CVM* 19 (1911): 26.

19. *Minutes of the Fifth Annual Meeting and Reunion of the United Confederate Veterans* (1894), p. 12; Curry quoted in Richard M. Weaver, *The Southern Tradition at Bay: A History of Postbellum Thought* (New Rochelle, N.Y., 1968), p. 355.

20. Quoted in Pierce, *Public Opinion,* p. 162.

21. *CVM* 10 (1902): cover.

22. Herman Hattaway, "Clio's Southern Soldiers: The United Confederate Veterans and History," *Louisiana History* 12 (1971): 234–35; Lumpkin, *Making of a Southerner*, p. 127.

23. Pierce, *Public Opinion*, pp. 39, 66–69, 162–63 (quotation p. 66); Fitzgerald, *America Revised*, pp. 29, 35.

24. *Minutes of the Twenty-first Annual Meeting and Reunion of the United Confederate Veterans* (1910), p. 101.

25. *Minutes of the Twenty-second Annual Meeting and Reunion of the United Confederate Veterans* (1911), p. 15; *CVM* 19 (1911): 160.

26. *Minutes of the Sixth Annual Meeting and Reunion of the United Confederate Veterans* (1895), pp. 23–24.

27. *CVM* 19 (1911): 561.

28. Ibid., 533.

29. *CVM* 4 (1896): 362.

30. Mildred L. Rutherford, "Historical Sins of Omission and Commission," in *Four Addresses* (n.p., 1916), pp. 113–14.

31. Ibid., p. 112.

32. Mildred L. Rutherford, *A Measuring Rod to Test Text Books and Reference Books in Schools, Colleges, and Libraries* (n.p., 1919), pp. 2–3.

33. Ibid., p. 5.

34. All by Mildred L. Rutherford: *The Truths of History* (n.p., n.d.); *The South Must Have Her Rightful Place in History* (Athens, Ga., 1923), p. 19; "The South in the Building of the Nation" (Washington, 1912), in *Four Addresses*, p. 13; "Thirteen Periods of United States History" (New Orleans, 1912), in *Four Addresses*, p. 37.

35. Rutherford, *Truths of History*, p. 75.

36. In addition to holding several high offices in the UDC, Rutherford was a longtime teacher and administrator at a prominent Atlanta girls' school, the author of several textbooks on literature and history, and an officer or board member of several women's organizations, including the national YWCA. See Edward T. James, ed., *Notable American Women*, 3 vols. (Cambridge, Mass., 1971), 3:214–15.

37. William E. Dodd, "The Status of History in Southern Education," *Nation* 75 (Aug. 7, 1902): 110–11.

38. Riley quoted in Gaines M. Foster, *Ghosts of the Confederacy: Defeat, the Lost Cause, and the Emergence of the New South, 1865 to 1913* (New York, 1987), p. 185.

39. *CVM* 19 (1911): 365.

40. *Roanoke Times* quoted in ibid., 148, 316.

41. Ibid., 319, 148.

42. Ibid., 194, 196, 275 (first and second quotations); *CVM* 20 (1912): 443 (third quotation). See also Foster, *Ghosts of the Confederacy*, pp. 188–90.

43. Rollin G. Osterweis, *The Myth of the Lost Cause* (Hamden, Conn., 1973), p. 113.

44. In recent years the Sons of Confederate Veterans have revived the magazine as *Confederate Veteran.*

45. *CVM* 40 (1932): 128, 129, 157.


CHAPTER 9

1. Henry Adams, *The Education of Henry Adams: An Autobiography* (Boston, 1918), p. 266; Brooks D. Simpson, *Ulysses S. Grant: Triumph over Adversity, 1822–1865* (Boston, 2000), p. xvii.

2. J.F.C. Fuller, *Grant and Lee: A Study in Personality and Generalship* (London, 1933); T. Harry Williams, *Lincoln and His Generals* (New York, 1952); Kenneth P. Williams, *Lincoln Finds a General*, 5 vols. (New York, 1949–59); Bruce Catton, *Grant Moves South* (Boston, 1960) and *Grant Takes Command* (Boston, 1968).

3. John Y. Simon et al., eds., *Papers of Ulysses S. Grant*, 28 vols. (Carbondale, Ill., 1967– ); John Keegan, "Grant and Unheroic Leadership," in Keegan, *The Mask of Command* (New York, 1987), pp. 164–234; Geoffrey Perret, *Ulysses S. Grant: Soldier and President* (New York, 1997); Simpson, *Ulysses S. Grant;* Jean Edward Smith, *Grant* (New York, 2001).

4. Quoted in Simpson, *Ulysses S. Grant*, p. xvii.

5. *Personal Memoirs of U. S. Grant*, 2 vols. (New York, 1885), 1:276.

6. Ibid., 307.

7. Quoted in Simpson, *Ulysses S. Grant*, p. 134.

8. Horace Porter, *Campaigning with Grant* (New York, 1897), pp. 69–70.

9. Quoted in Simpson, *Ulysses S. Grant*, pp. 459–60.

10. *Personal Memoirs* 1:100, 139.

11. Simpson, *Ulysses S. Grant*, p. 466.

12. *Personal Memoirs* 1:248–50.

13. Simpson, *Ulysses S. Grant*, p. 61.

14. Ibid., p. 108.

15. Charles Bracelen Flood, *Grant and Sherman: The Friendship That Won the Civil War* (New York, 2005), p. vii.

16. Steven E. Woodworth, *Nothing but Victory: The Army of the Tennessee, 1861–1865* (New York, 2005), pp. 568, ix.

17. Ibid., p. ix.

18. Ibid., p. x.

19. Ibid., p. 465.

20. Ibid., p. 492.

21. Sherman to Ellen Ewing Sherman, April 11, 1862, in Brooks D. Simpson and Jean V. Berlin, eds., *Sherman's Civil War: Selected Correspondence of William T. Sherman, 1800–1865* (Chapel Hill, N.C., 1999), p. 202.

22. Grady McWhiney and Perry D. Jamieson, *Attack and Die: Civil War Military Tactics and the Southern Heritage* (University, Ala., 1982), pp. 22–23.

23. Basil H. Liddell Hart, *Sherman: Soldier, Realist, American* (New York, 1929); see also Liddell Hart, *Sherman: The Genius of the Civil War* (London, 1930).

24. Basil H. Liddell Hart, *Strategy: The Indirect Approach* (New York, 1954).

25. Jay Luvaas, *The Military Legacy of the Civil War: The European Inheritance* (Chicago, 1959; rpt. Lawrence, Kans., 1988), pp. 213n., 224–225.

26. Ibid., pp. 217–22.

27. Dunbar Rowland, ed., *Jefferson Davis, Constitutionalist: His Letters, Papers, and Speeches,* 10 vols. (Jackson, Miss., 1923), 6:386, 341–42.

28. Porter, *Campaigning with Grant,* p. 313.

29. Liddell Hart, *Sherman: Soldier Realist, American,* p. 383.

30. Quoted in Lloyd Lewis, *Sherman: Fighting Prophet* (New York, 1932), pp. 484, 490.

31. Quoted in Bell Irvin Wiley, *The Life of Billy Yank: The Common Soldier of the Union* (Indianapolis, 1952), pp. 321–23.

32. Quoted in Woodworth, *Nothing but Victory,* p. 465.

33. Compiled from Thomas L. Livermore, *Numbers and Losses in the Civil War in America, 1861–1865* (Boston, 1900) and William F. Fox, *Regimental Losses in the American Civil War, 1861–1865* (Albany, N.Y., 1898).

34. Compiled from Livermore, *Numbers and Losses,* and Fox, *Regimental Losses.*


CHAPTER 10

1. Mark Grimsley, *The Hard Hand of War: Union Military Policy Toward Southern Civilians, 1861–1865* (Cambridge, Mass., 1995), p. 1.

2. Joseph T. Glatthaar, *The March to the Sea and Beyond: Sherman's Troops in the Savannah and Carolinas Campaigns* (New York, 1985); John F. Marszalek, *Sherman: A Soldier's Passion for Order* (New York, 1993); Brooks D. Simpson and Jean V. Berlin, eds., *Sherman's Civil War: Selected Correspondence of William T. Sherman, 1860–1865* (Chapel Hill, N.C., 1999); Stanley P. Hirshson, *The White Tecumseh: A Biography of William T. Sherman* (New York, 1997); Charles Bracelen Flood, *Grant and Sherman: The Friendship That Won the Civil War* (New York, 2005).

3. Grimsley, *Hard Hand of War,* pp. 2, 186, 219.

4. Ibid., p. 223.

5. John Bennett Walters, *Merchant of Terror: General Sherman and Total War* (Indianapolis, 1973); James Reston Jr., *Sherman's March and Vietnam* (New York, 1984); Harry S. Stout, *Upon the Altar of the Nation: A Moral History of the Civil War* (New York, 2005).

6. Sherman to Henry W. Halleck, Dec. 24, 1864, *War of the Rebellion . . . Official Records of the Union and Confederate Armies,* 128 vols. (Washington, 1880–1901), ser. 1, vol. 44, p. 799. Hereinafter cited *O. R.*

7. *Memoirs of General William T. Sherman,* 2nd ed., 2 vols. (New York, 1886), 2:249; Sherman to Ulysses S. Grant, Oct. 4, 1862, *O. R.,* ser. 1, vol. 17, pt. 2, p. 261, Sherman to Halleck, Sept. 17, 1863, ibid., vol. 30, pt. 3, p. 698.

8. Mark E. Neely Jr., "Was the Civil War a Total War?" *Civil War History* 37 (1991): 14–15, 27.

9. Grimsley, *Hard Hand of War,* pp. 2–3, 157, 222, and passim.

10. Sherman to Ellen Ewing Sherman, July 28, 1861, in Simpson and Berlin, *Sherman's Civil War,* p. 125.

11. Sherman to General Stephen A. Hurlbut, July 10, 1862, *O. R.,* ser. 1, vol. 17, pt. 2, pp. 88–89; second quotation from Grimsley, *Hard Hand of War,* p. 100.

12. John to William T. Sherman, Aug. 24, 1862, in Michael Fellman, *Citizen Sherman: A Life of William Tecumseh Sherman* (New York, 1995), pp. 138–39.

13. Sherman to Salmon P. Chase, Aug. 11, 1862, in Simpson and Berlin, *Sherman's Civil War,* p. 269; Sherman to John Sherman, Aug. 26, Sept. 22, 1862, in ibid., pp. 292, 301.

14. A. Fisk Gore to "Sister Katie," Aug. 5, 1862, A. Fisk Gore Papers, Missouri Historical Society; *O. R.,* ser. 1, vol. 17, pt. 2, p. 150.

15. *O. R.,* ser. 1, vol. 11, pt. 3, p. 362.

16. Lincoln to Cuthbert Bullitt, July 28, 1862, and to August Belmont, July 31, 1862, in Roy P. Basler, ed., *The Collected Works of Abraham Lincoln,* 9 vols. (New Brunswick, N.J., 1953–55), 5:346, 350.

17. Gideon Welles, "The History of Emancipation," *Galaxy* 14 (1872): 842–43.

18. *O. R.,* ser. 1, vol. 24, pt. 3, p. 157.

19. Grimsley, *Hard Hand of War,* pp. 98–119.

20. Ibid., pp. 163, 185.

21. Reston, *Sherman's March and Vietnam,* esp. chap. 4.

22. Sherman to Henry W. Halleck, Dec. 24, 1864, *O. R.,* ser. 1, vol. 44, p. 799; soldier quoted in Lloyd Lewis, *Sherman: Fighting Prophet* (New York, 1932), p. 489.

23. Grimsley, *Hard Hand of War,* pp. 200, 202–3.


CHAPTER 11

1. David Dixon Porter, *Incidents and Anecdotes of the Civil War* (New York, 1885), pp. 95–96.

2. Lincoln to Buell, Jan. 6, 1862, in Roy P. Basler, ed., *The Collected Works of Abraham Lincoln,* 9 vols. (New Brunswick, N.J., 1953–55), 5:91; McClellan to Buell, Jan. 6, 1862, *War of the Rebellion . . . Official Records of the Union and Confederate Armies,* 128 vols. (Washington, 1880–1901), ser. 1, vol. 5, p. 531. Hereinafter cited *O. R.*

3. Lincoln to Samuel Treat, Nov. 19, 1862, in Basler, *Collected Works of Lincoln* 5:501.

4. Halleck to Banks, Nov. 9, 1862, *O. R.*, ser. 1, vol. 15, pp. 590–91.

5. John Niven, ed., *The Salmon P. Chase Papers*, vol. 1, *Journals, 1829–1872* (Kent, Ohio, 1993), pp. 358–59, entry of Aug. 3, 1862.

6. Yates persuaded seven other governors to sign a letter to Lincoln urging McClernand's appointment to this position: Yates et al. to Lincoln, Sept. 26, 1862, Abraham Lincoln Papers, Library of Congress. See also Steven E. Woodworth, *Nothing but Victory: The Army of the Tennessee* (New York, 2005), pp. 249–50, and Richard L. Kiper, *Major General John Alexander McClernand: Politician in Uniform* (Kent, Ohio, 1999), pp. 133–36.

7. *O. R.*, ser. 1, vol. 17, pt. 2, p. 282.

8. Col. William S. Hillyer to William T. Sherman, Oct. 29, 1862, ibid., pp. 307–8; Grant to Halleck, Nov. 10, 1862, Halleck to Grant, Nov. 11, 1862, Grant to Sherman, Nov. 14, 1862, Grant to Halleck, Dec. 9, 1862, all in John Y. Simon et al., eds., *Papers of Ulysses S. Grant*, 28 vols. so far (Carbondale, Ill., 1967– ), 6:288, 288n., 310, 7:6.

9. T. Harry Williams, *Lincoln and His Generals* (New York, 1952), p. 193.

10. McClernand to Lincoln, Dec. 29, 1862, Jan. 7, 16, 1863, Lincoln Papers; Lincoln to McClernand, Jan. 22, 1863, in Basler, *Collected Works of Lincoln* 6:70.

11. Lorenzo Thomas to Halleck, March 10, 1862, Halleck to Thomas, March 15, 1862, *O. R.*, ser. 1, vol. 7, pp. 683–84; Edwin M. Stanton to Halleck, April 23, 1862, Halleck to Stanton, April 24, May 2, 1862, ibid., ser. 1, vol. 10, pt. 1, pp. 98–99.

12. Don E. Fehrenbacher and Virginia Fehrenbacher, eds., *Recollected Words of Abraham Lincoln* (Stanford, Calif., 1996), pp. 11, 292.

13. Washburne to Grant, Jan. 24, 1864, in Simon et al., *Papers of Grant* 9:522n.

14. Medill to Washburne, Feb. 19, 1863, in Simon et al., *Papers of Grant* 7:317–18n.; Cadwalader Washburn to Elihu Washburne (the brothers spelled their last name differently), March 28, 1863, in Jean Edward Smith, *Grant* (New York, 2001), p. 230.

15. Albert Richardson to Sydney H. Gay, March 20, 1863, Gay Papers, Columbia University Library; John Dahlgren, diary entry of March 29, 1863, in Madeleine Vinton Dahlgren, *Memoir of John A. Dahlgren* (Boston, 1882), p. 389; Halleck to Grant, April 2, 1863, *O. R.*, ser. 1, vol. 24, pt. 1, p. 25.

16. Charles Bracelen Flood, *Grant and Sherman: The Friendship That Won the Civil War* (New York, 2005), pp. 154–55; Brooks D. Simpson, *Ulysses S. Grant: Triumph over Adversity, 1822–1865* (Boston, 2000), pp. 184–85.

17. Halleck to Grant, April 2, May 11, 1863, Halleck to Nathaniel P. Banks, May 23, 1863, *O. R.*, ser. 1, vol. 24, pt. 1, pp. 25, 36; vol. 26, pt. 1, pp. 500–501.

18. James S. Rusling, *Men and Things I Saw in Civil War Days* (New York, 1899), pp. 16–17; *Diary of Gideon Welles*, ed. Howard K. Beale, 3 vols. (New York, 1960), 1:364, entry of July 7, 1863.

19. Basler, *Collected Works of Lincoln* 6:326.
20. Lincoln to James C. Conkling, Aug. 26, 1863, ibid., 409.

CHAPTER 12

1. Wickham is quoted from a conversation I had with Edwin Bearss, chief historian emeritus of the National Park Service, who guided General Wickham's tour of Antietam.
2. Oxford University Press (New York, 1997).
3. Richard F. Miller, *Harvard's Civil War: A History of the Twentieth Massachusetts Volunteer Infantry* (Hanover, N.H., 2005); Carol Bundy, *The Nature of Sacrifice: A Biography of Charles Russell Lowell, Jr., 1835–1864* (New York, 2005).
4. Miller, *Harvard's Civil War*, p. 20.
5. Bundy, *Nature of Sacrifice*, p. 186.
6. Adams quoted in Bundy, *Nature of Sacrifice*, p. 186; Mrs. Revere quoted in Miller, *Harvard's Civil War*, p. 274.
7. Miller, *Harvard's Civil War*, p. 218.
8. Bundy, *Nature of Sacrifice*, p. 314.
9. Lowell quoted in Bundy, *Nature of Sacrifice*, p. 186; Putnam quoted in ibid., p. 197, and Miller, *Harvard's Civil War*, p. 28.
10. Quoted in William F. Fox, *Regimental Losses in the American Civil War, 1861–1865* (Albany, N.Y., 1898), p. 164.
11. Calculated from ibid., passim.
12. Miller, *Harvard's Civil War*, p. 244.
13. Bundy, *Nature of Sacrifice*, p. 206.
14. Ibid., pp. 408–15, quotation p. 409.
15. Ibid., p. 464.
16. Ibid., p. 470.
17. Ibid., p. 11.

CHAPTER 13

1. *The Diary of George Templeton Strong*, vol. 3, *The Civil War, 1860–1865*, ed. Allan Nevins and Milton Halsey Thomas (New York, 1952), p. 449; James M. McPherson, *Battle Cry of Freedom: The Civil War Era* (New York, 1988), p. viii.
2. Louis M. Starr, *Reporting the Civil War: The Bohemian Brigade in Action, 1861–1865* (orig. pub. as *The Bohemian Brigade*; New York, 1962), p. 44; W. Fletcher Thompson Jr., *The Image of War: The Pictorial Reporting of the American Civil War* (New York, 1960), p. 137.
3. Comte de Paris, *History of the Civil War in America*, quoted in Belle Becker Sideman and Lillian Friedman, eds., *Europe Looks at the Civil War* (New York, 1960), pp. 52–53.

4. Gustave Paul Cluseret, *Armée et democratie* (Paris, 1869), pp. 101–2, trans. Philip Katz.

5. Bell Irvin Wiley, *The Life of Billy Yank: The Common Soldier of the Union* (Indianapolis, 1952), pp. 153–54; Phillip Knightley, *The First Casualty* (New York, 1975), pp. 17, 24.

6. "Robert A. Moore: The Diary of a Confederate Private," ed. James W. Silver, *Louisiana Historical Quarterly* 39 (1956): 312, entry of Jan. 28, 1862; Ted Barclay to his sister, March 6, 1864, in Ted Barclay, *Liberty Hall Volunteers: Letters from the Stonewall Brigade,* ed. Charles W. Turner (Rockbridge, Va., 1992), p. 131; William J. Mims to his wife, Sept. 22, 1864, in "Letters of Major W. J. Mims, C.S.A.," *Alabama Historical Quarterly* 3 (1941): 223.

7. James G. Theaker to his brother, Aug. 10, 1863, in Paul E. Rieger, ed., *Through One Man's Eyes: The Civil War Experiences of a Belmont County Volunteer* (Mount Vernon, Ohio, 1974), p. 49.

8. J. Cutler Andrews, *The South Reports the Civil War* (Princeton, N.J., 1970), p. 89; J. Cutler Andrews, "The Confederate Press and Public Morale," *Journal of Southern History* 32 (1966): 463.

9. All quotations from Starr, *Reporting the Civil War,* p. 202.

10. Thompson, *Image of War,* pp. 83, 137–38.

11. Hamilton Branch to his mother, July 20, 1861, in "Three Brothers Face Their Baptism of Battle, July 1861," ed. Edward G. Longacre, *Georgia Historical Quarterly* 61 (1977): 163; William G. Morris to his wife, Feb. 15, 1862, Morris Papers, Southern Historical Collection, Wilson Library, University of North Carolina at Chapel Hill; Leonidas Torrence to his father, July 20, 1861, in "The Road to Gettysburg: The Diary and Letters of Leonidas Torrence of the Gaston Guards," ed. Haskell Monroe, *North Carolina Historical Review* 36 (1959): 480.

12. William Ames to his father, June 28, 1861, "Civil War Letters of William Ames, from Brown University to Bull Run," ed. William Greene Roelker, *Rhode Island Historical Society Collections* 33 (1940): 82; James Goff to his father, Jan. 23, 1862, Goff Papers, Huntington Library, San Marino, Calif.; Stephen Keyes Fletcher, diary entry of Oct. 16, 1861, in "The Civil War Journal of Stephen Keyes Fletcher," ed. Perry McCandless, *Indiana Magazine of History* 54 (1958): 145–46.

13. Joseph Diltz to Mary Diltz, Jan. 19, Sept. 21, 1862, Diltz Papers, Perkins Library, Duke University; James Overcash to Joseph Overcash, Aug. 11, 1861, Joseph Overcash Papers, Perkins Library, Duke University.

14. James Binford to Carrie and Annie, Aug. 13, 1862, Binford Papers, Virginia Historical Society, Richmond; John McCreery to his mother and father, Oct. 13, 1864, McCreery Letters, John Sickles Collection, U.S. Army Military History Institute, Carlisle, Pa.

15. Josiah Chaney to his wife, July 28, 1862, Chaney Papers, Minnesota Historical Society, St. Paul; Charles H. Brewster to Mary Brewster, April 30, 1864, in David

W. Blight, ed., *When This Cruel War Is Over: The Civil War Letters of Charles Harvey Brewster* (Amherst, Mass., 1992), p. 291; Samuel F. Tenney to Alice Toomer, April 18, 1863, in "War Letters of S. F. Tenney, a Soldier of the Third Georgia Regiment," *Georgia Historical Quarterly* 57 (1973): 293.

16. Henry H. Orendorff to Washington Orendorff, March 3, 1864, and to parents, June 20, 1864, in William M. Anderson, ed., *We Are Sherman's Men: The Civil War Letters of Henry Orendorff* (Macomb, Ill., 1986), pp. 75, 92; Charles Brewster to Mary Brewster, Nov. 25, 1863, in Blight, *When This Cruel War is Over*, p. 348.

17. Andrews, *South Reports the Civil War*, pp. 189–90; Douglas Southall Freeman, *Lee's Lieutenants: A Study in Command*, 3 vols. (New York, 1942–44), 1:664–68.

18. Carol Reardon, *Pickett's Charge in History and Memory* (Chapel Hill, N.C., 1997).

19. Roswell H. Lamson to Catherine Buckingham, April 24, 30, 1863, in James M. McPherson and Patricia R. McPherson, eds., *Lamson of the Gettysburg: The Civil War Letters of Lieutenant Roswell H. Lamson, U.S. Navy* (New York, 1997), pp. 101, 104.

20. John Euclid Magee, diary, undated entry, Perkins Library, Duke University; Cyrus F. Boyd, diary entry of July 7, 1862, in "The Civil War Diary of C. F. Boyd, Fifteenth Iowa Infantry," ed. Mildred Throne, *Iowa Journal of History* 50 (1952): 170–71.

21. Daniel B. Sanford to his sister, July 25, 1863, Sanford letters in the possession of Sanford Pentecost, quoted with permission; John A. Everett to his mother, Aug. 4, 1863, Everett Papers, Emory University Library; Thomas T. Taylor to his wife, July 15, 1863, Taylor Papers, Ohio Historical Society, Columbus.

22. Robert A. McClellan to his sister, May 13, 1863, McClellan Papers, Perkins Library, Duke University; Joab Goodson to Nannie Clements, Aug. 18, 1863, in "The Letters of Captain Joab Goodson, 1862–1864," ed. W. Stanley Hoole, *Alabama Review* 10 (1957): 146–47; Peter McDavid to Nellie McDavid, Aug. 15, 1863, McDavid Papers, Perkins Library, Duke University.

23. W. Buck Yearns and John G. Barrett, eds., *North Carolina Civil War Documentary* (Chapel Hill, N.C., 1980), pp. 298–99.

24. Charles M. Coit to his family, Jan. 5, 1863, Coit Papers, Gilder Lehrman Collection, New-York Historical Society; Charles Wills to his sister, Feb. 7, 1863, *Army Life of an Illinois Soldier: Letters and Diary of the Late Charles Wills* (Washington, 1906), pp. 153–54; Osiah Moser to his wife, March 22, 1863, Civil War Collection, Missouri Historical Society, St. Louis.

25. Enos B. Lewis to his parents, April 21, 1863, in "The Civil War Letters of Enos Barret Lewis," *Northwest Ohio Quarterly* 57 (1985): 90; Alexander Caldwell to his brother, March 7, 1863, Caldwell Papers, U.S. Army Military History Insitute; Bela Zimmerman to Minnie Zimmerman, June 14, 1863, Zimmerman letters in possession of Samuel F. Abernethy, quoted with permission.

26. Nelson Chapin to his wife, March 6, 1864, Chapin Papers, U.S. Army Military History Institute.

27. Wiley, *Life of Billy Yank*, pp. 179–83, 402; Emil Rosenblatt and Ruth Rosenblatt, eds., *Anti-Rebel: The Civil War Letters of Private Wilbur Fisk, 1861–1865* (Croton-on-Hudson, N.Y., 1983) and *Hard Marching Every Day: The Civil War Letters of Private Wilbur Fisk, 1861–1865* (Lawrence, Kans., 1992).

28. Delos Van Deusen to Henrietta Van Deusen, Aug. 21, 1864, Van Deusen Papers, Huntington Library, San Marino, Calif.

29. Abner E. McGarity to Franinia McGarity, March 6, 1865, in "Letters of a Confederate Surgeon: Dr. Abner Embry McGarity, 1862–1865," ed. Edmund Cody Burnett, *Georgia Historical Quarterly* 30 (1946): 62.

30. *London Daily News*, Sept. 27, 1864, quoted in Allan Nevins, *The War for the Union*, vol. 4, *The Organized War to Victory, 1864–1865* (New York, 1971), pp. 141–42.

## CHAPTER 14

1. Paul Glass and Louis C. Singer, *Singing Soldiers: A History of the Civil War in Song* (New York, 1975), pp. 152–53, 267–69; Willard A. Heaps and Porter W. Heaps, *The Singing Sixties: The Spirit of Civil War Days Drawn from the Music of the Times* (Norman, Okla., 1960), pp. 159–60, 224–26.

2. See essay 5 in this volume, "The Saratoga That Wasn't: The Impact of Antietam Abroad."

3. *New York Times*, Jan. 29, 1863. See also *New York Tribune*, Jan. 9, 14, 22, 1863.

4. Seward quoted in *The Diary of George Templeton Strong*, vol. 3, *The Civil War, 1860–1865*, ed. Allan Nevins and Milton Halsey Thomas (New York, 1952), p. 293, entry of Feb. 1, 1863. This affair is analyzed at length in Lynn M. Case and Warren F. Spencer, *The United States and France: Civil War Diplomacy* (Philadelphia, 1970), pp. 384–97.

5. Roy C. Basler, ed., *The Collected Works of Abraham Lincoln*, 9 vols. (New Brunswick, N.J., 1953–55), 7:53–56.

6. *New York Times*, May 9, 1864; *New York Herald*, May 14, 1864; *New York Tribune*, May 14, 1864.

7. *New York Tribune*, May 31, 1864.

8. *New York World*, July 12, 30, Aug. 6, 1864.

9. Basler, *Collected Works of Lincoln* 7:448–49; *New York World*, July 19, 1864.

10. *Diary of Gideon Welles*, 3 vols., ed. Howard K. Beale (New York, 1960), 2:44, 73, entries of June 2 and July 11, 1864; Adam Gurowski, *Diary*, 3 vols. (Boston, 1862–66), 3:254, entry of Aug. 19, 1864.

11. *Diary of George Templeton Strong* 3:474, entry of Aug. 19, 1864; Sarah Butler to Benjamin Butler, June 19, 1864, in Jesse A. Marshall, ed., *Private and Official*

*Correspondence of General Benjamin F. Butler During the Period of the Civil War,*
5 vols. (Norwood, Mass., 1917), 4:418.

12. *Columbus Crisis,* Aug. 24, 1864, quoted in Wood Gray, *The Hidden Civil War: The Story of the Copperheads* (New York, 1942), p. 174; *Boston Pilot,* quoted in Thomas H. O'Connor, *Civil War Boston: Home Front and Battlefield* (Boston, 1997), p. 202.

13. Clement C. Clay to Judah P. Benjamin, Aug. 11, 1864, in *War of the Rebellion . . . Official Records of the Union and Confederate Armies,* 128 vols. (Washington, 1880–1901), ser. 4, vol. 3, p. 585 (hereinafter cited as *O. R.*). For the activities of Confederate agents in Canada, see Oscar A. Kinchen, *Confederate Operations in Canada and the North* (North Quincy, Mass., 1970), esp. pp. 35–103.

14. *Richmond Dispatch,* July 23, 1864; *Diary of George Templeton Strong* 3:470, entry of Aug. 6, 1864; Weed to Seward, Aug. 22, 1864, in Abraham Lincoln Papers (Robert Todd Lincoln Collection), Library of Congress.

15. Greeley to Lincoln, July 7, 1864, Lincoln Papers.

16. Lincoln to Greeley, July 9, 1864, in Basler, *Collected Works of Lincoln* 7:435.

17. Basler, *Collected Works of Lincoln* 7:440–42, 451; *Inside Lincoln's White House: The Complete Civil War Diary of John Hay,* ed. Michael Burlingame and John R. Turner Ettlinger (Carbondale, Ill., 1997), pp. 224–29, two memoranda written by Hay circa July 21 and after July 22, 1864; John G. Nicolay and John Hay, *Abraham Lincoln: A History,* 10 vols. (New York, 1890), 9:184–92.

18. Clement C. Clay and James Holcombe to Greeley, July 21, 1864, in *New York Times,* July 22. This letter was published in many Northern newspapers on July 22 or 23 and appeared in Southern newspapers soon after, with extensive editorial commentary. In a letter to Jefferson Davis on July 25, Clay and Holcombe explained that their purpose in this affair had been to "throw upon the Federal Government the odium of putting an end to all negotiations." Clement C. Clay Papers, Perkins Library, Duke University, quoted in Larry E. Nelson, *Bullets, Ballots, and Rhetoric: Confederate Policy for the United States Presidential Contest of 1864* (University, Ala., 1980), p. 67.

19. *New York Times,* July 23, 1864; Clay to Benjamin, Aug. 22, 1864, in *O. R.,* ser. 4, vol. 3, pp. 585–86.

20. *Independent,* July 26, 1864; *New York Tribune,* Aug. 5, 1864.

21. Greeley to Lincoln, Aug. 9, 1864, Lincoln Papers; *New York Times,* July 25, 1864.

22. No official record of this meeting was kept. This account and the quotation are taken from Gilmore's article in *Atlantic Monthly* 8 (Sept. 1864): 372–83. Gilmore wrote a briefer version describing the meeting for the *Boston Transcript* of July 22, 1864, and a longer one in his memoirs many years later. These versions vary slightly in detail but agree in substance, as does Judah Benjamin's account in a circular sent to Confederates abroad after Gilmore's article was published in the *Atlantic.* Benjamin to James M. Mason, Aug. 25, 1864, in *Official Records of the*

*Union and Confederate Navies,* 30 vols. (Washington, 1894–1922), ser. 2, vol. 3, pp. 1190–94.

23. James R. Gilmore, "A Suppressed Chapter of History," *Atlantic Monthly* 59 (April 1887): 435–46.

24. *New York Times,* Aug. 20, 1864.

25. *Semi-Weekly Richmond Enquirer,* Aug. 26, 30, 1864.

26. *New York World,* Aug. 15, 1864.

27. *Columbus Crisis,* Aug. 3, 1864; *New York News,* quoted in *Washington Daily Intelligencer,* July 25, 1864.

28. *New York World,* July 25, 1864; *New York Herald,* Aug. 7, 1864.

29. *Newark Daily Advertiser* and *Ann Arbor Journal,* quoted in *Washington Daily Intelligencer,* Aug. 8, 1864.

30. *New York Tribune,* July 28, 1864; *Diary of George Templeton Strong* 3:474, entry of Aug. 19, 1864.

31. *New York Times,* Aug. 18, 1864.

32. Lincoln to Charles D. Robinson, dated Aug. 17, 1864, in Basler, *Collected Works of Lincoln* 7:499–501.

33. Ibid., 500, 506–7.

34. William Frank Zornow, *Lincoln and the Party Divided* (Norman, Okla., 1954), p. 112; Basler, *Collected Works of Lincoln* 7:514.

35. Raymond to Lincoln, Aug. 22, 1864, Lincoln Papers.

36. Basler, *Collected Works of Lincoln* 7:517; Nicolay and Hay, *Abraham Lincoln* 9:220.

37. Nicolay to Hay, Aug. 25, 1864, Nicolay to Theresa Bates, Aug. 28, 1864, in *With Lincoln in the White House: Letters, Memoranda, and Other Writings of John G. Nicolay, 1860–1865,* ed. Michael Burlingame (Carbondale, Ill., 2000), pp. 152–53.

38. On this matter see Burlingame, *Inside Lincoln's White House,* 238, Hay's diary entry of Oct. 11, 1864; and Charles A. Dana to Henry J. Raymond, date not specified, in Francis Brown, *Raymond of the Times* (New York, 1951), p. 260n.

39. For the platform see Edward McPherson, *The Political History of the United States During the Great Rebellion,* 2nd ed. (Washington, 1865), pp. 406–7.

40. Ibid., pp. 419–20.

41. *Harper's Weekly* 8 (Aug. 30, 1864): 530; *New York Times,* Aug. 17, 1864; *New York Tribune,* Sept. 2, 1864.

42. McClellan struggled to strike a balance between the platform and his own commitment to reunion as a prerequisite for negotiations. For an analysis of the successive drafts of McClellan's acceptance letter, see Charles R. Wilson, "McClellan's Changing View on the Peace Plank of 1864," *American Historical Review* 38 (1933): 498–505. Drafts of McClellan's letter are in the McClellan Papers, Library of Congress, and in the Samuel L. M. Barlow Papers, Huntington Library, San Marino, Calif.

43. *O. R.*, ser. 1, vol. 38, pt. 5, p. 777; *Diary of George Templeton Strong* 3:480–81, entry of Sept. 3, 1864.

44. *Richmond Examiner,* Sept. 5, 1864. The sermon was published in the *New York Times,* Sept. 19, 1864.

45. Delos Lake to his mother, July 12, Nov. 1, 1864, Lake Papers; John Berry to Samuel L. M. Barlow, Aug. 24, 1864, Barlow Papers; both collections in the Huntington Library.

46. Basler, *Collected Works of Lincoln* 8:149, 151.

47. *The Journals of Josiah Gorgas, 1857–1878,* ed. Sarah Woolfolk Wiggins (Tuscaloosa, Ala., 1995), pp. 147–49, entries of Jan. 6, 18, 1865.

48. John B. Jones, *A Rebel War Clerk's Diary,* ed. Earl Schenck Miers (New York, 1958), pp. 489–90, entry of Jan. 30, 1865; *Richmond Enquirer,* Jan. 19, 1865; *Richmond Sentinel,* rpt. in *New York Herald,* Jan. 24, 1865; *New York World,* Jan. 23, 1865; *New York Herald,* Jan. 25, 1865.

49. Basler, *Collected Works of Lincoln* 8:275.

50. Ibid., 275–76. Italics added.

51. William J. Cooper Jr., *Jefferson Davis, American* (New York, 2000), pp. 510–11.

52. Grant to Edwin M. Stanton, Feb. 2, 1865, in Basler, *Collected Works of Lincoln* 8:282.

53. "Memorandum of the Conversation at the Conference in Hampton Roads," in John A. Campbell, *Reminiscences and Documents Relating to the Civil War During the Year 1865* (Baltimore, 1877), pp. 11–17; Seward to Charles Francis Adams, Feb. 7, 1865, in *O. R.*, ser. 1, vol. 46, pt. 2, pp. 471–73; Alexander H. Stephens, *A Constitutional View of the Late War Between the States,* 2 vols. (Philadelphia, 1870), 2:598–619. The best study of the Hampton Roads conference is William C. Harris, "The Hampton Roads Peace Conference: A Final Test of Lincoln's Presidential Leadership," *Journal of the Abraham Lincoln Association* 21 (2000): 31–61.

54. Basler, *Collected Works of Lincoln* 8:279.

55. Stephens, *Constitutional View* 2:613.

56. In his account, Stephens maintained that Lincoln had urged him to go home to Georgia and persuade the legislature to take the state out of the war and to ratify the Thirteenth Amendment prospectively, to take effect in five years. This claim cannot be accepted; Lincoln was too good a lawyer to suggest any such absurdity as a "prospective" ratification of a constitutional amendment. The president had just played a leading part in getting Congress to pass the Thirteenth Amendment, and he was using his influence to get every Republican state legislature as well as those of Maryland, Missouri, and Tennessee to ratify it. Stephens, *Constitutional View* 2:611–12. See also Harris, "Hampton Roads Peace Conference," p. 51.

57. *Richmond Examiner,* Feb. 6, 1865; Dunbar Rowland, ed., *Jefferson Davis, Constitutionalist: His Letters, Papers, and Speeches,* 10 vols. (Jackson, Miss., 1923), 6:465–67.

58. Jones, *War Clerk's Diary,* p. 493, entry of Feb. 6, 1865; *Richmond Dispatch,* Feb. 7, 1865; *Richmond Whig,* Feb. 6, 1865.

59. *New York Tribune,* Feb. 7, 1865; *New York Times,* Jan. 18, Feb. 13, 1865. See also *Harper's Weekly* 9 (Feb. 4, 1865): 66: "The government does insist on an unconditional surrender. That was the exact issue before the people in the late election. There was to be no compromising, no compounding, no convention, no waving of olive boughs."

60. Basler, *Collected Works of Lincoln* 8:332–33.

61. *Journals of Josiah Gorgas,* p. 167, entry of May 4, 1865.

CHAPTER 15

1. Douglas L. Wilson, *Lincoln Before Washington: New Perspectives on the Illinois Years* (Urbana, Ill., 1997); Wilson and Rodney O. Davis, eds., *Herndon's Informants: Letters, Interviews, and Statements About Abraham Lincoln* (Urbana, Ill., 1998); Wilson, *Honor's Voice: The Transformation of Abraham Lincoln* (New York, 1998).

2. Wilson and Davis, *Herndon's Informants,* p. xiv.

3. Wilson, *Honor's Voice,* p. 3. Lincoln did, however, write a 3,400-word autobiography for the biographer, John L. Scripps. Roy P. Basler, ed., *The Collected Works of Abraham Lincoln,* 9 vols. (New Brunswick, N.J., 1953–55), 4:60–67.

4. Quotation from Charles B. Strozier, *Lincoln's Quest for Union: Public and Private Meanings* (New York, 1981), p. xvi.

5. *Abraham Lincoln, 1809–1858,* 2 vols. (Boston, 1928).

6. Wilson, *Lincoln Before Washington,* p. x.

7. See especially Michael Burlingame, *The Inner World of Abraham Lincoln* (Urbana, Ill., 1994) and Burlingame's forthcoming three-volume biography of Abraham Lincoln.

8. Wilson, *Lincoln Before Washington,* p. 75. See also Carl Sandburg, *Abraham Lincoln: The Prairie Years,* 2 vols. (New York, 1926), 1:140–41, 185–90.

9. James G. Randall, *Lincoln the President,* 4 vols., vol. 4 completed by Richard N. Current (New York, 1945–55); Ruth Painter Randall, *Mary Lincoln: Biography of a Marriage* (Boston, 1953); David Donald, *Lincoln's Herndon* (New York, 1948); Jean H. Baker, *Mary Todd Lincoln* (New York, 1987).

10. Wilson, *Lincoln Before Washington,* p. x.

11. Randall, *Lincoln the President* 2:325.

12. Wilson, *Lincoln Before Washington,* p. 91.

13. *Herndon's Life of Lincoln* (rpt. of *Herndon's Lincoln*), ed. Paul M. Angle (New York, 1949), p. 304; Joshua Speed to Herndon, Feb. 7, 1866, in Wilson and Davis, *Herndon's Informants,* p. 197.

14. Quoted in Wilson, *Honor's Voice,* p. 301.

15. Ibid., p. 302.

16. Lincoln to Joshua Speed, March 27, July 4, 1842, in Basler, *Collected Works of Lincoln* 1:282, 289.

17. Wilson, *Honor's Voice*, p. 319.

18. Ibid., p. 320.

19. Basler, *Collected Works of Lincoln* 7:500.

20. John A. Corry, *Lincoln at Cooper Union: The Speech That Made Him President* (New York, 2003); Harold Holzer, *Lincoln at Cooper Union: The Speech That Made Abraham Lincoln President* (New York, 2004).

21. Garry Wills, *Lincoln at Gettysburg: The Words That Remade America* (New York, 1992); Ronald C. White Jr., *Lincoln's Greatest Speech: The Second Inaugural* (New York, 2002).

22. Corry, *Lincoln at Cooper Union*, pp. 97–98; Holzer, *Lincoln at Cooper Union*, p. 109.

23. Holzer, *Lincoln at Cooper Union*, p. 114.

24. Ibid., p. 113; Corry, *Lincoln at Cooper Union*, p. 112.

25. *New York Tribune*, Feb. 28, 1860, quoted in Corry, *Lincoln at Cooper Union*, pp. 157–58.

26. Harvard student quoted in Holzer, *Lincoln at Cooper Union*, p. 173; *New York Herald*, Feb. 28, 1860, quoted in Corry, *Lincoln at Cooper Union*, p. 151.

27. Basler, *Collected Works of Lincoln* 3:535, 546–47.

28. Ibid., 550.

29. Mario M. Cuomo, *Why Lincoln Matters Today More than Ever* (New York, 2004).

30. Don E. Fehrenbacher, "Words of Lincoln," in *Abraham Lincoln and the American Political Tradition*, ed. John L. Thomas (Amherst, Mass., 1986), p. 39.

31. James M. McPherson, "Abraham Lincoln and the Second American Revolution," in ibid., pp. 142–60.

32. Fehrenbacher, "Words of Lincoln," in ibid., pp. 42, 39.

33. Don E. Fehrenbacher and Virginia Fehrenbacher, eds., *Recollected Words of Abraham Lincoln* (Stanford, Calif., 1996).

34. Ibid., p. 428.

35. Ibid., p. 1.

36. Ibid., pp. lii–liii.

37. Ibid., p. liii.

38. Ibid., pp. 98, 311.

39. Ibid., p. 369. See Horace Porter, *Campaigning with Grant* (New York, 1897), pp. 218–19.

40. Fehrenbacher and Fehrenbacher, *Recollected Words*, pp. 20, 36–37, 134, 207, 335, 390, 410.

41. Basler, *Collected Works of Lincoln* 7:376–77.

42. Michael F. Holt, "Abraham Lincoln and the Politics of Union," in Thomas, *Abraham Lincoln and the American Political Tradition,* p. 135. For an interpretation similar to Holt's, see Randall and Current, *Lincoln the President* 4:130–34.

43. Fehrenbacher and Fehrenbacher, *Recollected Words,* pp. 291, 316–17.

44. David Herbert Donald, *Lincoln* (New York, 1995), pp. 505–6.

45. Basler, *Collected Works of Lincoln* 4:24, 5:52. See Eric Foner, *Free Soil, Free Labor, Free Men: The Ideology of the Republican Party Before the Civil War* (New York, 1970).

46. Basler, *Collected Works of Lincoln* 2:461, 4:24.

47. Ibid., 7:282.

48. Donald, *Lincoln,* pp. 14, 354, 15, 337.

49. Basler, *Collected Works of Lincoln* 7:282.

50. Donald, *Lincoln,* p. 14.

51. For an incisive analysis of the Hodges letter, see Ronald C. White, *The Eloquent President: A Portrait of Lincoln Through His Words* (New York, 2005), pp. 260–75.

52. Lincoln to William Kellogg, Dec. 11, 1860, to John D. Defrees, Dec. 18, 1860, to James T. Hale, Jan. 11, 1861, in Basler, *Collected Works of Lincoln* 4:150, 155, 172.

53. Donald, *Lincoln,* pp. 285–86.

54. John G. Nicolay and John Hay, *Abraham Lincoln: A History,* 10 vols. (New York, 1890), 4:62.

55. Donald, *Lincoln,* p. 449.

56. Ibid., pp. 547–48.

CHAPTER 16

1. *Inside Lincoln's White House: The Complete Civil War Diary of John Hay,* ed. Michael Burlingame and John R. Turner Ettlinger (Carbondale, Ill., 1997), pp. 217–18, entry of July 4, 1864.

2. Roy P. Basler, ed., *The Collected Works of Abraham Lincoln,* 9 vols. (New Brunswick, N.J., 1953–55), 5:421, Sept. 13, 1862.

3. See especially Dean Sprague, *Freedom Under Lincoln* (Boston, 1965); Mark E. Neely Jr., *The Fate of Liberty: Abraham Lincoln and Civil Liberties* (New York, 1991); Daniel Farber, *Lincoln's Constitution* (Chicago, 2003); and Michael Stokes Paulsen, "The Civil War as Constitutional Interpretation," *University of Chicago Law Review* 71 (Spring 2004): 691–727.

4. Abel Upshur, *A Brief Enquiry into the True Nature and Character of Our Federal Government,* p. 116, quoted in Wilfred E. Binkley, *The Man in the White House: His Powers and Duties* (Baltimore, 1958), p. 189.

5. 50 U.S. (9 Howard) 614–15 (1850).

6. Basler, *Collected Works of Lincoln* 4:338–39, April 19, 1861.

7. Ibid., 331–32, 353–54.

8. Ibid. 5:241–42.

9. Ibid. 4:353, 5:241.

10. Ibid. 5:242; Paulsen, "Civil War as Constitutional Interpretation," 720.

11. Basler, *Collected Works of Lincoln* 4:426, 440.

12. Clinton Rossiter, *The American Presidency*, rev. ed. (New York, 1960), p. 99, makes the same point.

13. 67 U.S. 635.

14. Basler, *Collected Works of Lincoln* 4:429; *U.S. Statutes at Large* 12:326, Aug. 6, 1861.

15. Basler, *Collected Works of Lincoln* 4:347, 419, 554, 5:436–37.

16. *Ex parte Merryman,* 17 F. Cas. 148–53 (1861).

17. Basler, *Collected Works of Lincoln* 4:430–31.

18. Ibid., 430.

19. Paulsen, "Civil War as Constitutional Interpretation," 721.

20. Lincoln to Albert G. Hodges, April 4, 1864, in Basler, *Collected Works of Lincoln* 7:281.

21. "Opinion of Attorney General Bates, July 5, 1861," in *War of the Rebellion . . . Official Records of the Union and Confederate Armies*, 128 vols. (Washington, 1880–1901), ser. 2, vol. 2, pp. 20–30 (hereinafter cited as *O. R.*); Reverdy Johnson, *Power of the President to Suspend the Habeas Corpus Writ* (New York, 1861); Horace Binney, *The Privilege of the Writ of Habeas Corpus Under the Constitution* (Philadelphia, 1862). See also Edward Bates to Lincoln, July 5, 1861, Abraham Lincoln Papers, Library of Congress.

22. *O. R.*, ser. 2, vol. 5, pp. 633–46.

23. Quoted in William B. Hesseltine, *Lincoln and the War Governors* (New York, 1948), p. 331.

24. In 1866, after the passions of war had partly cooled, the Supreme Court over-turned a similar military conviction in 1864 of an Indiana Copperhead, Lambdin P. Milligan, on the grounds that when the civil courts are functioning, civilians must be tried therein even in wartime. *Ex parte Milligan,* 71 U.S. 2, 120–42.

25. Erastus Corning et al. to the President, in Frank Freidel, ed., *Union Pamphlets of the Civil War*, 2 vols. (Cambridge, Mass., 1967), 2:740–43; Matthew Birchard et al., Resolutions presented to Lincoln," in Basler, *Collected Works of Lincoln* 6:300–301n.

26. Basler, *Collected Works of Lincoln* 6:260–69, 300–306.

27. Lincoln to Frémont, Sept. 1, 1861, in ibid. 4:506.

28. Lincoln to Browning, Sept. 22, 1861, in ibid., 531–32.

29. Ibid. 5:434, 6:29–30.

30. Whiting, *The War Powers of the President . . .* , 7th ed. (Boston, 1863), passim. Whiting and Lincoln became personal friends. See James M. McPherson, *The*

*Struggle for Equality: Abolitionists and the Negro in the Civil War and Reconstruction* (Princeton, N.J., 1964), pp. 68–69, and Lincoln to Edwin M. Stanton, March 25, 1865, in Basler, *Collected Works of Lincoln* 8:373.

31. Basler, *Collected Works of Lincoln* 5:222–23.

32. Gideon Welles, "The History of Emancipation," *Galaxy* 14 (Dec. 1872): 842–43.

33. Lincoln to James C. Conkling, Aug. 26, 1863, in Basler, *Collected Works of Lincoln* 6:408.

34. Francis B. Carpenter, *Six Months at the White House with Abraham Lincoln* (New York, 1866), pp. 76–77. Carpenter spent six months in 1864 painting a picture of Lincoln and his cabinet at the first reading of the Emancipation Proclamation. He was present when Lincoln spoke these words to an antislavery delegation on April 7, 1864.

35. Lincoln to the committee that notified him of his nomination, June 9, 1864, in Basler, *Collected Works of Lincoln* 7:380.

36. Ibid., 301–2.

# Index

*Ableman vs. Booth*, 9

Abolitionists, 13, 30–31, 148

Adams, Charles Francis, 9; minister to Britain, 65; issue of British recognition of Confederacy, 67, 68, 73

Adams, Charles Francis Jr., 147

Adams, Henry, 67, 71, 155; on impact of Emancipation Proclamation, 75; on Grant, 109

Adams, John, 147

African Americans. *See* Blacks

Ames, Adelbert, 91

Anderson, "Bloody Bill," 88–89, 90

Andrew, John A., 35, 149, 150

Antietam, battle of, 48, 49, 59, 79–81; forestalls European intervention, 65, 72–74, 168; and Emancipation Proclamation, 74–75, 219; casualties in, 145

Appomattox, surrender at, 63, 110, 120

Armstrong, Jack, 192

Army of Northern Virginia, embodies Confederate nation, 62–63, 120, 165

Army of the Potomac, compared with Army of the Tennessee, 115–16, 119–21

Army of the Tennessee: success of, 114–18, comparison with other Union armies, 119–21

Atlanta: military campaign of, 49, 59, 60, 61, 117–18; capture of, 166, 178–79

Baker, Jean H., 191

Balch, Emily, 146

Balch, Francis, 146

Ballard, Colin, 52

Ball's Bluff, battle of, 67, 148, 149

Banks, Nathaniel P., 134–35, 139–40, 142

Beard, Charles A., 5

Beauregard, Pierre G. T., 19, 44, 61, 82; and Jefferson Davis, 51; and Confederate strategy, 58, 60, 63

Beecher, Henry Ward, 35

Belmont, battle of, 111

Benét, Stephen Vincent, 37

Benjamin, Judah P., 172, 173; on benefits of European recognition, 65–66; and peace initiatives, 174, 244n. 22

Benning, Henry L., 164

Bentonville, battle of, 123

Beveridge, Albert J., 188–89

Blacks, and John Brown, 30, 32, 37–38

Black soldiers: in Union army, 28, 46, 147–48; Lincoln praises, 177

Blair, Francis Preston, 179–81

Blight, David, 38

Bradford, Sarah, 23, 25

Bragg, Braxton, 82, 142; and Jefferson Davis, 51, 52; and Confederate strategy, 58, 60, 61, 63, 80; invasion of Kentucky, 134

Bright, John, 70

Brooks, Preston, 31

Brown, John: hatred of slavery, 29–30; Pottawatomie massacre, 31; Harpers Ferry raid, 29, 32–33; martyrdom of, 34–36; conflicting images of, 37–39

Brown, Kent Masterson, 77

Brown, Owen, 30

Browning, Orville, 217, 219

Buchanan, James, 9, 17

Buell, Don Carlos, 132–33, 134

Bull Run, battles of. *See* Manassas

Bundy, Carol, 147, 151

Burns, Ken, 4

Burns, Ric, 4

Burnside, Ambrose E., 52, 81
Butler, Benjamin, 91, 134, 171
Butler, Sarah, 171

Calhoun, John C., 7, 13
Campbell, John A., 180–81
Carpenter, Francis B., 251n. 34
Carroll, Kenneth, 33
Catton, Bruce, 37, 109
Cecil, Lord Robert, 66
Cedar Creek, battle of, 152
Chancellorsville, battle of, 60, 61, 81, 83
Chandler, Zachariah, 209
*Charleston Mercury*, 11
Chase, Salmon P., 195–96, 210
Chattanooga, battles at, 115–16, 142
Cheney, Lynne, 22
Chickamauga, battle of, 49, 59, 60, 119, 142
Chickasaw Bluffs, battle of, 138
Child, Lydia Maria, 27
Children of the Confederacy, 96
Chiniquy, Charles, 202
Clausewitz, Karl von, 52
Clay, Clement C., 171, 173, 244n. 18
Clement, Archie, 88, 90
Clinton, Catherine, 22–23, 25, 29
Cluseret, Gustave Paul, 156
Cobden, Richard, 70, 75
Cold Harbor, battle of, 113
*Confederate Veteran Magazine*, 105; and
    Lost Cause, 96; textbook crusade of, 99,
    105; revival of, 236n. 44
Conrad, Earl, 22
Cooper Union address, Lincoln's, 195–99
Copperheads. *See* Peace Democrats
Corinth, Mississippi, capture of, 68, 162
Craven, Avery, 6
Cunningham, Sumner A., 96
Curry, Jabez L. M., 98–99
Cushing, William B., 162

Dana, Charles A., 139
Daniel, Peter, 16
Davis, Charles C., 133, 134
Davis, Jefferson, 101; on causes of
    secession, 3–4, 5; and Fugitive Slave Law,
    9; and Fort Sumter, 18–19, 207; and
    internal Confederate divisions, 46;

relations with generals, 51–52, 54, 161;
    and Confederate strategies, 54–56,
    58–63, 79–80; and Gettysburg campaign,
    81–84; and fall of Atlanta, 118; restores
    Johnston to command, 119; and peace
    initiatives, 169, 172, 174–77, 179–83,
    244n. 22
Davis, Rodney O., 189
Davis, Varina, 54
Davis, William C., 46–47
*De Bow's Review*, 36;
Dew, Charles B., 11–12
Disease mortality, in Eastern and Western
    Union armies, 120
Dix, John A., 60
Dodd, William E., 103
Donald, David Herbert (Lincoln
    biographer), 191, 204–6; Lincoln
    passivity thesis of, 206–8
Douglas, Stephen A., 35, 195, 196, 197–98
Douglass, Frederick, 13, 30, 32
Dred Scott decision, 9, 31, 198, 214
Du Bois, William E. B., 37–38

Early, Jubal, 58, 59, 60, 63; in Gettysburg
    campaign, 85; 1864 raid of, 151; battle of
    Cedar Creek, 152
Edwards, John Newman, 90
Edwards, Matilda, 193
Elson, Henry W., 104–5
Elections: presidential, 1860, 9, 16, 36, 195,
    205; Northern congressional elections,
    1862, 80; Northern presidential election
    of 1864, 113, 118, 165, 173–79, 207
Emancipation: and "hard war" policy, 124,
    126–27; and 20th Massachusetts, 148;
    and peace issue in 1864, 175–78, 182. *See
    also* Slavery.
Emancipation Proclamation, 169, 206, 209,
    251n. 34; impact in Europe, 74–75, 168;
    Mildred Rutherford on, 103; Lincoln's
    decision to issue, 126–27, 207; and war
    powers, 217–20
Emerson, Ralph Waldo, 34–35, 36
Ewell, Richard, 83, 85

Fabius, Quintus, 55
Farragut, Daniel Glasgow, 133–34

Faust, Drew Gilpin, 45
Fehrenbacher, Don E., 199–204
Fehrenbacher, Virginia, 200–204
Fisk, Wilbur, 165
Foote, Andrew H., 133
Foote, Shelby, 43
Ford, Bob, 92
Ford, Charley, 92
Fort Donelson, capture of, 57, 67, 110, 111, 116, 133, 138
Fort Fisher, capture of, 179
Fort Henry, capture of, 67, 116, 133
Fort Sumter: firing on, 18–19, 128, 202–3, 211; Lincoln's decision to resupply, 207–8
France, and issue of Confederate recognition, 65, 67, 69–73, 75, 168
Fredericksburg, battle of, 59, 79, 80, 83
Freehling, William W., 45, 50
Fremont, John C., 156, 217
French, Daniel Chester, 153
Fugitive Slave Law, 9, 21, 25
Fuller, J.F.C., 52, 109

Gallagher, Gary W., 47–49
Garrett, Thomas, 25
Garrison, William Lloyd, 13, 34
Gasparin, Count Agenor-Etienne, 70
Gettysburg: campaign and battle of, 49, 58, 60, 61, 62, 63, 233n. 17; Lee's goals in, 77–86; 50th anniversary commemoration, 93; Meade and, 141; casualties in, 145; Pickett's charge, 161; and Northern morale, 163, 169, 217
Gettysburg Address, Lincoln's, 147, 189, 196
Gilbert, James N., 38
Gilmore, James R., 174–75, 244n. 22
Gladstone, William, 72, 73
Gone with the Wind, 6
Gorgas, Josiah, 180, 183
Grand Army of the Republic, 98
Grant, Ulysses S., 49, 52, 58, 96, 164; Vicksburg campaign of, 82, 134, 135–42; as president, 91; compared with Lee, 94; reputation of, 109; qualities of character and generalship, 110–15; on Georgia campaign, 118; strategy of, 120–21; and

"hard war," 126, 127, 129; capture of Fort Donelson, 133; 1864 overland campaign of, 170; and Hampton Roads conference, 181
Great Britain: and question of Confederate recognition, 65–74, 168; and Emancipation Proclamation, 75
Greeley, Horace: on John Brown, 34; Lincoln's letter to on slavery, 74; and peace negotiations, 169, 172–74, 183; despair of, 170; on emancipation and peace negotiations, 176
Grierson, Benjamin, 140
Grimsley, Mark, on Union war policies, 123–25, 127–29
Guderian, Heinz, 117

Habeas Corpus, Lincoln's suspension of, 213–15, 216
Halleck, Henry W.: Union general in chief, 71; on "hard war," 126, 127; and Western rivers, 133; and Vicksburg campaign, 135–39, 141
Hamilton, Alexander, 210
Hamlin, Hannibal, 203, 204
Hammond, Scott John, 38
Hampton Roads peace conference, 181–82
Harpers Ferry, John Brown's raid on, 29, 32–34
Harper's Weekly, 157–59
Harrison, James (Henry?), 85
Harvard University, army officers from, 146, 152–53
Hattaway, Herman, 52
Hay, John: and Niagara Falls meeting, 172–73; and Raymond mission, 178; quotations of Lincoln, 200, 203; on Fort Sumter, 208
Herndon, William, on Lincoln, 187–93
Higginson, Thomas Wentworth, 26
Hill, A. P., 83, 161
History, Southern efforts to shape teaching and writing of, 97–106
Hobsbawm, Eric J., 87
Hodges, Albert, 206
Holden, William W., 164
Holmes, Oliver Wendell, 155
Holmes, Oliver Wendell Jr., 146, 147, 150

Holt, Michael, 203
Homer, Winslow, 158
Hood, John Bell, 59, 60, 63, 83, 118; and
    Jefferson Davis, 51, 61
Hooker, Joseph, 52; and Lee's invasion of
    Pennsylvania, 77, 81, 83–84, 85
Hotchkiss, Jedediah, 80
Howe, Julia Ward, 36
Humez, Jean, 23
Humphreys, Andrew A., 148
Hunter, David, 218
Hunter, Robert M. T., 180–82

*I'll Take My Stand*, 5

Jackson, Andrew, 9
Jackson, Thomas J. ("Stonewall"), 46, 52,
    62, 80, 135, 161; Shenandoah Valley
    Campaign, 68, 69; battle of Cedar
    Mountain, 71; battle of Chancellorsville,
    81
Jacobs, Harriet, 26–27, 28
James, Frank: and guerrilla war, 88–89;
    Northfield raid, 91–92
James, Jesse: interpretations of, 87–88; as
    Confederate guerrilla, 88–89; as
    Reconstruction outlaw, 90; Northfield
    raid, 91–92
Jaquess, James, 174–75
Jefferson, Thomas, 9, 13, 189
*John Brown's Body*, 37
Johnson, Andrew, 203
Johnson, Lyndon, 52
Johnston, Albert Sydney, 57, 60
Johnston, Joseph E., 44, 82; and Jefferson
    Davis, 51, 54, 56–57, 61; and
    Confederate strategy, 58, 59, 61, 63; in
    Georgia campaign, 118; restored to
    command, 119; and Vicksburg, 141
Jones, Archer, 52
Jones, John, 182
Juarez, Benito, 90

Kansas-Nebraska Act, 14, 30, 107
Keegan, John, 52
Kelliher, John, 150
King, Martin Luther Jr., 38
Kutuzov, Mikhail, 55

Lamon, Ward Hill, 188, 203
Lamson, Roswell H., 162
Larson, Kate Clifford, 23, 25
Lawrence, Kansas: burned by border
    ruffians, 31; Quantrill's raid, 88–89
Lee, Mary Custis, 97
Lee, Robert E., 46, 48, 50, 52, 96, 97, 120,
    180; and John Brown's raid, 32;
    compared to John Brown, 38–39; on
    cause of Confederate defeat, 43, 94;
    strategy of, 49, 57–63; and Jefferson
    Davis, 51, 59–61; Seven Days battles, 68,
    162; Second Manassas, 71; in Antietam
    campaign, 79–81; goals in Gettysburg
    campaign, 77–86; compared with Grant,
    109, 111, 112, 113; high casualties of,
    116; irony of his success, 128–29
Lee, Susan Pendleton, 99
Lee, William Raymond, 147, 149
Leopold, King, 74
Lewis, Sir George Cornewall, 74
Liddell Hart, Basil H., 52, 117–18
Lincoln, Abraham, 51, 103, 153; on cause of
    war, 3; election of as president, 9, 16, 36,
    205; house divided speech, 10–11; on
    slavery, 13, 125; resists secession, 17; and
    Fort Sumter, 18–19; on John Brown, 35;
    second inaugural address, 37, 183; and his
    generals, 51–52; and McClellan, 54;
    Emancipation Proclamation of, 74–75,
    103, 126–27, 168, 169, 206, 209, 217–20,
    251n; and Stephens peace mission of 1863,
    85–86; reelection of, 113, 118, 165, 179;
    and Grant in the Vicksburg campaign,
    131, 134–42; and East Tennessee, 132, 134;
    Gettysburg Address of, 147, 189, 196; and
    issue of peace negotiations, 168–69,
    172–83, 246n. 56; proclamation of
    amnesty and reconstruction, 170; and
    Herndon's research, 187–92; antebellum
    years, 193–95, 204–5; Cooper Union
    address, 195–99; misquotations of,
    199–203; alleged passivity of, 206–8; and
    presidential war powers, 209–12;
    suspension of habeas corpus, 213–15;
    and Vallandigham trial, 215–16
Lincoln, Mary Todd, 188, 190–91, 193–95,
    204

Lincoln, Robert, 190
London Daily News, on Northern
    determination, 166
London Morning Post, on Confederate
    independence, 70
London Times: anti-Americanism of, 66,
    70; on Northern success, 67; urges
    mediation, 69; on Antietam, 73
Longstreet, James, 61; and Gettysburg
    campaign, 82–83, 85, 233n. 17; quarrel
    with A. P. Hill, 161
Lovejoy, Elijah, 30
Lowell, Charles Russell: commander of 2nd
    Massachusetts Cavalry, 146, 150–51;
    motives for enlisting, 147–48; death of,
    152–53
Lowell, James Russell, 146, 148
Lowell, Josephine Shaw, 148
Lumpkin, Katharine Du Pre, 95–96

MacArthur, Douglas, 53
McClellan, George B., 156; and Lincoln, 51,
    54; Peninsula campaign of, 56–57, 68,
    71, 79, 129, 134; Antietam campaign, 81;
    fear of failure, 112; and ethos of Army of
    the Potomac, 115; and East Tennessee,
    132–33; presidential candidate, 175, 178,
    179, 245n. 42
McClernand, John A., 135–37, 239n. 6
McClure, Alexander, 203
McDowell, Irvin, 56
McFeely, William, 109
McMurry, Richard, 61
Macon, Nathaniel, 7
Macy, George, 150
Madison, James, 9, 104, 147, 210
Malcolm X, 38
Manassas: first battle of, 56, 67, 159; second
    battle of, 57, 59, 60, 71–72, 79
Martineau, Harriet, 104
Mason, James, 67–68, 71, 74
Maximilian, Ferdinand, 80, 180
Maynard, Nettie, 202
Meade, George Gordon, 51, 62, 160
Medill, Joseph, 139
Memphis, capture of, 68
Merryman, John, and ex parte Merryman,
    213–15

Mill Springs, battle of, 133
Miller, Richard F., 149
Milligan, Lambdin P., and ex parte
    Milligan, 250n. 24
Milroy, Robert, 77, 81
Missouri: guerrilla war in, and James gang,
    88–89; postwar climate of violence,
    90–91; changes in, 92
Missouri Compromise, 13
Moran, Benjamin, 72, 73
Mosby, John Singleton, 151
Murfreesboro, battle of, 60
Muzzey, David, 106

Napoleon Bonaparte, 79, 118, 167
Napoleon, Louis (Napoleon III): and
    recognition of Confederacy, 66, 67, 70,
    73, 168; and Maximilian, 90, 180
Nashville, battle of, 59
Nast, Thomas, 158
Neely, Mark E. Jr., 124
New Bern, battle of, 67
New Orleans, capture of, 67–68, 69, 134
New York Herald: on Union victories, 170;
    on peace terms, 176; on Lincoln's
    Cooper Union address, 197
New York Times: on unconditional
    surrender, 169, 174, 183; on Union
    victories, 170; on peace moves, 173, 175,
    176
New York Tribune: on foreign policy, 67; on
    Union victories, 170; on peace terms,
    176; on Lincoln's Cooper Union address,
    197
New York World: on Northern
    demoralization, 170–71; on Northern
    war aims, 175.
Newspapers, and morale of soldiers,
    155–66
Niagara Falls "peace negotiations," 172–73
Nicolay, John, 178, 203, 208

Owens, Mary, 193
Owsley, Frank, 6

Palmerston, Viscount, and issue of
    recognizing Confederacy, 66, 68, 70,
    71–74

Paris, comte de, 156
Paris *Constitutionnel*, urges mediation, 69, 70
Pea Ridge, battle of, 67
Peace Democrats, 80, 84; and Northern morale, 163–65; arrests of, 213; and 1864 election, 171–72, 174–75, 178; and Vallandigham trial, 215–17
Pemberton, John C., 82, 138, 140
Pender, Dorsey, 83
Perryville, battle of, 48
Petersburg, siege of, 113
Peterson, Merrill, 36
Phillips, Wendell, 13
Pickett, George, 63, 82, 85; and "Pickett's Charge," 93, 161
Polk, James K., 210
Polk, Leonidas, 131
Pollard, Edward, 94
Pope, John, 52, 57, 71
Porter, David Dixon, 131, 140
Port Hudson: campaign of, 135, 139; surrender of, 141, 163, 217
Pottawatomie massacre, John Brown and, 31, 39
Price, Sterling, 60, 134
*Prize Cases* (1863), 212
Putnam, George, 152
Putnam, William Lowell, 148

Quantrill, William Clarke, 88, 90

Ramsdell, Charles W., 44–45
Randall, James G., 6, 191–92
Randall, Ruth Painter, 191
Raymond, Henry, 169, 176–78
Reagan, John, 82
Reagan, Ronald, 199
Reston, James Jr., 128
Revere, Paul, 146, 147, 150
Reynolds, Davida S., 34, 39
Rhodes, James Ford, 103
Richards, Leonard, 8, 9
*Richmond Dispatch*: on European intervention, 69; on peace prospects, 172
*Richmond Enquirer*, fires up Southern war party, 175
*Richmond Examiner*: on invasion of

Pennsylvania, 85; and Longstreet, 161; on fall of Atlanta, 179; on peace terms, 182
Riley, Franklin L., 104
Roanoke Island, battle of, 67
Roanoke College, textbook war at, 104–5
Rosecrans, William S., 60, 81, 82
Ruffin, Edmund, 69, 155
Russell, Lord John, and issue of Confederate recognition, 68, 71–73
Rutherford, Mildred L., and writing of history, 101–3, 235n. 36
Rutledge, Ann, 190–93, 204

Sandburg, Carl, 190
Schofield, John, 112
Scott, Winfield, 131, 133
Sears, Stephen W., 81, 82
Second Massachusetts Cavalry, officers of, 146, 150–51; service of, 152
Seddon, James, 82
Seven Days battles, 57, 59, 60, 62, 68, 69, 74, 79, 85, 129, 161, 162
Seward, William H., 67, 68, 172; and irrepressible conflict, 10; and Harriet Tubman, 26, 28; warns British, 65; on cotton exports, 69; counsels Lincoln to postpone Emancipation Proclamation, 74, 219; on French intervention, 169; and Hampton Roads conference, 181–82; and 1860 election, 195
Seymour, Horatio, 215
Sharpsburg. *See* Antietam
Shaw, Robert Gould, 28, 147–48
Shelby, Joseph, 90
Shenandoah Valley, campaigns and battles in, 49, 57, 60, 68, 69, 77, 81, 151–52, 179
Sheridan, Philip, 151–52, 179
Sherman, John, 125
Sherman, William T., 52, 60, 170, 180; on Grant, 110, 112; partnership with Grant, 114–15, 120–21; strategy of indirect approach, 116–18; marches through Georgia and Carolinas, 118–19, 121, 123, 142; and "hard war," 124–29; and Vicksburg campaign, 136–38, 140; dislikes press, 160; capture of Atlanta, 166, 178

Shields, James, 193–94
Shiloh, battle of, 57, 59, 60; Grant and, 111, 114, 116, 133, 138
Simon, John Y., 109
Simpson, Brooks D., 109, 112, 113–14
Slave Power, issue of, 7–10, 14
Slavery: and issue of war causation, 3–13; controversy over expansion of, 13–16, 197–99; and Harriet Tubman, 21–26; and Harriet Jacobs, 26–27; John Brown's hatred of, 29–30, 39; and Confederacy, 44–46, 49, 94, 97; historical controversies about, 99, 100, 104; 13th Amendment abolishes, 182, 220. *See also* Emancipation; Emancipation Proclamation
Slidell, John, 70, 71
Smith, Edmund Kirby
Smith, Gerrit, 30
Sons of Confederate Veterans: and issue of war causation, 4, 7, 16; and Lost Cause, 94–95; and writing of history, 105–6, 123–24, 128
Sorrel, G. Moxley, 161
Speed, Joshua, 193
Spotsylvania, battle of, 113
Stanton, Edwin M., 63, 219; and Vicksburg campaign, 136, 139
State's rights, and issue of war causation, 4, 7–9
Stephens, Alexander H., on slavery and the Confederacy, 3–4, 11; and Confederate divisions, 46; aborted peace mission in 1863, 84–85, 86; Hampton Roads conference, 180–81, 246n. 56
Still, William, 25
Stiles, T. J., on Jesse James, 87–89, 92
Stone's River, battle of. *See* Murfreesboro
Stowe, Harriet Beecher, 21, 201
Strategy: definitions of, 52–53; Confederate strategies, 54–63; of indirect approach, Sherman's, 116–18
Stuart, James E. B. ("Jeb"), 85
Strong, George Templeton: on peace sentiment in 1864, 171, 172, 176; on fall of Atlanta, 178
Sumner, Charles, 31, 63, 70
Symonds, Craig, 51, 56

Taney, Roger B.: and Dred Scott decision, 9, 168; and *ex parte Merryman*, 213–15
Tariff, and sectional conflict, 5–6, 10, 15
Taylor, Zachary, 112
Thelen, David, 87
Thomas, Emory, 59–61
Thomas, George, 133, 179
Thompson, Joseph T., 179
Thoreau, Henry David, 34
Thorstenberg, Herman J., 104
Trimble, Isaac, 83–84
Truman, Harry, 53, 112
Tubman, Harriet: fame of, 21–23; "Moses" of fugitive slaves, 23–29; and John Brown, 29, 30
Twentieth Massachusetts Infantry: officers of, 146, 149–50; and slavery, 148, casualties of, 148–49

*Uncle Tom's Cabin*, 21, 201
Underground railroad, 24–26
United Confederate Veterans: and Lost Cause, 94, 95; and writing of history, 97–105
United Daughters of the Confederacy: and Lost Cause, 94–96; and writing of history, 98–106
Upshur, Abel, 210

Vallandigham, Clement L., 165, 215–16
Van Dorn, Earl, 134, 138
Vicksburg: campaign of, 49, 59, 61, 80, 82, 114, 116, 217; capture of, 110, 163, 169; Lincoln and, 131–32, 134–42

Walker, William, 14
Warren, Robert Penn, 37
Washburn, Cadwalader, 139
Washburne, Elihu, 110, 138, 139
Washington, George, 55, 57
Waud, Alfred, 158
Webster, Fletcher, 146
Weed, Thurlow, 172, 175
Weik, Jesse W., 188
Weld, Theodore, 13
Welles, Gideon, 141, 171, 219
White, Richard, 87
White, Ronald C., 196

Whiting, William, 218, 219
Wickham, John A., 145
Wigfall, Louis, 82
Wilderness, battle of, 111, 155
Wiley, Bell Irvin, 156
Williams, Kenneth P., 52, 109
Williams, T. Harry, 52, 56, 109
Wills, Brian Steel, 50
Wills, Garry, 196
Wilmot, David, and Wilmot Proviso, 15
Wilson, Douglas L.: on Lincoln and Herndon, 189–92; on Lincoln's values, 193–95

Wilson, Woodrow, 93, 100–101, 105, 167
Wilson's Creek, battle of, 67
Winchester, third battle of, 152
Wise, Henry A., 33
Wyatt-Brown, Bertram, 16
Woodworth, Steven: on Confederate strategy, 59–61; on Army of the Tennessee, 115

Yates, Richard, 136, 239n.
Younger brothers: part of James gang, 89, 90; Northfield raid, 91–92